Between Truth and Falsity
Liberal Education and the Arts of Discernment

Edited by

Karim Dharamsi
Mount Royal University, Canada
and
David Ohreen
Mount Royal University, Canada

Series in Education

Copyright © 2021 by the authors.

All rights reserved. No part of this publication may be reproduced, stored in a retrieval system, or transmitted in any form or by any means, electronic, mechanical, photocopying, recording, or otherwise, without the prior permission of Vernon Art and Science Inc.

www.vernonpress.com

In the Americas:
Vernon Press
1000 N West Street, Suite 1200
Wilmington, Delaware, 19801
United States

In the rest of the world:
Vernon Press
C/Sancti Espiritu 17,
Malaga, 29006
Spain

Series in Education

Library of Congress Control Number: 2020950202

ISBN: 978-1-64889-251-6

Also available: 978-1-62273-937-0 [Hardback]; 978-1-64889-183-0 [PDF; E-Book]

Product and company names mentioned in this work are the trademarks of their respective owners. While every care has been taken in preparing this work, neither the authors nor Vernon Art and Science Inc. may be held responsible for any loss or damage caused or alleged to be caused directly or indirectly by the information contained in it.

Every effort has been made to trace all copyright holders, but if any have been inadvertently overlooked the publisher will be pleased to include any necessary credits in any subsequent reprint or edition.

Cover design by Vernon Press. Cover photo by Drew Graham on Unsplash.

This volume is dedicated to the hard work of Dr James Zimmer, former Vice President and Vice Provost of Teaching and Learning at Mount Royal University and Dr Terry Chapman, former Vice President Academic of Medicine Hat College in Medicine Hat, Alberta.

Table of Contents

	Acknowledgements	vii
	Foreword Bruce Umbaugh Webster University President of the Association of General and Liberal Studies	ix
Chapter 1	**Introduction** Karim Dharamsi Mount Royal University and David Ohreen Mount Royal University	1
Chapter 2	**Metaphors for Higher Education in Our Public Discourse** Andrew Moore St Thomas University	13
Chapter 3	**The Discourse of Crisis in Liberal Education: Real Emergency or Fake News?** Jason Openo Medicine Hat College	33
Chapter 4	**Detecting Bullshit in a Culture of Fake News and Lies** David Ohreen Mount Royal University	53
Chapter 5	**Liberal Education and Truth in the Ages of Plato's Culture Industry** James Cunningham Mount Royal University	77
Chapter 6	**How to 'Handle' the Truth from a Liberal Arts Perspective** Ronald Peter Glasberg University of Calgary	93

Chapter 7	**Black Criminality: A Matter of 'Truth' and our Acquiescence**	119

Navneet Kumar
Medicine Hat College

Chapter 8	**Complexity, Chaos, Collaboration: Untangling Strands of Truth; Teaching/Learning/Teaching in the 21st Century**	131

Deborah Forbes
Medicine Hat College

Chapter 9	**Truth and Awe**	151

Robert M. Randolph
Waynesburg University

	About the Authors	163
	Index	167

Acknowledgements

On May 3-5, 2018, we held our fourth liberal education conference in Calgary, Alberta, Canada. Held at the Calgary Westin Downtown, this collection of papers is selected from those delivered at the conference. A joint committee of dedicated faculty form Mount Royal University and Medicine Hate College helped to organize the meeting. We would like to thank Diane Bennett, Sean Carleton, Marty Clark, Elizabeth Evans, Cynthia Gallop, Mark Gardiner, Charles Helper, Navneet Kumar, Rob Platts, Brenda Quantz, and Archie Maclean. We extend a special thanks to James (Jim) Zimmer and Terry Chapman, colleagues to whom we have dedicated this volume. Of course, we thank the many authors and our anonymous reviewers for their constructive feedback—and Bruce Umbaugh for his foreword to this volume. Finally, we thank Vernon Press for their commitment and support of our work in liberal education.

Foreword

Bruce Umbaugh
Webster University
President of the Association of General and Liberal Studies

The essays collected here address a range of issues about higher education in general, liberal education in particular, and contemporary concerns about expertise, truth, propaganda, and illiberal disdain for the difference between truth and falsehood. They are timely and at once foundational and applied.

Some of these essays take up views of the role of higher education: is it a private good that allows students to accumulate a kind of capital? Is it a public good intended to benefit the citizenry broadly? Is it something else or more?

Students attend universities for many reasons, but especially for credentials to land 'good jobs' and for social mobility. Universities, though, promise in addition that we will offer a 'liberal education' that gives students more than a degree.

A liberal education is the education of free people. It is also a *liberating* education—an education that frees people. Liberal education prepares people for meaningful participation in democracy and for leading flourishing lives.

Several essays take up liberal education in relation to being able to distinguish among truth, made up 'news,' and bullshit offered without regard for whether it is true or false. In Plato's *Meno*, Socrates and Meno agree that true opinions are useful—just as useful as real knowledge—but Socrates insists that knowledge is the more valuable of the two. Socrates offers a metaphor to illustrate the difference between genuine knowledge and mere belief that happens to be true. Mere opinion, he says, is like the statues of Daedalus that were said to be incredibly lifelike—so much so that they would run away if not tied down. Knowledge is such a statue tied down by the ability to give a justification for it.

Here is a place for liberal education. Liberal education frees people to think for themselves, to seek out and to evaluate information, to reason ethically about alternatives, and to advance justifications. It helps people to make themselves knowers and not mere opinion-havers and thereby to enhance democratic processes and practices as a citizen.

As the volume documents, these skills are in obvious demand today. Consider, for example, all-too-common media representations of blackness. As one essay discusses, such representations have served racial oppression over centuries. This and other examples of pressing challenges we face in the 21st century—including a viral pandemic, global climate change, and movements such as #metoo and #blacklivesmatter—call on us to interpret, reason, and act together. Moreover, each of these problems and associated movements has behind it deep, professional expertise. As individuals, we cannot know all of it, but liberal education prepares us to make sense of it as needed. To do that, we must discern truth and falsity, likely and unlikely, cogent and incoherent—and do so in awareness of our own limitations and biases.

Liberal education is good for democratic society at large, and liberal education is good for the economic well-being of individuals. More than that, it helps people live genuinely good and flourishing lives.

Dave Pollard has suggested that a flourishing life involves work that a person loves, does well, and that makes a positive difference in the world. Liberal education assists students with all three of those.[1] By addressing breadth of learning, liberal education helps students find things they love. In developing knowledge and skills, it helps them be effective at what they undertake to do. Liberal education informs one's understanding of how the world works and improves ethical reasoning abilities to help people make choices that improve the world. In these ways, universities' liberal education programs prepare our students to live rich, meaningful, flourishing lives.

Finally, some essays here address pedagogy, relationships, and collaboration. I have argued elsewhere that the best pedagogies depend on something like ethics of care.[2] Ethics of care focus not on abstract principles, but on relationships between persons and on meeting the particular needs of—in the pedagogical case—actual students. In one formulation, we recognize a need for care, take responsibility to meet that need, do the work of meeting it, and evaluate how well the care provided met the caring need.[3] A wealth of literature documents practices that are now well understood to improve student learning, agency, and well-being.[4] All of them require that instructors identify

---

[1] Dave Pollard, *Finding the Sweet Spot: The Natural Entrepreneur's Guide to Responsible, Sustainable Joyful Work* (White River Junction Vt.: Chelsea Green, 2008).
[2] Bruce Umbaugh "The Imperative of Care Over Contract," Association of American College and Universities Annual Meeting. Washington, D.C., 2020; Bruce Umbaugh, "Care for Students to Build Democratic Citizenship," Orlando, Florida: Association of General and Liberal Studies, 2019.
[3] Joan Tronto, "Creating Caring Institutions: Politics, Plurality, and Purpose," *Ethics and Social Welfare* 4 (2) (2010): 158–71. https://doi.org/10.1080/17496535.2010.484259.
[4] See, for example, George Kuh, "High-Impact Educational Practices: What They Are, Who Has Access to Them, and Why They Matter," Association of American Colleges and Universities, 2008, https://www.aacu.org/node/4084; Mary-Ann Winkelmes, David E.

students' needs and act in their interests—hallmarks of care ethics. Thinking about this in the context of the present volume, I recognize that care, too, depends on discernment, for if we are mistaken about students' needs and interests, then we will make poor and potentially destructive choices in our relationships with them. It's discernment all the way down.

The papers collected in this volume address the urgent imperative to think outside partisan identity or prejudice, to discern and utilize genuine expertise, and to draw on the disciplines, methods, and pedagogies of liberal education. They make clear that liberal education is of both private and public benefit. It improves students' economic prospects—a private good— as it also prepares them for citizenship. By cultivating discernment, it makes flourishing lives more readily attainable. Liberal education enhances both agency and caring, and so prepares one not just to be a worker (as students expect), or even a citizen (as governments might desire), but to be full persons who can understand and collaborate with diverse other persons to improve the world. It is easy to discern the value in all that.

References

Kuh, George. "High-Impact Educational Practices: What They Are, Who Has Access to Them, and Why They Matter," *Association of American Colleges and Universities*, September 30, 2008, https://www.aacu.org/node/4084.

Pascarella, Blaich. "Lessons from the Wabash National Study of Liberal Arts Education." *Change (New Rochelle, N.Y.)* 45, no. 2 (March 1, 2013): 6–15. https://doi.org/10.1080/00091383.2013.764257.

Pollard, Dave. *Finding the Sweet Spot: The Natural Entrepreneur's Guide to Responsible, Sustainable Joyful Work.* White River Junction Vt.: Chelsea Green, 2009.

Tronto, Joan. "Creating Caring Institutions: Politics, Plurality, and Purpose." Ethics and Social Welfare 4, no. 2 (July 1, 2010): 158–71. https://doi.org/10.1080/17496535.2010.484259.

Umbaugh, Bruce. "The Imperative of Care Over Contract." *Association of American College and Universities Annual Meeting.* Washington, D.C., 2020.

Umbaugh, Bruce. "Care for Students to Build Democratic Citizenship." Orlando, Florida: *Association of General and Liberal Studies*, 2019.

Copeland, Ed Jorgensen, Alison Sloat, Anna Smedley, Peter Pizor, Katharine Johnson, and Sharon Jalene, "Benefits (Some Unexpected) of Transparently Designed Assignments." *The National Teaching & Learning Forum*, 2015, https://doi.org/10.1002/ntlf.30029; Ernest Pascarella, and Charles Blaich, "Lessons from the Wabash National Study of Liberal Arts Education." *Change: The Magazine of Higher Learning*, 2013, https://doi.org/10.1080/00091383.2013.764257.

Winkelmes, Copeland. "Benefits (some Unexpected) of Transparently Designed Assignments." *The National Teaching & Learning Forum 24*, no. 4 (May 2015): 4–7. https://doi.org/10.1002/ntlf.30029.

Chapter 1

Introduction

Karim Dharamsi
Mount Royal University

and

David Ohreen
Mount Royal University

I

Perhaps our curiosity began with the first flickers of conscious awareness. We might well have come to recognize early in our natural history the world as being independent of our thoughts and that our unfettered desires may be thwarted by an uncooperative mind-independent order. In our coming of age with our capacities for language and symbol use, we likely came to understand other minds as having their own *independent* inner-lives—and that *potentially* the world for another person may well be conceptualized differently, that what they named and how it figured in their view of the world might be distinctively their own. Perhaps a confederation of interests and ontological commitments seemed less a challenge between those we recognized as part of our community, while, conversely, we came to understand the sometimes seemingly insurmountable challenges presented by the 'stranger', the 'outsider', *perhaps even the 'intruder.'*

From our first encounters with those unlike our compatriots, rational agents subject to different norms, we might have come to understand that our world is not shared—that our assumptions about the universalizability of our beliefs may well be naïve. Perhaps more importantly, we may have come to understand well that those we are now encountering may work on a similar epistemic assumption, namely, that their beliefs are universalizable, that differences are ultimately superficial. Our hopes for intersubjective agreement, objectivity, and *truth*—comprehensive ideals that regulate our understanding of the world and ourselves—may have been frustrated at the realization that a plurality of interests, sometimes incommensurable, were intrinsic to the human condition. With this watershed, we likely wondered then, as we wonder now, how well do our ideas represent the world *as it really is*? How can we ever know? Are all kinds of knowledge *the same*? Do the methods used to secure *truths* in biology resemble the methods used to secure the *truths* of politics? Are there many *truths*, appropriate to the questions being answered, or is there a single unified truth no matter the methods or *kinds of questions*?

For those committed to privileging their own thoughts and beliefs and the primacy of their own vocabularies, another question might have arisen then as it arises now: is there even a world *as it really is*? While answering these questions has often presented recalcitrant challenges to the philosopher, the scientist, and indeed, the theologian, these questions and our responses have helped shape our public vocabularies and subsequently, our diverse and complex public squares. Those who have maintained a comprehensive ideal have sometimes claimed answers to how our *thoughts* and *reality* are aligned and how truth and objectivity are not merely convenient (or, indeed, inconvenient) myths.

Of course, we are familiar with those in power defending self-serving myths—*or even explicit falsehoods*. Recurrent, sometimes these myths are consanguineous, fearfully erecting seemingly impervious borders in aid of rationing or inventing 'facts' and protecting loyalties. Such loyalties depend on thinking that 'my' group's beliefs align *better* with 'reality' than the alternatives available. And my fealty for the principles of this community over that is grounded largely on birthright and tradition. In this sense, it seems a commonplace for idiosyncratic, incommensurable worldviews to clash over our most fundamental values—ideas core to who we think we are and how we ought to be—*and live*.

In recent years, pseudo-scientific 'experts' have defended against vaccinations. Others with vested interests in a particular kind of economy have denied the relationship between human activities and the climate crisis. Sometimes such defenses have ignored territorial issues, both side-stepped claims to *national* sovereignty, and have defended such claims when convenient. Others, still, have elided histories of the less powerful and disadvantaged. Questions once thought under the jurisdiction of 'experts' in relevant fields are sometimes adjudicated in the court of public opinion, arguments dissected and reassembled on Twitter, Facebook, and Instagram. This court's pernicious intentions can be camouflaged by the pretense of respectability and the broad protection of free speech. Defective reasoning can be easily masked; favouring of hasty generalization, ad hominem, and the seductive forces of consensus has become a toolkit for political conformity and the possibility that a 'shared world' is not epistemically justifiable, but a political imperative to be imposed.

Entering this maelstrom of conflicting vocabularies and values presents significant challenges to those working in colleges and universities. It is also a challenge to those defending the efficacy of liberal learning. This collection of papers brings together academics who have been tasked to address the following question: can a liberal education make you a better discerner of truth? Their investigations represent different disciplinary methodologies and perspectives. This means that, taken together, these papers do not provide a signal unified view but attempt to capture the range and diversity of liberal learning in higher education.

II

Christian Smith argues that academic 'bullshit', the stuff of the academy's exclusive status, is eroding the foundations of academia itself. He writes, "BS is the university's loss of capacity to grapple with life's Big Questions, because of our crisis of faith in truth, reality, reason, evidence, argument, civility, and our common humanity."[1] According to Smith, the forces which seek to undermine higher education have ultimately usurped the pursuit of truth in favour of a chimera substituting for reality. No opinion or belief is considered to represent some objective reality or truth about the world; everything is in doubt and questionable—a world in which fake news and alternative facts hold equal intellectual weight as science and mathematics. It's not a hyperbole to suggest that reason itself is under attack. Birthers, flat earthers, holocaust deniers, and Internet trolls rejoice. But the forces that undermine academia's pursuit of truth, as Smith notes, "is mortally corrosive of our larger culture and politics."[2] The latter of which is best embodied by the lies of Donald Trump.

The election of the President of the United States in 2016 has brought to light the very idea of fake news or alternative facts into mainstream consciousness. For example, Trump's tweet on November 20, 2019, in which he claims to have opened a major Apple manufacturing plan in Austin, Texas for Mac Pro desktop computer, is not true…fake news; it's a lie. The plant opened in 2013, six years before the claim was made.[3] Or consider his claim, speaking at the International Association of Chiefs of Police in Chicago, that the city's murder rate has gone up since 2018 compared to the 10% drop across America. Again, the statement is fake news; it's a lie. Chicago's murder rate has decreased by 26%

---

[1] Christian Smith, "Higher Education Is Drowning in BS: And It's Mortally Corrosive to Society," *The Chronicle Review*, January 9, 2018, para. 3, https://www.chronicle.com/article/Higher-Education-Is-Drowning/242195.
[2] Ibid.
[3] Madlin Mekelburg, "Did Trump Open a 'Major Apple Manufacturing Plant' in Austin? No," *Politifact*, November 21, 2019, https://www.politifact.com/texas/statements/2019/nov/21/donald-trump/did-trump-open-apple-plant-austin-no/.

and the national murder rate decreased by 6.9%.[4] Since taking office and up to Dec 16, 2019, Trump has made 15,413 documented false or misleading claims and, according to critics, is leading the charge for the dissemination of misinformation and lies.[5] But Trump is not the only political leader to engage in the blurring of truth and reality, facts with fiction. The Brexit referendum and Russian denial of interfering in the 2016 U.S. election, has ushered in a 'post-truth leadership' style which places emotional appeals above facts as a means to winning the hearts and minds of voters.[6]

However, news conferences and stump speeches, can only spread lies so far; social media has become the vehicle of choice to spread misleading information. For example, a recent Facebook post on December 2, 2019 shows former President Barack Obama looking through the wrong end of binoculars. The photo produced numerous comments calling him a clown; others expressed dismay he was voted into office.[7] Of course, the photo was faked; doctored to intentionally create fake news, created no doubt to cast doubt on the President's intelligence. Facebook, Twitter, and other social media platforms allow sharing of content, ensuring that content can be consumed by all. Unfortunately, research shows fake news can spread farther and faster than accurate news stories. In part, this is because social media allows information to be sent with the click of a button.[8] Its sensational claims are also seductive.

But lies and fake news are just part of the problem. 'Bullshit' has also increasingly crept into our society. Unlike lies, says philosopher Harry Frankfurt, the bullshitter does not care whether their claims are true or false;

---

[4] Kiannah Sepeda-Miller, "Trump 'Dead Wrong' about the Change in Murders in Chicago," *Politifact*, 2019, https://www.politifact.com/illinois/statements/2019/oct/29/donald-trump/trump-dead-wrong-about-change-murders-chicago/.
[5] Greg Kessler, Salvador Rizzo, and Meg Kelly, "President Trump Has Made 15,413 False or Misleading Claims over 1,055 Days," *The Washington Post*, December 16, 2019, https://www.washingtonpost.com/politics/2019/12/16/president-trump-has-made-false-or-misleading-claims-over-days/.
[6] Spoelstra, Sverre. "The Truths and Falsehoods of Post-Truth Leaders." Leadership (London, England), July 9, 2020, 174271502093788–. https://doi.org/10.1177/1742715020937886; Rose, Jonathan. 2017. "Brexit, Trump, and Post-Truth Politics." Public Integrity 19 (6): 555–58. doi:10.1080/10999922.2017.1285540; Kristiansen, Lars J. et Kaussler, Bernd "The Bullshit Doctrine: Fabrications, Lies, and Nonsense in the Age of Trump *Informal Logic* 38, no. 1 (2018): 13–52. https://doi.org/10.22329/il.v38i1.5067.
[7] O'Rourke, "A Doctored Photo Appears to Show Obama Using Binoculars Wrong," *Politifact*, January 7, 2020, https://www.politifact.com/facebook-fact-checks/statements/2020/jan/07/viral-image/doctored-photo-appears-show-obama-using-binoculars/.
[8] Soroush Vosoughi, Deb Roy, and Sinan Aral, "The Spread of True and False News Online." *Science (New York, N.Y.)* 359, no. 6380 (March 9, 2018): 1146–51, https://doi.org/10.1126/science.aap9559.

they exaggerate and state nonsense to create a false belief in others either to sell something, vote for someone, prevent bad public relations, or have others think they know what they are doing or talking about, when they do not.[9] As Barry Eisler writes:

> There's so much bullshit, we don't even notice it anymore. Every movie, no matter how trivial, is a Major Motion Picture. Every business plan ever written boasts a World Class Management Team; every alliance is a Strategic Alliance. Toys r Us calls its customers "guests." ...Domestic prisons are called Correctional Facilities (are the prisoners "correctees"?). A detainee, on the other hand, is a prisoner we're holding indefinitely without charge, trial, or conviction...Nasty countries assassinate; we engage in sanitary Targeted Killings. Establishment is our word for what we call an oligarchy when it happens in Russia. Only dictatorships have show trials and kangaroo courts; we employ military commissions. Where others have tribes, we have factions. And of course, we don't torture, preferring enhanced interrogation, instead.[10]

From the pungent to the mild, bullshit stinks in many different ways but we all contribute to its stench, more or less, in our own way says Harry Frankfurt. But with the increased influence of social media, hackers and algorithms, which automatically recommend our reinforced prejudices, truth has become increasingly difficult to detect.

III

Despite the criticisms leveled against liberal education and predictions of its impending demise, its place in higher learning is important. In Part 1, "Roots of the Crisis," the authors explore how the supposed crisis in higher education began and why liberal education still plays an important role in public discourse.

In Part II, "Liberal Education: It's Value in a Culture of Fake News and Lies," the papers presented analyze liberal education's value to society and how such learning can attenuate our susceptibility to fake news, unjustified claims, and lies. Most importantly, they argue the essence of post-secondary education is to welcome debate and discussion in the search for truth—or, indeed, the

---

[9] Henry G Frankfurt, *On Bullshit* (Princeton, N.J: Princeton University Press, 2005).
[10] Barry Eisler, "Advertising Bullshit," The Heart of the Matter (blog), April 8, 2010, . http://barryeisler.blogspot.com/2010/04/advertising-bullshit.html.

truths revealed by our different disciplines and their methodological commitments.

In Part III, "Liberal Education: Pedagogical Approaches to Truth," the authors explore a number of pedagogical, practical ways by which a liberal education reveals *truths* from the vantage of a range of disciplinary perspectives, including chaos theory, architecture, and artistic imagery.

Part I: Liberal Education: Roots of the Crisis

Andrew Moore introduces the volume in Part 1. In Chapter 2, his paper "Metaphors for Higher Education in Our Public Discourse," explores the fake crisis associated with liberal education stems, in part, from the commodification of education itself. For Moore, universities have been co-opted by faulty wealth-based metaphors to undermine liberal education's broader importance. The comparison of education to financial investments is ubiquitous. Similar to individuals investing in stocks or bonds, government investments in education should get a return on investment at the least possible cost. That is, an education's worth is judged by how a graduate is employed or what kinds of skills she has to meet employer or economic demand. However, the focus on education to provide skills training or meet market demand undermines the more holistic values inculcated by liberal education itself. The financialization of universities turns them into mere vocational institutions and, as a result, diminishes the value they create in knowledge dissemination, creativity, critical thinking, and human inspiration, to name a few benefits. For Moore, liberal education helps people flourish, to make good decisions in life, and to become a well-educated person. However, disruptive forces are at work to reset the foundations of academia. Technological changes could allow professors to reach a wider audience beyond local institutions. After all, there is no point duplicating lectures in philosophy, say critics, if a professor can upload lectures to streaming services in order to reach a wider audience and make education more efficient and cost-effective. As Moore argues, education is more than mere content; it is relational, and students often need help making sense of ideas, concepts, and information and this means professors are crucial to interpret, guide, respond, and aid student learning. Education, says Moore, is more like a party; they are ends in themselves. Good parties, like education, do not serve any other ends than being good parties or being well-educated. Universities provide value because they enrich and expand the concept of human life beyond a mere job. To reduce the educational experience to content reduces their intrinsic value—and, indeed, their role in serving, in the broadest sense, the common good.

The commodification of post-secondary education rests, in part, on a false discourse. In Chapter 3, Jason Openo's paper "The Discourse of Crisis in Liberal

Education: Real Emergency or Fake News?" argues liberal education suffers from a discourse of crisis rather than a crisis itself. Neoliberalist forces have created an artificial crisis that suggests radical change must be had in order to save post-secondary education from itself. The crisis is underscored by the fact that many liberal arts degrees in North America are increasingly underfunded or are under threat of elimination because they are seen as having little economic value. The public perceives professors using arcane theory and jargon with no relevance to society, and stories abound with liberal arts graduates working in low-income and unfulfilling jobs with little future. But this, he argues, is just 'fake news.' Openo argues that students who graduate with a liberal education are doing just fine; they tend to be gainfully employed, have relatively high incomes, and, perhaps most importantly, are better poised to prosper in the new tech economy than many other professional degrees. *There is no crisis*. Policymakers have created a crisis in order to disrupt and alter post-secondary education in ways that are inimical to its aspirational goals. The consequences of such a 'made-crisis' are far-reaching. Addressing climate change, amongst other pressing social issues, will require a number of academic disciplines, including those represented by the sciences, our business majors, and the broad range of liberal arts. The artificial crisis has also created a loss of trust between society and academia to the point where experts are often disparaged as intellectual 'elites' or 'snobs' unworthy of being heard. Finally, the manufactured crisis perpetuates the myth that higher education is a waste of money and time. Solutions to the post-secondary crisis usually involve some kind of technology-as-savor approach. But, says Openo, we must resist this impulse. Technological solutions will inevitably undermine the liberal arts, rather than serve them, and ultimately short circuit the humanist's motives for a better world.

Part II: Liberal Education's Value in a Culture of Fake News and Lies

The supposed crisis in liberal education might merely be a manifestation of how smart algorithms, social media platforms, and tech giants, such as Google, undermine academia itself. Never before in human history has technology enabled us to access so much information instantaneously while sitting in our bathrobes having breakfast or sitting on a bus or debating with friends in a pub. And never before in human history have companies been able to collect so much personal information about us and our lives, which are then thrown back to us in self-justifying memes and videos to reinforce personal preferences. This, while companies rake in profits. Exposure to debate, discussion and opposing views has been usurped by fake news, alternative facts, and *bullshit* designed to echo what you already think.

In Chapter 4, "Detecting Bullshit in a Culture of Fake News and Lies," David Ohreen argues that lies and bullshit permeate our culture and liberal education can play an important role in detecting the truth. In a post-truth era of fake news, determining what is true can become increasingly difficult. Unfortunately, fake news culture has only become more prominent and exacerbated by the President of the United States. For Ohreen, Trump's lies and bullshit are emblematic of deeper cultural worries about the search for truth. From a philosophical point of view, Ohreen sees the difference between bullshit and lies as important and uses the work of Harry Frankfurt to make his case. In his book, *On Bullshit*, Frankfurt argues, in the liar's case, that he or she misrepresents their own mind; they misrepresent what they are talking about. If someone lies, say, about getting an *A* in philosophy class, they not only misrepresent their own mind—they know they did not get an *A*—but they also try to create a false belief in someone else. In the case of bullshit, the bullshitter need not create a false belief in the other's mind; that is not their intent. As Frankfurt explains, bullshit's "primary intention is…to give its audience a false impression concerning what is going on in the mind of the speaker."[11] The bullshitter, in other words, does not need to lie but merely has no regard for the truth value of their statements. Given the amount of lies and bullshit in society, Ohreen argues, liberal education is more important than ever. The hope rests in inculcating critical thinking into a broad liberal education program and in creating a healthy dose of scepticism in students' minds. Together, Ohreen believes liberal education can provide light against the darkness of bullshit and lies. Liberal education can help those who study it be better truth discerners—or at least better bullshit detectors.

In Chapter 5, Ronald Glasberg suggests the very idea of truth is up to question and debate. Glasberg argues in his paper, "How to 'Handle the Truth from a Liberal Arts Perspective," the very idea of what is 'true' or 'real' is up for grabs when it's interpreted from different personal, class, or cultural perspectives. If truth is an object of contestation, resolving it becomes an exercise in futility. Such futility is often fueled by erroneous attribution errors, which tend to make finding a way past an impasse seem impossible. Glasberg outlines four 'attributions of folly': ignorance or innocence due to being too young or old or because of lack of education; willful stupidity, whereby intellectual shortcuts are taken (*ad hominem* attacks) to circumvent the debate necessary to reach conclusions; using language or jargon (linguistic insularity) to obfuscate and confuse the debated issue; and finally, appealing to the spiritual, mystical or religious realm as a bridge to truth. Liberal education, says Glasberg, can play an important role in circumventing such attributive follies. With regard to

---

[11] Frankfurt, *On Bullshit*, 15.

ignorance, liberal education can play an important role in educating people. It can introduce them to the capacious range of human thought about our most fundamental concerns. And, by virtue of this, students can develop a better understanding of reality and thus grow as persons. Willful stupidity can be compromised by liberal arts educators guiding people the long-way-around by pointing out the key ideas, arguments, faulty reasoning, and logic to topics discussed. Understanding concepts and their etymology is the heart of many liberal arts traditions, such as philosophy; its analysis can shed critical insight into the origin of our ideas and how some create impervious barriers. As for those who appeal to mystical or spiritual truths, liberal education can be the catalyst to deepen a person's understanding by having mystical experiences (prayer, meditation, and the like) incorporated in curricular exercises. The 'ugly truth' is that social media, Facebook, Instagram, and the like, often create a reality which is preferred to our own messy lived truths of financial stress, work, and unhappy marriages. Liberal education, Glasberg argues, can be used to reveal and understand worldly truths if we are willing to broach them directly through literature, mythology, classic texts, and even hallucinogenic drug use. As Glasberg concludes, we must come to understand truth in all its dimensions.

However, the internet can spread lies quicker than truth; creating constellations of lies and a 'need for speed' over depth of argument and truth. In Chapter 6, in his paper "Liberal Education and Truth in the Ages of Plato's Culture Industry," James Cunningham presents arguments for liberal education as an antidote to our technological driven mass media culture where algorithms echo back our own voices and biases in an endless self-referential loop. Using Hans-Georg Gadamer's critical theory, Cunningham draws parallels between our current culture industry and the Greek Sophists who equally drowned out dissenting voices through the amplification of their voices to sway the crowd and get their way. Following Gadamer's analysis of the *Republic*, Cunningham demonstrates how Plato asked his students to look beyond appearances in order to seek the truth. By engaging students in the dialectic enterprise, they learned to make distinctions, to understand the meaning of things, and step towards a reality not distorted by sensible experience. But the most important distinction students must make is between the good and other forms of reality. Knowledge of the good is not only intellectual but also normative. The good, however, can only be known through a dialectic process of argument and debate. The dialectician can achieve the good only through testing themselves against the Sophist's claims. Whereas the Sophists care nothing of the good, the dialectician's possession of the good provides immunity against them. Similarly, like the Sophists, modern culture, driven by economic priorities and social media, equally cares nothing for the good or truth but only can be subdued through debate and dialogue. Moreover, the allegory of the cave is used by Cunningham to show how the current cultural industry is merely presenting shadows to its citizens. Social media posts and claims by the President of the United States are often shadows; a world of appearances which do not represent reality. Professors of liberal education must ask their students to seek the good/truth, for its own sake and for the sake of our society.

The shadows of truth are often fuel by propaganda. In Chapter 7, "Black Criminality: A Matter of 'Truth' and Our Acquiescence," Navneet Kumar outlines the harms such propaganda played in shaping the idea of black criminality. The result of which lead to specific polices that discriminated and thus incarcerated thousands of black citizens in the United States over decades of misinformation. Black criminality, as a work of propaganda, erodes the principles of liberal democracies and allows demagogues to use these values to achieve their undemocratic reality. For Kumar, the 1960's propaganda about the laziness of black youth fueled much of the discriminatory policies related to crime and its subsequent enforcement by police in racial neighbourhoods. In the 1970s, propaganda about black poverty and criminal drug use resulted in 'War on Drugs' policies by the Johnson administration. These policies, based on racialized notions of 'truth', produced discriminatory 'legislation and intensified incarceration and surveillance.' The consequences of such policies have been well documented, including significantly higher prison rates for blacks and repeal of various rights (housing, food stamps, voting, etc.) for individuals lucky enough to be released. In contemporary contexts, this kind of racialized demagogy is often spread by fake news claims, such as Muslims are terrorists, Mexicans are drug dealers, and immigrants are rapists. Liberal education, says Kumar, can help students understand such prejudicial policies and how they came into existence. Most importantly, liberal education can help students see the difference between at-issue-context and not-at-issue context. In other words, truths are often wrapped in fake or false claims which need to be unpacked, interrogated, and dissected to reveal their myths and related realities. Failure to separate myth from fact can lead to ill-informed or partially informed citizens and thus threaten democracy itself. Liberal education can be an important way to raise student consciousness, civic responsibility, and community engagement and activism as an antidote to widespread propaganda and fake news.

Part III: Liberal Education: Pedagogical Approaches to Truth

Pedagogical approaches to truth can be challenging and rewarding. Teaching is challenging because students often do not understand the methodology used or fail to grasp the objectives of the class. Teaching is rewarding because the student can come to new truths and realizations about the world around them and how the work they are doing in their classes helps them better understand the different modes of human experience shaping our understanding of both our natural and social worlds.

In Chapter 8, Deborah Forbes', "Complexity, Chaos, Collaboration: Untangling Strands of Truth; Teaching/Learning/Teaching in the 21st Century," argues for a particular pedagogical strategy based on collaboration, chaos and complexity. In this dynamic creative system, students use an interdisciplinary approach to sift through tangled and complex social issues to discover truths about the world and about themselves. Forbes thinks that linear approaches to liberal education often rely too heavily on mechanistic or instrumental approaches which sometimes miss essential elements necessary to our understanding and untangling complex issues. With the help from chaos and complexity theory, Forbes argues these can be used to foster a collaborative context within post-secondary classrooms to stimulate emergent learning. Using chaos/complexity theory as a theoretical foundation, Forbes argues that educators can use complexity as a means to illuminate for students the many uncertainties and simultaneities that do not fit comfortably into more conventional theories of learning. Complexity theory allows students to place greater emphasis on interpreting perspectives, which not only invites greater ambiguity and trans-disciplinary understanding than traditional educational approaches but can reveal important truths about today's most pressing social issues. Using student examples, Forbes demonstrates how active learning within a messy and non-linear classroom environment can help students untangle truth as a personal journey.

Finally, in Chapter 9, "Truth and Awe," Randolph suggests art and other imagery can be used to unlock truths for students. He argues that such truths are often not grasped by the conscious mind but require access to the unconscious. The unconscious mind reveals itself through imagery; it's so powerful it can elicit awe and change the perspective of the ego and in doing so reveal new truths about the world. As Randolph writes, unconscious manifestations of images can propagate new understandings of truth. And if these images are seen as symbolic, they can move us to a deeper holistic understanding and transformation of personality and, in some cases, whole cultures. The unconscious, for Randolph, is seen as an instrument of attaining truth because our conscious ego often perceives the world in restricted and polarizing ways. In this sense, the great artists and image creators are essential to revealing the truth because they often threaten conventional thinking, believes and values. Awe-inspiring images can move people beyond their narrow perspectives to reveal more holistic thinking, but this change might be difficult and painful for some but equally necessary. Liberal education, says Randolph, is the storehouse of images; their study, analysis, and critique by students can be painful, especially if cherished ideals or values are challenged or called into question. Liberal education can provide important contextualized understanding to students as they work towards uncovering unconscious truths to their conscious selves.

The editors would like to thank all those who have contributed to this volume and the reviewers who have commented on the papers.

References

Eisler, Barry. "Advertising Bullshit." The Heart of the Matter (blog), April 8, 2010, http://barryeisler.blogspot.com/2010/04/advertising-bullshit.html.

Frankfurt, Henry G. *On Bullshit*. Princeton, N.J: Princeton University Press, 2005.

Kessler, Greg, Salvador Rizzo, and Meg Kelly. "President Trump Has Made 15,413 False or Misleading Claims over 1,055 Days." *The Washington Post*, December 16, 2019. https://www.washingtonpost.com/politics/2019/12/16/president-trump-has-made-false-or-misleading-claims-over-days/.

Mekelburg, Madlin. "Did Trump Open a 'Major Apple Manufacturing Plant" in Austin? No.'" *Politifact*, November 21, 2019. https://www.politifact.com/texas/statements/2019/nov/21/donald-trump/did-trump-open-apple-plant-austin-no/.

O'Rourke. "A Doctored Photo Appears to Show Obama Using Binoculars Wrong." *Politifact*, January 7, 2020. https://www.politifact.com/facebook-fact-checks/statements/2020/jan/07/viral-image/doctored-photo-appears-show-obama-using-binoculars/.

Sepeda-Miller, Kiannah. "Trump 'Dead Wrong' about the Change in Murders in Chicago." *Politifact*, 2019. https://www.politifact.com/illinois/statements/2019/oct/29/donald-trump/trump-dead-wrong-about-change-murders-chicago/.

Smith, Christian. "Higher Education Is Drowning in BS: And It's Mortally Corrosive to Society." *The Chronicle Review*, January 9, 2018. https://www.chronicle.com/article/Higher-Education-Is-Drowning/242195.

Spoelstra, Sverre. "The Truths and Falsehoods of Post-Truth Leaders." *Leadership (London, England)*, July 9, 2020, 174271502093788–. https://doi.org/10.1177/1742715020937886.

Vosoughi, Soroush, Deb Roy, and Sinan Aral. "The Spread of True and False News Online." *Science (New York, N.Y.)* 359, no. 6380 (March 9, 2018): 1146–51. https://doi.org/10.1126/science.aap9559.

Chapter 2

Metaphors for Higher Education in Our Public Discourse

Andrew Moore
St Thomas University

Abstract

The public discourse surrounding higher education has become infested by wrongheaded metaphors and unimaginative analogies. These bad comparisons stultify our thinking about education, diminishing our sense of what education could or should be. This paper examines the figurative language deployed in the public discourse around education. It includes close readings of the metaphors of "investment" found in provincial government policy papers. It also interrogates the suggestion—found frequently in newspaper and magazine op-eds—that higher education is "ripe for disruption," a popular (though jarring) metaphor borrowed from Silicon Valley start-ups. I will demonstrate how our lazy and unthinking reliance on these ready-to-hand metaphors negatively affects the way we talk about educational priorities and goals. While the bulk of this paper will be taken up with analyses of "public texts," that is government documents and commentary pieces, throughout, I will also be drawing from works of literature by Homer, Virginia Woolf, Lorna Goodison, and Haruki Murakami in order to illustrate how figurative language shapes our thinking. Ultimately, I hope to contribute to the search for an alternative figurative language that might help us foster a healthier, more humane, and more liberal understanding of higher education.

Keywords: metaphors, higher education, public discourse, liberal education

***

Introduction

When we talk about universities — the benefits they confer on society, as well as the challenges they face — what kinds of comparisons present themselves? What metaphors, similes, and analogies do we rely on to make sense of the educational process? What images do we draw upon to help explain what universities do, or ought to do? Here I would like to examine certain tendencies in our public discourse. I want to explore some of the metaphors that figure prominently in discussions about higher education. My argument is that our educational discourse has become overrun by faulty comparisons that threaten to stultify our thinking and diminish our sense of what higher education could or should be. A set of very specific metaphors have become pervasive both in government policy documents and in the popular media. Over and over again, as I will illustrate, higher education is compared to a financial investment, and (usually unfavorably) to the 'disruptive' technologies emerging from Silicon Valley. The causes of this figurative consensus in our public discourse are no doubt varied and complex. However, we can say with certainty that these metaphors are premised upon and designed to instantiate a particular vision of higher education in which the university is understood to be, above all else, a generator of wealth. The metaphors that dominate our public discourse evidence a widespread commitment to prosperity as the highest human good; universities, we are told, must operate with singular focus in service of that good.

Metaphors are never neutral, especially when they are mobilized in discussions about public policy and government funding. Figurative language does not merely illuminate or explicate, it also generates and shapes. As David Ritchie notes, an educational metaphor "suggests and reinforces a distinct way of framing higher education, a distinct set of assumptions about higher education, and a distinct way of interpreting assertions about higher education."[1] In particular, the use of business metaphors in higher education contexts, as Judith Bessant argues, "makes other commercial metaphors and thus market-based solutions seem logical, and in many instances the only sensible option."[2] The purpose of this paper is to examine some of the most popular images of higher education in our public discourse, to explore their premises and their implications. I will explore how a figurative consensus in our public discourse on higher education constrains and restricts the ways we think and talk about universities. In particular, I will demonstrate how the logic of business and technology metaphors privilege and advance a very narrow conception of higher education. We will see how these metaphors consistently reinforce the idea that universities exist to generate wealth; the same images

---

[1] David Ritchie, "Monastery or Economic Enterprise: Opposing or Complementary Metaphors of Higher Education?," *Metaphor and Symbol* 17, no. 1 (2002): 46, https://doi.org/10.1207/S15327868MS1701_4.
[2] Judith Bessant, "Dawkins' Higher Education Reforms and How Metaphors Work in Policy Making," *Journal of Higher Education Policy and Management* 24, no. 1 (2002): 94, https://doi.org/10.1080/13600800220130789.

discredit and marginalize more expansive or holistic models of education, such as liberal education.

This paper builds upon an existing body of scholarship on the metaphors that circulate throughout and around higher education. There is a robust scholarship on pedagogical metaphors, examining how educators can use figurative language to help them develop their own teaching practice.[3] Other studies move beyond the classroom, exploring, for example, what the metaphors that circulate among faculty and administrators on a particular campus can tell us about institutional culture, or what the metaphors used by government officials reveal about policy agendas.[4] My analysis here will focus on the prevalence of certain educational metaphors in government documents and in the media. I will examine the premises and implications of these comparisons. I will also try to unsettle these images with some alternative images of my own. By demonstrating how alternative metaphorical formulations help us to think and talk about educational priorities differently, I hope to suggest how we might, as a public, re-evaluate our priorities with respect to universities.

---

[3] Anna Bager-Elsborg and Linda Greve, "Establishing a Method for Analysing Metaphors in Higher Education Teaching: A Case from Business Management Teaching," *Higher Education Research & Development*, 2017, 1–14, https://doi.org/10.1080/07294360.2017.1327945; Lynnette B Erickson and Stefinee Pinnegar, "Consequences of Personal Teaching Metaphors for Teacher Identity and Practice," *Teachers and Teaching* 23, no. 1 (2017): 106–22, https://doi.org/10.1080/13540602.2016.1203774; Emily O Gravett, "'Who Am I?': The Biblical Moses as a Metaphor for Teaching," *Teaching Theology & Religion* 18, no. 2 (2015): 159–69, https://doi.org/10.1111/teth.12276; Elizabeth Claire Reimer and Louise Whitaker, "Exploring the Depths of the Rainforest: A Metaphor for Teaching Critical Reflection," *Reflective Practice* 20, no. 2 (2019): 175–86, https://doi.org/10.1080/14623943.2019.1569510; Cheryl J Craig, Jeongae You, and Suhak Oh, "Pedagogy through the Pearl Metaphor: Teaching as a Process of Ongoing Refinement," *Journal of Curriculum Studies* 49, no. 6 (2017): 757–81, https://doi.org/10.1080/00220272.2015.1066866; Elisabeth Wegner and Matthias Nückles, "Knowledge Acquisition or Participation in Communities of Practice? Academics' Metaphors of Teaching and Learning at the University," *Studies in Higher Education* 40, no. 4 (n.d.): 624,643, http://www.tandfonline.com/doi/abs/10.1080/03075079.2013.842213; Diane M Enerson, "Mentoring as Metaphor: An Opportunity for Innovation and Renewal," *New Directions for Teaching and Learning*, no. 85 (2001): 7.

[4] Robert Gregory and George Noblit, "The 'Coal Miner' University: Explorations into Metaphors on Education Organizations," *The High School Journal* 82, no. 1 (1998): 43; Nidia Bañuelos, "Dangerous Metaphors: The Consequences of Treating Higher Education Like a Consumer Good," *Change: The Magazine of Higher Learning* 51, no. 1 (2019): 14–21, https://doi.org/10.1080/00091383.2019.1547064.

Education as Investment

The most common trope we see in the public discourse on education is the language of financial investment. We talk about students 'investing' in their education, and governments talk about making 'investments' in colleges and universities. These comparisons of education to investment are so common that we may no longer even recognize them as comparisons at all. Politicians seem almost compelled to justify government expenditures on education by describing them as investments. For example, in a press release issued on April 10, 2018, the Government of Saskatchewan described how the new budget "reflects the government's plan to invest in programs and services Saskatchewan people value."[5] The release redeploys the investment image in its conclusion: "Over more than a decade, the province has invested $9.1 billion in post-secondary institutions and student supports."[6] Similar language can be found in a press release issued by the government of New Brunswick on May 11, 2017 announcing "funding to support post-secondary education students."[7] The announcement begins by stating, "The provincial government will invest $3.4 million to help more students access post-secondary education."[8] This lead is followed by a statement from the former premier of the province, Brian Gallant, "Education is the key to unlocking a prosperous economy and an even better quality of life here in New Brunswick... Investments in education and training help increase the competitiveness of New Brunswick businesses and industries."[9]

The comparison of education to a financial investment is not absurd. Education is like an investment insofar as it produces benefits. Governments or individuals who spend money on education should get something valuable in return. And it is true that the benefits received from a good education are worth more than the money governments and students spend. However, we have come to use the language of investment so reflexively and unthinkingly that we now assume the comparison is even more exact. We speak as if the

---

[5] Government of Saskatchewan, "Stable Funding for Post-Secondary Institutions to Keep Saskatchewan On Track," accessed October 28, 2019, https://www.saskatchewan.ca/government/news-and-media/2018/april/10/budget-advanced-education.

[6] We should note the peculiarity of the phrase "over more than a decade." "More than a decade" could mean 11 years or 101 years; 9.1 billion divided over 11 years may be a significant amount but divided over 15 or 21 years the number would be significantly smaller.

[7] Office of the Premier and Post-Secondary Education, Training and Labour, "Government Announces Funding to Support Post-Secondary Education Students," 2017, https://www2.gnb.ca/content/gnb/en/news/news_release.2017.05.0684.html.

[8] Ibid.

[9] Ibid.

benefits produced by university education, both for the student and the government, will be exclusively financial. We hardly ever speak of cultural, political, intellectual, or moral benefits. Consequently, we try to justify the cost of tuition on the grounds that students will get more money back in the future once they have a high-paying job, that is, a 'return on investment.'

A brief survey of some government policy documents further illustrates how common the image of education-as-investment has become in our public discourse. In 2013, Ontario's government published *Ontario's Differentiation Policy Framework for Post-secondary Education*, the first sentence of which is, "Over the past decade, the Government of Ontario has increased investment in post-secondary education significantly."[10] The *Manitoba Fiscal Performance Review* prepared by KPMG in 2017 also begins with a statement on investment: "Investing in education benefits not only the present day student, it is an investment in our province's collective future."[11] The 2010 *Report on the University System in Nova Scotia* repeatedly describes students as investors stating, "The economic returns to the individual student from investment in a university education are high and rising."[12] However, the report cautions us that "the value of a university education" needs to be measured against the student's "investment of both direct financial resources and forgone income."[13] Predictably, these policy papers on education are nearly unanimous in their proposed solutions to the challenge of funding post-secondary education: make funding contingent on graduation rates, and specifically on graduating people who work in the specific fields that the current government thinks will benefit the economy most immediately—return on investment.[14] This new formulation means that money will go into post-secondary institutions on the condition that a certain number of students will come out with the right kind of skills; skills thought likely to boost economic productivity. Such policies obviously prioritize a vocational education rather than, say, a civic, moral, or holistic education. By this logic, forms of education that do not obviously and immediately improve a province's short-term economic outlook are less deserving of funding than those projects that promise quick gains. This conception of education has become so dominant that even universities

---

[10] Government of Ontario Ministry of Training, Colleges and Universities. "Ontario's Differentiation Policy Framework for Post-secondary Education," 2013, http://www.tcu.gov.on.ca/pepg/publications/PolicyFramework_PostSec.pdf.
[11] Ibid.
[12] Tim O'Neil, Report on the University System in Nova Scotia, 2010, 5.
[13] Ibid., 81.
[14] Mike Crawley, "How the Ford Government Will Decide on University, College Funding," *CBC*, May 2019. In 2019 the Ford Government in Ontario announced they planned to tie post-secondary funding to employment outcomes for graduates among other metrics.

themselves have become accustomed to speaking of education as an investment. For instance, Universities Canada, a lobby group that describes itself as "the voice of Canadian universities" has adopted investment rhetoric.[15] In a 2018 document prepared for the House of Commons Standing Committee on Finance entitled, *Investing in Talent to Drive a Prosperous, Inclusive and Innovative Canadian Economy*, Universities Canada argues that "investments in skills training will build a Canadian economy that thrives in the face of automation and digitization," and "investment in work-integrated learning provides students with the skills needed to build Canada's economy."[16] Government fixation on financial metaphors has thus prompted universities themselves to speak of their missions and purposes in terms of return on investment.

As the image of the university as wealth-generator spreads, our sense of what universities are and can be is diminished. As Italian philosopher Nuccio Ordine writes, our fixation on "exclusively economic interest," threatens to destroy "the memory of the past, the classical disciplines and languages, education, free research, imagination, art, critical thinking, and the civil horizon that ought to inspire all human activity."[17] Most distressingly, the emphasis on investment subordinates the ends of higher education to the ends of the private sector, as if to suggest that corporate interests ought to dictate what citizens should study. However, if we can recognize and clearly articulate the limitations of these images—students are investors, education is an investment—we might be able to free ourselves of their grip. We can more clearly recognize the limitations and inadequacy of financial imagery if we apply the language of investment to another field of human endeavour.

Take, for example, parenting. What is the role of a parent? What are the parent's responsibilities? How can we tell if a person is a good or bad parent? What metrics can we use to measure success? The answers to these questions are obviously complicated but permit me to engage in a thought experiment.

---

[15] Universities Canada, "About Us," accessed May 30, 2019, https://www.univcan.ca/about-us.

[16] Universities Canada, "Investing in Talent to Drive a Prosperous, Inclusive and Innovative Canadian Economy," 2018, https://www.univcan.ca/media-room/publications. In fairness, Universities Canada's proposal to the House Finance Committee does advocate a wide variety of policies which will benefit students, such as increasing funds for study abroad opportunities and increasing supports for Indigenous students. However, the document consistently claims that such initiatives are good because they will reap economic benefits for Canada. Variations of the word 'invest' appear no fewer than 35 times in the five-page document.

[17] Nuccio Ordine, *The Usefulness of the Useless*, ed. Alasair McEwen (Philadelphia: Paul Dry Books, 2017), 4.

Suppose we were to say that the only meaningful measure of parental success was prosperity. Our position will be that a person is a good parent if her children grow up to make $70,000 a year or more. In fact, if they make more—say, six or seven figures—then she must be a very good parent. If we applied only this metric to parenting, how might it pervert and distort our sense of the activity? If we only cared about producing children who grew up to make high salaries, how might it alter parenting practice? What would strike us immediately is the inefficiency of parent-child relationships, the wasted time reading nonsensical stories, playing games, and visiting with older relatives. How, after all, do these activities prepare children for success in the digital economy? Are there ways we could streamline childrearing, and make parenting more productive? How, for example, might we link our children's activities more directly to the needs of the provincial economy? Parents invest an incredible amount of resources into their young. How can they be sure they are going to receive the highest possible return on investment?

The point of this little exercise is merely to demonstrate the absurdity of taking a complex and fundamental human activity like parenting and describing it as if its only purpose were to increase prosperity. If one were to focus all of her attention as a parent on producing the kind of skilled workers most admired by the New Brunswick Minister for Post-secondary Education, Training and Labor that would be ridiculous, perhaps even abusive. In the context of parenting, we recognize this intuitively. But in the context of education, we have become confused.

As a second thought experiment, let us compare higher education to parenting rather than investing. If we compare education to parenting, other attributes of the process are illuminated. A whole new set of priorities and standards start to suggest themselves. Prosperity is, of course, one of the aspirations of parenting. We all would like our children to be financially secure and self-sufficient. But there are other goods we desire and seek for our children. We want them to learn to foster good friendships, to pursue their passions and develop their talents—even if those passions and talents do not correspond to the current fashions and interests of society. We want our children to make good decisions in love, to be thoughtful and engaged citizens. Good parents raise their children to deal with heartbreak, professional failure, stress, and grief. If we take good parenting, as opposed to prudent investing as the model for education, a different framework for education emerges. The case for liberal education appears far stronger, and the case for a strictly vocational education appears far weaker.

Liberal education, like parenting, is about helping a person to flourish in a fuller sense. It is a transformative process that involves encouragement, attention, discipline, enticement, instruction, and inspiration. It takes time.

The end result of both processes—liberal education and parenting—is not merely a taxpayer, but a more complete person. The purpose of parenting is not only to satisfy the needs of the provincial economy, and the purpose of education is not only to fill cubicles. By comparing education to parenting we begin to see the potential for a university to produce a more self-aware, resilient, capable, happy person; not just someone with a job.

Education is Ripe for Disruption

The idea that higher education is 'ripe for disruption' circulates frequently in the media.[18] A 2012 *Globe and Mail* column by Margaret Wente, for example, invoked the image in the title: "We're ripe for a great disruption in higher education."[19] A 2013 piece for *Forbes* written by Naveen Jain, had a similar headline: "Rethinking Education: Why Our Education System is Ripe for Disruption."[20] In 2014, the *Wall Street Journal*'s website likewise queried, "Is the College Model Ripe for Disruption?"[21] A 2016 editorial in *The American Interest* answered in the affirmative, echoing the assessment of a multinational investment firm, "Goldman Sachs: Higher Ed Ripe for Disruption."[22] Just so, in 2017 in the now-defunct *Weekly Standard*, Andy Smarick began an article with

---

[18] Léo Charbonneau, "The Top Three Hoary Metaphors of the Higher-Ed Apocalypse," *University Affairs*, June 5, 2012, https://www.universityaffairs.ca/opinion/margin-notes/the-top-three-hoary-metaphors-of-the-higher-ed-apocalypse. In 2012 Léo Charbonneau identified several metaphors commonly associated with "the higher-ed apocalypse." The notion of a "Great Disruption" was among them.

[19] Margaret Wente, "We're Ripe for a Great Disruption in Higher Education," *The Globe and Mail*, February 4, 2012, https://www.theglobeandmail.com/opinion/were-ripe-for-a-great-disruption-in-higher-education/article543479/. This piece was updated on May 3, 2018.

[20] Naveen Jain, "Rethinking Education: Why Our Education System Is Ripe for Disruption," *Forbes*, March 24, 2013, https://www.forbes.com/sites/naveenjain/2013/03/24/disrupting-education/#2fd90fd623ef.

[21] Jason Bellini, "Is the College Model Ripe for Disruption?," *The Wall Street Journal*, November 28, 2014, https://www.wsj.com/video/is-the-college-model-ripe-for-disruption/ 0F344350-3A44-4C7B-9F45-B9CF3972555F.html.

[22] "Goldman Sachs: Higher Ed Ripe for Disruption," The American Interest, accessed January 6, 2016, https://www.the-american-interest.com/2016/01/06/goldman-sachs-higher-ed-ripe-for-disruption; Robert D. Boroujerdi and Christopher Wolf, "Emerging Theme Radar: What If I Told You…," *Goldman Sachs*, December 2, 2015, https://www.goldmansachs.com/insights/pages/macroeconomic-insights-folder/what-if-i-told-you/report.pdf.

the sentence, "It's widely accepted that traditional colleges and universities are ripe for some kind of disruption."[23]

This image of ominous ripeness is a sort of mixed metaphor. It appears at first to be a vegetative or horticultural metaphor. Higher education is here likened to a fruit or vegetable. 'Ripeness' suggests a kind of natural readiness. However, in contemporary business-speak ripeness does not indicate the time for harvesting or eating, but for 'disruption.' The image takes a sudden turn. Colleges and universities have reached a point of readiness that culminates in some sort of fracturing or agitation. This language of vegetative crisis comes to us from the technology sector. The idea of economic 'disruption' was coined by Clayton M. Christensen, Professor at Harvard Business School. In his book *The Innovator's Dilemma*, he writes:

> Disruptive technologies bring to a market a very different value proposition than had been available previously. Generally, disruptive technologies underperform established products in mainstream markets. But they have other features that a few fringe (and generally new) customers value. Products based on disruptive technologies are typically cheaper, simpler, smaller, and frequently, more convenient to use.[24]

A disruptive technology is a technology that wholly upends the old way of doing things and establishes new orders and expectations. Netflix's video streaming service is a good example of such a technology. Netflix disrupted the home entertainment industry, effectively destroyed the video rental business, and challenged the dominance of traditional cable companies. Uber, the ride-sharing service, has similarly disrupted the taxi industry. Airbnb, which allows property owners to rent out private residential spaces to travellers has disrupted the hotel industry. In the wake of such successes, established industries and institutions have become targets of tech start-ups as ambitious entrepreneurs seek out fields that are 'ripe for disruption.' Higher education has become a prime target because universities attract large amounts of both public and private money. Tech start-ups hope that by outmaneuvering traditional universities they can redirect the flow of that money—including taxpayer money—in their direction. Essential to this strategy is a particular

---

[23] Andy Smarick, "Mitch Daniels Shows How Higher-Ed Reform Can Be Entrepreneurial," *The Weekly Standard,* May 2, 2017, https://www.weeklystandard.com/andy-smarick/mitch-daniels-shows-how-higher-ed-reform-can-be-entrepreneurial.
[24] Clayton M. Christensen, *The Innovator's Dilemma* (New York: Harper Business, 2011), xvii.

narrative about what universities are and what classrooms are like. In particular, we frequently see comparisons of traditional university classrooms to outmoded or arcane media technologies. This 2018 column in *The Boston Globe* by Kenneth Rogoff provides a representative example:

> [W]hat sense does it make for each college in the United States to offer its own highly idiosyncratic lectures on core topics like freshman calculus, economics, and US history, often with classes of 500 students or more?… At least for large-scale introductory courses, why not let students everywhere watch highly produced recordings by the world's best professors and lecturers, much as we do with music, sports, and entertainment?[25]

A slightly modified version of this narrative can be found in a 2015 piece for *The Guardian*, in which Donald Clark writes with contempt of the traditional lecture-based classroom: "Imagine if a movie were shown only once. Or your local newspaper was read out just once a day in the local square. Or novelists read their books out once to an invited audience. That's face-to-face lectures for you: it's that stupid."[26] Just as Blockbuster Video was an inefficient video streaming service, the traditional university classroom is here imagined as an inefficient education streaming service. However, this comparison of a university to an 'outmoded medium' depends on the reduction of education to 'content,' which can be delivered faster or more reliably in a digital, pre-recorded package. Here again we can see the potential dangers in figurative language. Attending a lecture is something like attending a movie or watching a documentary. However, education cannot simply be understood as content. The analogy falls apart under scrutiny. For starters, education is relational. While university faculty may teach subjects or lessons (biology, Canadian history, etc.), faculty also think of themselves as teaching students. What is happening in the classroom is not simply an exchange of information. Students are not simply 'downloading' from a professor a lesson on Descartes, for instance. If that were the case, students could just read books. Libraries would have made universities redundant long ago. Instead we have a common belief that people need help—human help—in order to sort through information and learn how to test its validity. Students need the guidance of teachers to

---

[25] Kenneth Rogoff, "When Will Technology Disrupt Higher Education?," *The Boston Globe*, February 9, 2018, https://www.bostonglobe.com/opinion/2018/02/09/when-will-technology-disrupt-higher-education/RDqq0tsJufA0dG2VEiRFgI/story.html.

[26] Donald Clark, "Ten Reasons We Should Ditch University Lectures," *The Guardian*, May 15, 2014, https://www.theguardian.com/higher-education-network/blog/2014/may/15/ten-reasons-we-should-ditch-university-lectures.

understand how to judge, evaluate, and critique the 'content' of a course. Teaching, properly speaking, is not merely the oral dissemination of information to a group of people sitting in chairs; teaching involves interaction between educators and learners. It is a process through which the educator develops the capacities and abilities of the learner. Education is built on a relationship and depends for its success on factors like trust, respect, attentiveness, responsiveness, and compassion. Teaching and learning are activities that work best when we share the same time and space. Recall our parenting thought experiment from before. Can parenting be performed remotely? Could we reduce the number of parents so that all children could simply access—on demand—video recordings of life lessons or words of encouragement whenever they needed? Such technology would no doubt make parenting less labour intensive, but it would also damage the child. Just as parenting cannot be reduced to job-training, education cannot be reduced to content.

The advocates of disruption also posit a false dilemma, a fictitious either/or: a choice between stadium-sized lecture halls filled with bored-stiff students on the one hand and, on the other hand, exciting, highly responsive apps that are personalized, faster, cheaper, and accessible to anyone anywhere at any time. Advocates of disruption neglect to mention the seminar; they downplay the virtues of in-class discussion; they highlight the problem of dull teachers without ever addressing the effects of inspiring, caring, enthusiastic teachers. And they do not acknowledge the importance of mentorship in class, the conversations that happen in the hall after class, or the questions fielded during office hours. Consider, for example, a 2012 column for *Forbes*, by Bill Fischer titled, "Disruption: Coming Soon to a University Near You" in which Fischer denounces traditional universities for their, "impractical learning, out-of-touch faculty, exorbitant tuitions, time-wasting requirements and diminishing probabilities of employment."[27] Such rhetoric is necessary to persuade decision-makers—taxpayers, students, and members of government—that universities are a kind of outmoded technology, dead-weight that should be innovated out of existence. However, the argument that universities can be easily replaced by apps is only believable if we subscribe to a reductive account of what education actually is. Universities do face substantial challenges: financial, structural, demographic, and pedagogical challenges. Those challenges are real. But it is a mistake to assume that all of those problems are

---

[27] Bill Fischer, "Disruption: Coming Soon to a University Near You," *Forbes*, January 19, 2012, para. 1, https://www.forbes.com/sites/billfischer/2012/01/19/disruption-coming-soon-to-a-university-near-you/#cf72194239cb.

technical—or rather technological problems. Not everything in life can be hacked.

Moreover, we should not simply accept the premise that technological innovation is an unqualified good, that it increases efficiency without any associated costs. In other arenas, we can see how the adoption of new technologies has produced many unintended and unwanted consequences. A few decades on, it is becoming clear how the public has been served by the replacement of local newspapers with online media. Is the public better informed now that we have access to the Internet? Surely information is more available than ever before, but there is also a huge amount of misinformation. Some of that misinformation is spread unintentionally; some of it is spread deliberately by interested parties. In the wake of the 2016 United States Presidential election we are grappling with the problem of 'fake news' and more specifically the problem of hostile foreign governments using social media in order to manipulate the outcomes of democratic elections.[28] The record of the Internet and its ability to disseminate knowledge is, at best, checkered. Similarly, researchers are only now beginning to grapple with the consequences of our dependence on mobile phones.[29] New technologies often come with unanticipated consequences, and before we decide to redesign every classroom, and higher education itself, to better serve the digital economy, we should consider carefully the 'terms and conditions' to which we are agreeing, and the possible effects of the transformation.

---

[28] Shane Harris, Ellen Nakashima, and Craig Timberg, "Through Email Leaks and Propaganda, Russians Sought to Elect Trump, Mueller Finds," *The Washington Post*, April 2019; Scott Shane, "These Are the Ads Russia Bought on Facebook in 2016," *The New York Times*, November 2017; Jane Mayer, "How Russia Helped Swing the Election for Trump," *The New Yorker*, September 2018; John Swaine, "Russian Propagandists Targeted African Americans to Influence 2016 US Election," *The Guardian*, December 2018.

[29] Joshua Harwood et al., "Constantly Connected – The Effects of Smart-Devices on Mental Health," *Computers in Human Behavior* 34, no. C (2014): 267–72, https://doi.org/10.1016/j.chb.2014.02.006; Andree Hartanto and Hwajin Yang, "Is the Smartphone a Smart Choice? The Effect of Smartphone Separation on Executive Functions," *Computers in Human Behavior* 64 (2016): 329–36, https://doi.org/ 10.1016/j.chb.2016.07.002; Bill Thornton et al., "The Mere Presence of a Cell Phone May Be Distracting," *Social Psychology* 45, no. 6 (2014): 479–88, https://doi.org/10.1027/1864-9335/a000216; Joël Billieux, Martial Van Der Linden, and Lucien Rochat, "The Role of Impulsivity in Actual and Problematic Use of the Mobile Phone," *Applied Cognitive Psychology* 22, no. 9 (2008): 1195–1210, https://doi.org/10.1002/acp.1429.

Education as Party

I would like to conclude with a very brief reading of Virginia Woolf's stream-of-consciousness novel *Mrs. Dalloway*. Published in 1925, the novel is primarily concerned with the pursuit of meaning in human life. More specifically, it explores how we can defend or justify human activities that do not serve obviously utilitarian ends. What is the point, exactly, of buying flowers or discussing emigration over tea? Throughout her career Woolf demonstrated how certain value systems—capitalist, imperialist, and patriarchal—foster priorities and goals that are ultimately destructive to human life.[30] "The patriarchal code; the world of finance and acquisition; the Empire: all these three [...] are intimately linked in Woolf's writings and in her analysis of the world."[31] In *Mrs. Dalloway*, Woolf also explores alternative value systems, ways of justifying human activities that are not directed towards acquisition and power. Her novel, I believe, helps us to think about modes of human life that do not depend on profit. Thus, *Mrs. Dalloway* can provide us with pathways by which we might think ourselves out of the restrictive metaphors which dominate our public discourse on higher education.

Mrs. Dalloway is set in London a few years after the end of the Great War. The whole of the novel takes place in a single day; however, over the course of the story we slip from one character's consciousness into another, and we are exposed to a plethora of memories and reminiscences. Woolf's narrative technique is used to special effect with the character Septimus Smith, a WWI veteran suffering from shellshock, or what we would now recognize as PTSD. Septimus is a broken man whose suicide "is a direct result of his inability to communicate his experiences to others and thereby give those experiences meaning and purpose."[32] The novel's main character, however, is Clarissa Dalloway, a fifty-something London housewife married to a parliamentary back-bencher named Richard. Clarissa spends most of the novel preparing to host a party. She shops and gets her dress ready; she bumps into friends on the

---

[30] Jane Marcus, *Virginia Woolf and the Language of Patriarchy* (Bloomington: Indiana University Press, 1987); Naomi Black, *Virginia Woolf as Feminist* (Ithaca: Cornell University Press, 2004); Kathryn. Simpson, *Gifts, Markets and Economies of Desire in Virginia Woolf* (London: Palgrave Macmillan UK, 2009), https://doi.org/10.1057/9780230228436.

[31] Helen Carr, "Virginia Woolf, Empire and Race," in *The Cambridge Companion to Virginia Woolf*, ed. Susan Sellers, 2nd ed. (Cambridge, MA: Cambridge University Press, 2010), 197.

[32] Karen DeMeester, "Trauma, Post-Traumatic Stress Disorder, and Obstacles to Postwar Recovery in Mrs. Dalloway," in *Virginia Woolf and Trauma: Embodied Texts*, ed. Suzette Henke and David Eberly (New York: Pace University Press, 2007), 77.

street and confirms their attendance. Amidst these preparations, Clarissa is herself bothered by memories of an old boyfriend named Peter Walsh (another one of the novel's main characters):

> But Peter—however beautiful the day might be, and the trees and the grass, and the little girl in pink—Peter never saw a thing of all that. He would put on his spectacles, if she told him to; he would look. It was the state of the world that interested him; Wagner, Pope's poetry, people's characters eternally, and the defects of her own soul. How he scolded her! How they argued! She would marry a Prime Minister and stand at the top of a staircase; the perfect hostess he called her (she had cried over it in her bedroom), she had the makings of the perfect hostess, he said.[33]

This 'perfect hostess' insult comes up multiple times throughout the novel. Clarissa meditates upon it again later, and Peter recalls how he said it in a fit of jealousy to hurt Clarissa.[34] The image of the 'perfect hostess' was meant to demean Clarissa as a teenager, to warn her that her sphere of influence would be small, domestic, and insignificant. On the day of her party, Clarissa is clearly concerned that Peter's insult was prophetic. She, has, in fact, become a perfect hostess: she spends the whole novel preparing to host a party. Remembering Peter's putdown, Clarissa struggles with regret and roads not taken. However, she also tries to work out a justification for her choices, for the life she has lived. In doing so, I contend, she is able to reclaim the label of the perfect hostess for herself.

For example, at one point in the novel she considers how her husband, Richard, and her old boyfriend, Peter, both condescend to her and fail to take her party-planning seriously. Peter thinks Clarissa does it to hob-knob with elites. Richard thinks she just likes the excitement. "Well, how was she going to defend herself?" Clarissa thinks. And then she mounts a case. She realizes that both Peter and her husband, Richard "were quite wrong."

What she liked was simply life. "That's what I do it for," she said, speaking aloud, to life……But suppose Peter said to her, "Yes, yes, but your parties — what's the sense of your parties?" all she could say was (and nobody could be expected to understand): They're an offering; which sounded horribly vague…[35] Clarissa's vagueness, her difficulty articulating the value of something to a skeptical audience should be familiar to anyone who has ever

---

[33] Virginia Woolf, *Mrs. Dalloway*. (New York: Penguin, 2016), 7.
[34] Ibid.
[35] Ibid., 120–21.

tried to articulate the value of a liberal education. Still, in trying to understand Clarissa's defense—and I think Woolf's defense—of parties, I believe we might find a model for a defense of liberal education. I think we might find a way of articulating the benefits of higher education without recourse to financial and technological metaphors.

What is the case for parties? Why do we have them? What's the good of a party? Our initial impulse might be to say that parties are unimportant and unserious—even wasteful. However, Clarissa associates them with life itself, and describes them quasi-religiously as 'an offering.' The thing about a party is that it is an end unto itself. Good parties do not have to serve any purpose other than being good parties. The question "What purpose does a party serve?" does not actually make much sense. We have parties so that we can have parties—so that we can be together. Granted, people may use parties as means to other ends—to advance their careers, for example—but we tend not to judge parties by whether or not they advance our careers, but rather by whether or not they were good parties. What we find in Woolf's vision of Clarissa Dalloway's party is an account of a human good that cannot be explained in strictly utilitarian or monetary terms, but which is, obviously, irrefutably good. This gets us closer to the kinds of goods made available to us through liberal education.

Consider too the similarities between parties and traditional university courses. A party takes place in a particular space, for a certain span of time, with a particular group of people. It is not accessible anywhere, anytime, by anyone. Those who come to the party may have different interests, and they may engage and participate in different ways. But the guests at a party, like the students and teachers in a classroom, are engaged in a shared enterprise. Every gathering is different. But what is happening at the party and in the classroom—at least the very best classrooms—is very similar. We are not there so that we can do something else. We are there so that we can be there, together. Those of us who have been teachers and students in great courses know this feeling, the feeling that the class has become completely spontaneous and somehow perfect. People contribute and collaborate in ways that could not have been predicted or designed. Once we have felt it, we long to reproduce it. It is hard work to create the right conditions—to become the perfect hostess—but we also know, because we've experienced it, that it is worth doing.

To compare education to a party might be reckless—particularly in the current climate. Outside the walls of our classrooms there are premiers and parents who want to know what our students are going to do with their lives. Perhaps the provinces, perhaps the world can ill afford to allow us the luxury to spend four years 'partying.' There are hospitals closing and pipelines that need building. There may not be time to sit in a circle and talk about Virginia Woolf. The economy needs us! But we might also find in Clarissa Dalloway's account of the party—"What she liked was simply life"—an alternative way of speaking about the value of education and the benefits we expect from it. The good of a party is both obvious and obviously not profit. It is an example that can shake us free of the profit-centric arguments that recommend themselves to us so easily in our current public discourse. The value of a party is evident not when we ask, "What does the party produce?" A party might not produce anything. But the value of parties is clearly evident when we ask, "Would you choose to live in a world without parties? Without hospitality? Without friendship? Without togetherness?" A world without parties would be an unthinkable privation. The same is true of a world without liberal education.

Finally, if we are going to defend liberal education against the forces that threaten it, we need to populate our public discourse with alternative, persuasive accounts of the goods made possible through such an education. Such images and comparisons might be new, or they might be recovered from the past. But wherever we find them, we need them to disrupt the easy circulation of bad metaphors and false analogies, and we need to alert people and decision-makers to the consequences of unthinkingly adopting bad figurative language. Universities are valuable primarily because to promote free inquiry is to promote an enriched and expansive conception of human life, a life that is not slavish. When we have places of learning that promote such a life, we have to support them, fund them, and preserve them, because to lose liberal education is to deprive ourselves of innumerable, invaluable goods.

References

Bager-Elsborg, Anna, and Linda Greve. "Establishing a Method for Analysing Metaphors in Higher Education Teaching: A Case from Business Management Teaching." *Higher Education Research & Development*, 2017, 1–14. https://doi.org/10.1080/07294360.2017.1327945.

Bañuelos, Nidia. "Dangerous Metaphors: The Consequences of Treating Higher Education Like a Consumer Good." *Change: The Magazine of Higher Learning* 51, no. 1 (2019): 14–21. https://doi.org/10.1080/00091383.2019.1547064.

Bellini, Jason. "Is the College Model Ripe for Disruption?" *The Wall Street Journal*, November 28, 2014. https://www.wsj.com/video/is-the-college-model-ripe-for-disruption/0F344350-3A44-4C7B-9F45-B9CF3972555E.html.

Bessant, Judith. "Dawkins' Higher Education Reforms and How Metaphors Work in Policy Making." *Journal of Higher Education Policy and Management* 24, no. 1 (2002): 87–99. https://doi.org/10.1080/13600800220130789.

Billieux, Joël, Martial Van Der Linden, and Lucien Rochat. "The Role of Impulsivity in Actual and Problematic Use of the Mobile Phone." *Applied Cognitive Psychology* 22, no. 9 (2008): 1195–1210. https://doi.org/10.1002/acp.1429.

Black, Naomi. *Virginia Woolf as Feminist*. Ithaca: Cornell University Press, 2004.

Boroujerdi, Robert D., and Christopher Wolf. "Emerging Theme Radar: What If I Told You…" *Goldman Sachs*, December 2, 2015. https://www.goldmansachs.com/insights/pages/macroeconomic-insights-folder/what-if-i-told-you/report.pdf.

Canada, Universities. "About Us." Accessed May 30, 2019. https://www.univcan.ca/about-us.

———. "Investing in Talent to Drive a Prosperous, Inclusive and Innovative Canadian Economy," 2018. https://www.univcan.ca/media-room/publications.

Carr, Helen. "Virginia Woolf, Empire and Race." In *The Cambridge Companion to Virginia Woolf*, edited by Susan Sellers, 2nd ed., 197–213. Cambridge, MA: Cambridge University Press, 2010.

Charbonneau, Léo. "The Top Three Hoary Metaphors of the Higher-Ed Apocalypse." *University Affairs*, June 5, 2012. https://www.universityaffairs.ca/opinion/margin-notes/the-top-three-hoary-metaphors-of-the-higher-ed-apocalypse.

Christensen, Clayton M. *The Innovator's Dilemma*. New York: Harper's Business, 2011.

Clark, Donald. "Ten Reasons We Should Ditch University Lectures." *The Guardian*, May 15, 2014. https://www.theguardian.com/higher-education-network/blog/2014/may/15/ten-reasons-we-should-ditch-university-lectures.

Craig, Cheryl J, Jeongae You, and Suhak Oh. "Pedagogy through the Pearl Metaphor: Teaching as a Process of Ongoing Refinement." *Journal of Curriculum Studies* 49, no. 6 (2017): 757–81. https://doi.org/10.1080/00220272.2015.1066866.

Crawley, Mike. "How the Ford Government Will Decide on University, College Funding." *CBC*, May 2019.

DeMeester, Karen. "Trauma, Post-Traumatic Stress Disorder, and Obstacles to Postwar Recovery in Mrs. Dalloway." In *Virginia Woolf and Trauma: Embodied Texts*, edited by Suzette Henke and David Eberly, 77–93. New York: Pace University Press, 2007.

Enerson, Diane M. "Mentoring as Metaphor: An Opportunity for Innovation and Renewal." *New Directions for Teaching and Learning*, no. 85 (2001): 7.

Erickson, Lynnette B, and Stefinee Pinnegar. "Consequences of Personal Teaching Metaphors for Teacher Identity and Practice." *Teachers and Teaching* 23, no. 1 (2017): 106–22. https://doi.org/10.1080/13540602.2016.1203774.

Fischer, Bill. "Disruption: Coming Soon to a University Near You." *Forbes*, January 19, 2012. https://www.forbes.com/sites/billfischer/2012/01/19/disruption-coming-soon-to-a-university-near-you/#cf72194239cb.

"Goldman Sachs: Higher Ed Ripe for Disruption." *The American Interest*. Accessed January 6, 2016. https://www.the-american-interest.com/2016/01/06/goldman-sachs-higher-ed-ripe-for-disruption.

Government of Saskatchewan, "Stable Funding for Post-Secondary Institutions to Keep Saskatchewan On Track." Accessed October 28, 2019. https://www.saskatchewan.ca/government/news-and-media/2018/april/10/budget-advanced-education.

Gravett, Emily O. "'Who Am I?': The Biblical Moses as a Metaphor for Teaching." *Teaching Theology & Religion* 18, no. 2 (2015): 159–69. https://doi.org/10.1111/teth.12276.

Gregory, Robert, and George Noblit. "The 'Coal Miner' University: Explorations into Metaphors on Education Organizations." *The High School Journal* 82, no. 1 (1998): 43.

Harris, Shane, Ellen Nakashima, and Craig Timberg. "Through Email Leaks and Propaganda, Russians Sought to Elect Trump, Mueller Finds." *The Washington Post*, April 2019.

Hartanto, Andree, and Hwajin Yang. "Is the Smartphone a Smart Choice? The Effect of Smartphone Separation on Executive Functions." *Computers in Human Behavior* 64 (2016): 329–36. https://doi.org/10.1016/j.chb.2016.07.002.

Harwood, Joshua, Julian J Dooley, Adrian J Scott, and Richard Joiner. "Constantly Connected – The Effects of Smart-Devices on Mental Health." *Computers in Human Behavior* 34, no. C (2014): 267–72. https://doi.org/10.1016/j.chb.2014.02.006.

Jain, Naveen. "Rethinking Education: Why Our Education System Is Ripe for Disruption." *Forbes*, March 24, 2013. https://www.forbes.com/sites/naveenjain/2013/03/24/disrupting-education/#2fd90fd623ef.

Marcus, Jane. *Virginia Woolf and the Language of Patriarchy*. Bloomington: Indiana University Press, 1987.

Mayer, Jane. "How Russia Helped Swing the Election for Trump." *The New Yorker*, September 2018.

Ministry of Training, Colleges and Universities. Government of Ontario. "Ontario's Differentiation Policy Framework for Post-secondary Education," 2013.
http://www.tcu.gov.on.ca/pepg/publications/PolicyFramework_PostSec.pdf.

Office of the Premier and Post-Secondary Education, Training and Labour. "Government Announces Funding to Support Post-Secondary Education Students," 2017. https://www2.gnb.ca/content/gnb/en/news/news_release.2017.05.0684.html.

O'Neil, Tim. *Report on the University System in Nova Scotia*. Report prepared for Premier Darrell Dexter. September, 2010. https://novascotia.ca/lae/HigherEducation/documents/Report_on_the_Higher_Education_System_in_Nova_Scotia.pdf.

Ordine, Nuccio. *The Usefulness of the Useless*. Edited by Alasair McEwen. Philadelphia: Paul Dry Books, 2017.

Reimer, Elizabeth Claire, and Louise Whitaker. "Exploring the Depths of the Rainforest: A Metaphor for Teaching Critical Reflection." *Reflective Practice* 20, no. 2 (2019): 175–86. https://doi.org/10.1080/14623943.2019.1569510.

Ritchie, David. "Monastery or Economic Enterprise: Opposing or Complementary Metaphors of Higher Education?" *Metaphor and Symbol* 17, no. 1 (2002): 45–55. https://doi.org/10.1207/S15327868MS1701_4.

Rogoff, Kenneth. "When Will Technology Disrupt Higher Education?" *The Boston Globe*, February 9, 2018. https://www.bostonglobe.com/opinion/2018/02/09/when-will-technology-disrupt-higher-education/RDqq0tsJufA0dG2VEiRFgI/story.html.

Shane, Scott. "These Are the Ads Russia Bought on Facebook in 2016." *The New York Times*, November 2017.

Simpson, Kathryn. *Gifts, Markets and Economies of Desire in Virginia Woolf*. London: Palgrave Macmillan UK, 2009. https://doi.org/10.1057/9780230228436.

Smarick, Andy. "Mitch Daniels Shows How Higher-Ed Reform Can Be Entrepreneurial." *The Weekly Standard*, May 2, 2017. https://www.weeklystandard.com/andy-smarick/mitch-daniels-shows-how-higher-ed-reform-can-be-entrepreneurial.

Swaine, John. "Russian Propagandists Targeted African Americans to Influence 2016 US Election." *The Guardian*, December 2018.

Thornton, Bill, Alyson Faires, Maija Robbins, and Eric Rollins. "The Mere Presence of a Cell Phone May Be Distracting." *Social Psychology* 45, no. 6 (2014): 479–88. https://doi.org/10.1027/1864-9335/a000216.

Wegner, Elisabeth, and Matthias Nückles. "Knowledge Acquisition or Participation in Communities of Practice? Academics' Metaphors of Teaching and Learning at the University." *Studies in Higher Education* 40, no. 4 (n.d.): 624,643. http://www.tandfonline.com/doi/abs/10.1080/03075079.2013.842213.

Wente, Margaret. "We're Ripe for a Great Disruption in Higher Education." *The Globe and Mail*, February 4, 2012. https://www.theglobeandmail.com/opinion/were-ripe-for-a-great-disruption-in-higher-education/article543479/.

Woolf, Virginia. *Mrs. Dalloway*. New York: Penguin, 2016.

Chapter 3

The Discourse of Crisis in Liberal Education: Real Emergency or Fake News?

Jason Openo
Medicine Hat College

Abstract

A comically self-referential discourse of crisis has obfuscated focus on the greatest challenges now facing liberal education. The discourse of crisis is like the boy who cried wolf, laughing at the villagers who offer aid until the wolf finally attacks, kills, and slips away. False alarms create the conditions for real destruction. This paper examines the post-secondary press to explore the discourse of crisis within liberal education, to contemplate what it means to be in crisis, and to highlight a counter-narrative that liberal education is starkly practical as long as it serves the logic of technology. It demonstrates that shouting "Crisis!" is a rhetorical tool used to silence deliberation and force a course of action, to make the politically impossible the politically inevitable. It concludes with a consideration of the parties harmed by nonstop claims of crisis and suggests the real wolf may have already arrived in sheep's clothing.

Keywords: crisis, discourse analysis, ideology, technology, liberal education

***

A pervasive and decades-long discourse of crisis in higher education has created its own crisis and obfuscated focus on the greatest crises now facing humanity, most notably global warming and climate change. Higher education's persistent discourse of crisis has been like the boy who cried wolf. In the well-known fable, a young shepherd boy amuses himself by crying "Wolf!", only to repeatedly laugh at the villagers who come to his aid. After several false alarms, a wolf finally attacks. When the boy cries out for help this time, the villagers do not drop their work and run to the pasture to help the young boy protect his master's sheep. Instead, they say, "He cannot fool us again." The wolf then kills a great many sheep and slips away into the forest. The moral of the story is that liars are not believed even when they speak the truth. In the fable, the persistent claims of a false crisis eventually contribute to a real crisis, and this well-worn tale says something meaningful about the state of liberal education, which is now operating in a crowded square with many voices yelling, "Crisis!" Discourse analysis can be divided into two major approaches: language-in-use and sociopolitical.[1] Language-in-use is concerned with the micro dimensions of language (linguists), whereas sociopolitical approaches are more commonly used in the social and human sciences.[2] This contemplation aligns with the sociopolitical approach, which is concerned with how language forms and influences the social context, and how textual constructions maintain the social context. As Miles writes, discourse analysis always involves power, and:

> the role of power in a social context is connected to the past and the current context, and can be interpreted differently by different people due to various personal backgrounds, knowledge, and power positions. Therefore there is not one correct interpretation, but a range of appropriate and possible interpretations.[3]

Discourse analysis always involves the role of power and a range of possible interpretations. This particular interpretation draws heavily upon current articles in mainstream post-secondary news outlets to take a multi-perspective approach to consider who benefits and who is harmed by this discourse of crisis. This paper will outline multiple definitions of crisis and show that the discourse of crisis is a rhetorical convention often used to shut down deliberation and force action. It will also show that this discourse of crisis has harmed post-secondary education generally and the liberal arts, specifically. Finally, it will discuss how the discourse of crisis confuses and distracts attention that should be focused on the real crisis, the real wolf, that is now attacking the sheep.

Much like the boy who intentionally and consciously amuses himself by crying "Wolf!", the discourse of crisis has been deliberate and well-planned. A potential starting date is 1983, with the publication of Milton Friedman's *A Nation at Risk*. As Friedman wrote, "Only a crisis—actual or perceived—produces real change. When that crisis occurs, the actions that are taken depend on the ideas that are lying around."[4] Ramirez and Hyslop-Marginson

---

[1] Bart Miles, "Discourse Analysis," in *Encyclopedia of Research Design*, ed. Neil J Salkind (Los Angeles, [Calif.] ; SAGE, 2010), 367–70.
[2] Ibid., 367-370.
[3] Bart Miles, "Discourse Analysis," 370.
[4] Milton Friedman, *Capitalism and Freedom* (Chicago, Ill: University of Chicago Press, 1962), ix.

provide an excellent history of neoliberalism, its effect upon universities, and the role the discourse of crisis has played in their transformation. They argue that the rhetoric of crisis and austerity generated fear and urgency that provided neoliberals with opportunities to launch attacks on universities and challenge collegial governance and academic freedom.[5] What they fail to explain is why, if the discourse of crisis has so effectively worked against the aims of educators and liberal education, have higher education writers also broadly embraced Friedman's advice that only crisis produces real change.

A simple keyword search for 'crisis' in the main academic news outlets, including *The Chronicle of Higher Education, Inside Higher Ed*, and *Academica Top 10*, locates hundreds of articles suggesting higher education is awash in crises (Figure 3.1). These major crises include the student loan debt crisis, the crisis of adjunct labor, the free speech crisis, the outcomes crisis, the replication crisis, and the crisis of public perception. Hayashida describes a 'crisis-industrial complex' and *The Chronicle's Leadership Insights* includes the title *Managing a Crisis: What Every College Leader Needs to Know*.[6] The discourse of crisis in higher education has become comically self-referential.

Academica Top 10	Inside Higher Ed	The Chronicle of Higher Education
39	89	101

Figure 3.1. A count of the number 2019 articles within the major higher education news outlets containing the word *crisis*.

Mintz (2019) writes, "higher education has always been in crisis. Virtually every decade over the past century has seen the publication of books and articles on American colleges and universities with the word 'crisis' in the title,"[7] and he openly wonders if the wolf will really attack this time as a result of higher education's cost disease and mounting competition. Hayot (2018) agrees by saying, "I do not recall an era in which the language of crisis—pedagogical crisis, theoretical crisis, institutional crisis—was not the center of

---

[5] Andrés Ramírez and Emery Hyslop-Margison, "Neoliberalism, Universities and the Discourse of Crisis," *L2 Journal* 7, no. 3 (2015): 167–83, https://doi.org/10.5070/L27323492.
[6] Marcelle Hayashida, "The Crisis-Industrial Complex," *Inside Higher Ed*, January 31, 2019, https://www.insidehighered.com/views/2019/01/31/student-affairs-officers-should-avoid-always-operating-crisis-mode-opinion.
[7] Steven Mintz, "Is This Time Different?," *Inside Higher Ed*, April 8, 2019, para. 1, https://www.insidehighered.com/blogs/higher-ed-gamma/time-different.

our shared lexicon."[8] Goldie Blumenstyk, a reporter with *The Chronicle of Higher Education*, unequivocally states that "higher education is most assuredly in crisis,"[9] but she notes that this ubiquitous doomsday narrative is actually a collection of sub-narratives. One of these sub-narratives is the crisis in liberal education. The discourse of crisis in liberal education sounds something like this:

> At several universities, liberal arts degrees have been put under the microscope, especially in times of increased financial need. At the University of Wisconsin at Stevens Point, plans to cut liberal arts were initially put into place as a cost-saving measure until backlash from the community led to a reversal. In recent years, the University of Southern Maine, the University of Nebraska, the State University of New York at Stony Brook and the University of Central Missouri have all seen cuts to liberal arts.[10]

The humanities, which lie at the core of the traditional liberal arts education, desperately need a jolt of new energy. College course catalogs are filled with offerings like "The 18th-Century Novel" that no longer draw much of a crowd. But it's not just that these courses are stale or out of fashion. The periodic fights over whether literature professors deploy too much arcane theory or off-putting jargon aren't really the issue, either. More fundamentally, in a volatile higher-education marketplace, there is a widespread perception that the humanities are simply out of touch with the needs of a tech-driven workforce.[11]

Embedded in doubts about the economic value of a college degree are perceptions that many colleges and universities, especially those that

---

[8] Eric Hayot, "The Humanities as We Know Them Are Doomed. Now What?," *The Chronicle of Higher Review*, July 1, 2018, para. 1, https://www.chronicle.com/article/The-Humanities-as-We-Know-Them/243769.

[9] Goldie. Blumenstyk, *American Higher Education in Crisis? : What Everyone Needs to Know*, What Everyone Needs to Know (Oxford ; Oxford University Press, 2014), 1.

[10] Nick Hazelrigg, "Reorganizing Away the Liberal Arts," *Inside Higher Ed*, June 6, 2019, para. 15, https://www.insidehighered.com/news/2019/06/06/cuts-leave-concerns-liberal-arts-tulsa.

[11] Josh Macht, "Can Tech Save the Humanities?," *The*, April 6, 2018, para. 4, https://www.bostonglobe.com/ideas/2018/04/06/can-tech-save-humanities/brxHDGlDgSUUAm4VRRzkuO/story.html.

emphasize liberal education for undergraduates, do not take seriously their students' focus on preparing for a job after graduation.[12]

A liberal arts education is old, unpopular, theoretically insular and mainly preoccupied with itself. Most of all, a liberal education is luxuriously and indulgently irrelevant, and liberal educators are willfully ignorant of student desires for employment, explaining why the proportion of students awarded a bachelor's degree in the humanities has dropped 15 percent from 2008 to 2016 to 6 percent of majors,[13] at a time when the total number of bachelor's degrees awarded are on the rise[14]. Liberal education's reputation is not helped when skyrocketing debt loads for students are accompanied by accusations that students are indoctrinated with a radical leftist agenda and graduate as elitists and crybabies with junky degrees.[15] These accusations, along with accusations of archaic educational models ill-equipped to meet the new demands of the knowledge economy, add fuel to a decades' long assertion by neoconservatives and neoliberals alike that higher education has broken the public trust.[16] Considering some of the evidence, perhaps it is obvious; liberal education is in crisis.

But what if this is all 'fake news?' There is growing pushback to the discourse of crisis in liberal education and with good reason.[17] Many indicators suggest the liberal artsare doing just fine. At a high level, public opinion polls suggest most Americans and many Republicans still believe a post-secondary education is essential.[18] Furthermore, in a study of 7,000 undergraduates at more than 120 colleges, after two years in college, students gained an

---

[12] Richard Freeland, "Recovering Our Lost Public Esteem," *Inside Higher Ed*, January 22, 2018, para. 7, https://www.insidehighered.com/views/2018/01/22/three-ways-higher-ed-leaders-can-respond-declining-public-confidence-opinion.
[13] Macht, "Can Tech Save the Humanities?"
[14] Ben Felder, "How Colleges Are Adapting to the Decline in Liberal Arts Majors," *PBS News Hour*, November 30, 2018, https://www.pbs.org/newshour/education/how-colleges-are-adapting-to-the-decline-in-liberal-arts-majors.
[15] Kevin Sullivan and Mary Jordan, "Elitists, Crybabies and Junky Degrees: A Trump Supporter Explains Rising Conservative Anger at American Universities," *The Washington Post*, November 25, 2017, https://www.washingtonpost.com/sf/national/2017/11/25/elitists-crybabies-and-junky-degrees/?utm_term=.f302491ae710.
[16] Andrew F Wall, David Hursh, and Joseph W Rodgers III, "Assessment for Whom: Repositioning Higher Education Assessment as an Ethical and Value-Focused Social Practice," *Research & Practice in Assessment* 9 (2014): 5.
[17] Hayot, "The Humanities as We Know Them Are Doomed. Now What?"
[18] Doug Lederman, "Is Higher Education Really Losing the Public?," *Inside Higher Ed*, December 15, 2017, https://www.insidehighered.com/news/2017/12/15/public-really-losing-faith-higher-education.

appreciation of political viewpoints across the spectrum, not just liberal ones[19]. Humanities graduates tend to be gainfully employed, hold positions of authority, and are as satisfied with their level of income and career satisfaction as those who major in STEM fields.[20]

Perhaps the best news of all for educators is that liberal education is compatible with the demands of the new economy. Internal studies by Google found that top employees and top teams possess the qualities developed in the humanities, including communication, listening, problem-solving, critical thinking and empathy.[21] The more sophisticated economy, fueled by automation and technological advances, will also fuel a need for higher education to operate at an unprecedented scale, precisely in the area of liberal education. As Carnevale, Smith, and Strohl point out, the share of jobs requiring at least some college education has increased from 28 percent to at least 60 percent, and by 2020, it is estimated that 65 percent of all jobs in the United States will require some form of post-secondary education or training.[22] The fastest-growing sectors of the economy will be those that require post-secondary education. This growth is fueled, say the authors, by technology.[23] To adapt and participate in the technological-knowledge economy, more and more individuals will want and need what colleges and universities have to offer, including a liberal education.

This is the foundation of Aoun's argument in *Robot-Proof*; education, specifically liberal education, will be the "surest antidote to displacement by automation"[24]. He states:

---

[19] Matthew J. Mayhew et al., "Does College Turn People into Liberals?," *The Conversation*, February 2, 2018, https://theconversation.com/does-college-turn-people-into-liberals-90905.

[20] Scott Jaschik, "Shocker: Humanities Grads Gainfully Employed and Happy," *Inside Higher Ed*, February 7, 2018, https://www.insidehighered.com/news/2018/02/07/study-finds-humanities-majors-land-jobs-and-are-happy-them.

[21] Valerie Strauss, "The Surprising Thing Google Learned about Its Employees – and What It Means for Today's Students," *The Washington Post*, December 20, 2017, https://www.washingtonpost.com/news/answer-sheet/wp/2017/12/20/the-surprising-thing-google-learned-about-its-employees-and-what-it-means-for-todays-students/?utm_term=.68b573bf1b93.

[22] Anthony Carnevale, Nicole Smith, and Jeff Strohl, "Recovery: Job Growth and Eductional Requirements Through," 2016, https://cew.georgetown.edu/cew-reports/recovery-job-growth-and-education-requirements-through-2020/.

[23] Ibid., 16.

[24] Joseph Aoun, *Robot-Proof: Higher Education in the Age of Artificial Intelligence* (Cambridge, MA: The MIT Press, 2018), 17.

Intellectually, morally, and spiritually, the humanities are among the most fertile grounds on which to nurture a complete human being. They form the foundation of a life well-lived and the furnishings of a civilized mind. That is reason enough to study them. But they also happen to be starkly practical.[25]

A starkly practical liberal education provides students with opportunities to develop leadership, creativity, and social and human skills, such as persuasive communication. As Aoun puts it, "a computer can model climate change, but it takes human beings to devise and enact policies to stem it."[26] With this in mind, it seems that liberal education is far from being in a crisis state. It's fake news.

But again, if there is no crisis, why do so many within higher education and liberal education willingly participate in the propagation of the discourse of crisis? The best way forward is to contemplate what it means to be in crisis and then consider who benefits and who is harmed by this discourse.

The most elementary meaning of *crisis* comes from the Greek, meaning "a decisive point or moment."[27] To be in crisis is to make a decision, but this is clearly insufficient to understanding what it means to be in crisis or to understand how it is used in academic discourse because, it seems fairly obvious, that would imply we are always in crisis. We usually live at a point in time when we need to make decisive judgments about something, such as program curriculum. To be in crisis must mean more than simply making a decision. *Webster's Dictionary* provides further clues to the deeper meaning of crisis in its example, "This hour's the very crisis of your fate."[28] To be in crisis is not an ordinary state, but an extraordinary one. To state one is in crisis is to suggest that one exists in a moment in time when a rare and extraordinary decision must be made. Is the wolf at the door?

To be in crisis is also deeply related to the concept of progress or a sense of progression, which can be understood as the movement to a better and more desirable state.[29] This inevitable sense of movement towards better-ness is what Ronald Wright calls the myth of progress:

---

[25] Ibid., 59.
[26] Ibid., 43.
[27] Walter Skeat, *An Etymological Dictionary of the English Language* (London: Oxford University Press, 1963), 144.
[28] Webster's Dictionary, s.v. "Crisis," 1913. https://www.webster-dictionary.org/definition/Crisis
[29] Arvindus, "Crisis: Etymological Considerations," Contemplationem, 2012, http://www.contemplationem.com/publications/20120325.html.

Our practical faith in progress has ramified and hardened into an ideology – a secular religion which, like the religions that progress has challenged, is blind to certain flaws in its credentials. Progress, therefore, has become 'myth' in the anthropological sense. By this I do not mean a belief that is flimsy or untrue. Successful myths are powerful and often partly true. Myth is an arrangement of the past, whether real or imagined, in patterns that reinforce a culture's deepest values and aspirations . . . . Myths are so fraught with meaning that we live and die by them. They are the maps by which cultures navigate through time.[30]

The Myth of Progress is a time-map by which we will live and die. One way to conceive being in crisis, then, is that one's conception of progress towards a better and more evolved and enlightened state has ended. Arvindus employs the metaphor of a hike to explain the difference.[31] When the hiker knows the path and only experiences minor mundane obstacles, they are not in crisis because, normally, it is no crisis to step forward. To *move forward* happens always and most naturally. When the path becomes too difficult to see or too difficult to traverse, the hiker must halt. This is when the crisis has arrived, when the hiker can no longer move towards the goal on the chosen path and there is no clear way forward. As Arvindus writes, "Formerly the followed path was the one without a doubt."[32] To be in crisis means to be filled with doubt in the ability to progress on the current path, meaning a new path must be found. Finding this new way forward requires deliberate interpretation and judgment in a state of anxiety and suspense. Crises arises when our action has halted because we are insecure, uncertain and quite probably feeling unsafe, causing anxiety and requiring our next decisions to be made with the utmost care.

But what is the purpose of crisis or the purpose of claiming one is in a state of crisis? Returning to Friedman, he writes, "When that crisis occurs, the actions that are taken depend on the ideas that are lying around. That is, I believe, our basic function: to develop alternatives to existing policies, to keep them alive and available until the politically impossible becomes the politically inevitable."[33] To declare a crisis is to force movement towards alternative pathways. Crisis, in this case, is not a time of uncertainty and insecurity requiring deliberation; it functions as a rhetorical technique to drive action from the politically impossible towards the politically inevitable. Crisis functions to drive people towards a course of action, often the author's, an idea

---

[30] Ronald Wright, *A Short History of Progress* (Toronto: House of Anansi Press, Inc., 2004), 4.
[31] Arvindus, "Crisis: Etymological Considerations."
[32] Ibid., para. 7.
[33] Friedman, *Capitalism and Freedom*, ix.

that the author has conveniently 'lying around.' In most cases, crisis is used in a medical sense, where crisis is the turning point of a disease, when an important change takes place indicating either recovery or death. If the patient's heart fails, there is no longer time for deliberation about what action to take; action must be taken. The patient must be kept alive, and this forces commitment to a singular intervention—a specific and immediate course of action. If the intervention does not occur, then a severe consequence (life or death) will result from the decision or judgement. It is only in this medical sense of crisis that the observations of Wall, et al., make sense:

> It is not accidental that assessment in higher education emerged over a 25-year period in which a perceived educational crisis has undermined public trust, and displaced higher education's duty to serve learning for the public good with an increased emphasis on serving the needs of the market...A discourse of crisis frames assessment as a practice of control in which increased scrutiny is the answer to perceived limitations to higher education performance. The administrators and policy makers who framed higher education assessment practice are also the ones who identified the crisis. They have used the perceived crisis to call for examining educational expenditures and outcomes as part of an agenda to redefine the purpose of higher education.[34]

The perceived crisis, in a medical sense, displaces the need for deliberation. It requires action, specifically an action involving greater control over expenditures and increased scrutiny over outcomes. And it is those possessing that agenda, who's agenda will most likely benefit from the perception of crisis, and then yell the loudest. To declare a crisis, then, is often not to declare that the path forward is unclear or uncertain, and that one has reached a moment in time requiring careful discernment and thoughtful consideration. To declare a crisis is a rhetorical tactic suggesting that the time for debate is over or the patient will die.

To say higher education is in crisis is to say there is no longer time for debate, but it is also to drive people towards the action recommended by the author. To declare a crisis is to say, essentially, no other alternatives remain but the author's. Warner sums this approach up well when contemplating the crisis-related discourse of *disruptive innovation*.[35] He suggests that by insisting

---

[34] Wall, Hursh, and Rodgers, "Assessment for Whom, " 6–7.
[35] John Warner, "Disruptive Innovation? More like Destructive Innovation," *Inside Higher Ed*, November 20, 2017, https://www.insidehighered.com/blogs/just-visiting/ disruptive-innovation-more-destructive-innovation.

disruptive innovation is true, the authors hope to bring about the disruption—the discourse becomes a self-fulfilling prophecy.[36] Warner observes, "institutions can only exist as long as a sufficient number of people continue to believe in them...if belief in the value of the institution goes away, the institution ceases to exist."[37] Warner's accusation is that the only one who stands to benefit from the discourse of disruptive innovation is Clayton Christensen, the founder of the term. It becomes necessary, therefore, to consider who benefits and who is harmed by the consistent calls of crisis in post-secondary education.

In *The Boy Who Cried Wolf*, the first party that is harmed most directly (they are murdered and eaten) are the non-human participants in the story, the sheep. The sheep may be seen as the symbols of the non-human environment and the biosphere. The most pressing crisis facing humanity and the rest of the planet is climate change and global warming (crisis being used here to mean both a time when severe deliberation is required to find a different path forward for the culture and a time when extreme action is needed). There is a tremendous loss of biodiversity resulting from habitat destruction, invasive species, the intensive harvesting of timber, and creeping oceanic dead zones. There are compelling scientific, ethical, and theological reasons to stop the long march of human-caused extinction and make protecting biodiversity an organizing principle for liberal education. Ecological anxiety (*ecoanxiety*) is an emerging phenomenon, and the escalating scientific evidence for biodiversity loss is about real creatures suffering to the irreversible point of extinction, inducing a spiritual loneliness and longing because our lives are dependent on their flourishing.[38]

Climate change will also affect higher education directly in its physical environment and how it must adapt its curriculum. Myers and Lusk begin *Rising Threat, Threatened Campuses* with the dire warning for coastal colleges and universities in the United States:

> When the water comes, the familiar campus life will come to an end. Classes will be relocated or moved online; students will be forced to abandon the deluged library; campus construction plans will have to be overhauled, if not scrapped. The impact is almost unimaginable, but it is only a matter of time. That the climate is changing, and the seas will continue rising are no longer in question. The uncertainty now is how

---

[36] Ibid., para. 4.
[37] Ibid., para. 8.
[38] Celia Deane Drummond, "Why Should Christians Care about Biodiversity? [Webinar]," Youtube, 2019, https://www.youtube.com/watch?v=4wIsGlf6498.

much and how soon. For many colleges and universities on America's coasts, the threat is no longer theoretical.[39]

This particular expose focuses on only four institutions in the United States, but the disruption to those four universities and colleges represents 31,000 students and billions of dollars' worth of infrastructure, not to mention the larger damage that will occur to the cities and communities in which they reside. The impacts will be widespread, and climate change will eventually cause the biggest and most destructive difference in the United States' economic and social life. Post-secondary educational institutions from all over the world, and liberal educators, must meet this future head-on to survive and provide resilience to their communities. To its credit, higher education is responding; close to one thousand institutions worldwide are now participating in the Association for the Advancement of Sustainability in Higher Education's (AASHE) Sustainability Tracking, Assessment & Rating System (STARS).

The Intergovernmental Panel on Climate Change has warned that "rapid, far-reaching and unprecedented" changes are needed to keep the Earth's temperature from rising 1.5 degrees Celsius, and even though record numbers of Americans say that the global warming is personally important to them, 70 percent wouldn't pay $10 a month to help cool the warming planet.[40] The discourse of crisis in climate change has managed to convince people it is important, just not important to do anything. This then becomes a central challenge for liberal education, where the activity of imparting the knowledge and skills necessary to live a truly human life must include access to education, policy, sustainable actions, and the development of awareness of environmental systems, human impacts, and human reverence for life.[41] As Ursula Goodenough proclaims:

> I profess my Faith. For me, the existence of all this complexity and awareness and intent and beauty, and my ability to apprehend it, serves as the ultimate meaning and ultimate value. The continuation of life reaches around, grabs its own tail, and forms a sacred circle that requires

---

[39] Ben Myers and Erica Lusk, "Rising Threat: As the Climate Changes and Seas Swell, Coastal Colleges Struggle to Prepare," *The Chronicle of Higher Education*, December 6, 2017, paras. 1–3, https://www.chronicle.com/interactives/rising-threat.
[40] Robinson Meyer, "The Unprecedented Surge in Fear about Climate Change," *The Atlantic*, 2019, https://www.theatlantic.com/science/archive/2019/01/do-most-americans-believe-climate-change-polls-say-yes/580957/.
[41] Paul Hawken, *Blessed Unrest: How the Largest Movement in the World Came into Being and Why No One Saw It Coming* (New York: Viking, 2007).

no further justification, no Creator, no superordinate meaning of meaning, no purpose other than that the continuation continue until the sun collapses or the final meteor collides. I confess a credo of continuation. And in so doing, I confess as well as a credo of human continuation.[42]

Liberal education has long cultivated an appreciation for the collective human journey. It must now do so in an era of survival anxiety, and liberal educators must join their effort to the collective efforts underway to ensure that this journey continues to offer more learners the opportunity to appreciate the complexity and beauty of existence, and apprehend the meaning and value of being human.

The second party harmed by the discourse of crisis are the villagers. Their trust and faith in their community is damaged, and communal distrust undermines higher education and liberal education The Association of American Colleges and Universities (AAC&U) acknowledges that current challenges facing liberal education include "economic, racial, and ethnic segregation and an intolerance of difference" along with a "burgeoning loss of public trust" and the "notion of higher education as a public good has been displaced by a belief that a college education is a private commodity."[43] Evidence of this communal distrust can be found in Bennett, who writes that humanities professors are the problem.[44] Bennett argues that the democratization of the cannon turned beauty into ideology and poetry became a trick of power. This has also lead to the death of expertise: "if opinion is always contingent, why should we subsidize professionals to produce it?"[45] Expertise became power and power amounts to oppression and privilege, with the end result being "a culture in which business studies dominate" and legislatures are blind to the value of the liberal arts.[46]

---

[42] Ursula Goodenough, *The Sacred Depths of Nature* (New York: Oxford University Press, 1998), 171–72.
[43] American Association of Colleges and Universities, "Educating for Democracy: 2018-22 Stategic Plan" (Washington, 2018), 3, https://www.aacu.org/sites/default/files/files/about/AACU_StrategicPlan_2018-22.pdf.
[44] Eric Bennett, "Dear Humanities Profs: We Are the Problem," *The Chronicle of Higher Education*, April 13, 2018, https://www.chronicle.com/article/Dear-Humanities-Profs-We-Are/243100.
[45] Christian Smith, "Higher Education Is Drowning in BS: And It's Mortally Corrosive to Society," *The Chronicle Review*, January 9, 2018, para. 11, https://www.chronicle.com/article/Higher-Education-Is-Drowning/242195.
[46] Bennett, "Dear Humanities Profs: We Are the Problem," para. 14.

In the same vein as Bennett, Abrams accuses professors of contributing to the democratic deficit.[47] Abrams blames professors for the current civic deterioration because only 28 percent of more than 900 faculty members participating in his survey believed that helping to shape and condition the values of college undergraduates was essential, and "just 32 percent believed that engaging students in civil and balanced discourse around controversial issues of the day was significant."[48] Because professors do not see this as part of their role and responsibility, they are partially responsible for the loss in values, civility, and dialogue.

Christian Smith may have the strongest expression of this communal distrust when he pithily says higher education is drowning in bullshit that is mortally corrosive to society.[49] The bullshit includes "our crisis of faith in truth, reality, reason, evidence, argument, civility, and our common humanity,"[50] as well as rankings, ideologically infused jargon, tenure to lousy teachers, underpaid adjuncts, distance learning, the culture of offense, invisible self-censorship, the failure of leadership to champion the liberal-arts ideal, and the "grossly lopsided political ideology of the faculty of many disciplines."[51] In short, no one and nothing can be trusted. This bullshit has created a "disastrous political condition [that puts] at risk the very viability and character of decent civilization."[52]

Consequently, Smith has given up hope that education can resist the accumulated weight of all the bullshit, and his lament is similar to one originally issued by John Harvey Robinson almost 100 years ago:

> How indeed can a teacher be expected to explain to the sons and daughters of businessmen, politicians, doctors, lawyers, and clergymen—all pledged to the maintenance of the sources of their livelihood—the actual nature of business enterprise as now practiced, the prevailing method of legislative bodies and courts, and the conduct of foreign affairs? Think of a teacher in the public schools recounting the more illuminating facts about the municipal government under which he lives, with due attention to graft and jobs! So, courses in government,

---

[47] Samuel J. Abrams, "How Professors Contribute to the Democratic Deficit," *Inside Higher Ed*, 2018, https://www.insidehighered.com/views/2018/04/25/civic-engagement-and-social-change-not-priority-faculty-members-opinion.
[48] Ibid., para. 7.
[49] Smith, "Higher Education Is Drowning in BS: And It's Mortally Corrosive to Society."
[50] Ibid., para. 3.
[51] Ibid., para. 15.
[52] Ibid., para. 2.

political economy, sociology, and ethics confined themselves to inoffensive generalizations, harmless details of organization, and commonplaces of routine morality, for only in that way can they escape being controversial. Teachers are rarely able or inclined to explain our social life and its presuppositions with sufficient insight and honesty to produce any very important results. Even if they are tempted to tell the essential facts they dare not do so, for fear of losing their places, amid the applause of the righteously minded.

However we may feel on this important matter, we must all agree that the aim of education for citizenship as now conceived is a preparation for the same old citizenship which has so far failed to eliminate the shocking hazards and crying injustices of our social and political life. For we sedulously inculcate in the coming generation exactly the same illusions and the same ill-placed confidence in existing institutions and prevailing notions that have brought the world to the pass in which we find it.[53]

To teach the liberal arts, and to have the opportunity to study them, is a privilege-reinforcing activity that does not and cannot challenge the status quo. Liberal education does not teach students how to think; it teaches them how to think within the confines of maintaining an acceptable reality. This also becomes the quintessential challenge for liberal education (and perhaps always has been)—to be able to dismantle from within and transcend what Marcuse would have called *one-dimensional thought*, the pervasive mechanism of control outlined by Robinson that focuses solely on making the existing institutions to work better and perform more effectively.[54]

Finally, the boy himself is harmed by damaging his reputation, and this, too, has its implications for higher education. An analogous situation has recently arisen between Bryan Caplan and Margaret Spellings. Caplan, author of *The Case Against Education: Why the Education System is a Waste of Time and Money*, suggests that "the way our education system transforms student into paid workers seems like magic."[55] Education is little more than a bunch of signals and a credentialist arms race. Margaret Spellings, President of the University of North Carolina system and a former U.S. secretary of education,

---

[53] James Harvey Robinson, *The Mind in the Making: The Relation of Intelligence to Social Reform*. (Harper & Brothers, 1921), 21–22, https://doi.org/10.1037/10902-000.

[54] Stephen. Brookfield, *The Power of Critical Theory: Liberating Adult Learning and Teaching*, 1st ed. (San Francisco, Calif: Jossey-Bass, 2005).

[55] Bryan Douglas Caplan, *The Case against Education: Why the Education System Is a Waste of Time and Money* (Princeton: Princeton University Press, 2018), 12.

recognizes the perils of trashing the value of higher education.⁵⁶ This is the same kind of harm the boy brings on himself by calling, "Wolf!" Spellings makes this clear, writing:

> One of the unfortunate side effects of our endless wrangle over who should go to college is that it distracts from more urgent reform. I don't think every high-school graduate should proceed directly to the nearest university campus, and I don't know of any college president who does. The conversations I hear among policy makers aren't about "college for all" but about creating a much clearer set of options beyond high school — from apprenticeships to certifications to community college.⁵⁷

The discourse of crisis damages the reputation of higher education and prevents it from engaging in thoughtful deliberation and consideration of alternative paths of progress.

If the discourse of crisis in higher education harms human and environmental systems by distracting it from truly important developments like climate change, and the discourse of crisis also harms higher education by sowing discord and a lack of faith in the community and the institution itself, who benefits? Who is the shadowy predatory wolf who claims lives and escapes so stealthily into the forest? Canadian Dr. Tony Bates, in his recent 3-part series entitled *The Coming Crisis in Canadian Post-secondary Education*, provides some clues as to the culprit. The wolf is technology. Bates defines the threat, saying:

> The main threat comes from the semi-monopolistic power of large multinational Internet-based companies such as Amazon, Alphabet/Google, Apple, Facebook, Airbnb, Uber, etc. and new Internet-based companies that have yet to emerge. These are disrupting both the economy and society and have the potential to disrupt Canadian post-secondary education if it does not adapt quickly enough...Although these multinational Internet-based organizations offer many benefits, they also result in many negative consequences. On the economic side, they are destroying many physically-based businesses and thus killing jobs, they are avoiding taxation and thus reducing the power of the state to provide essential services such as health and education, and reducing

---

⁵⁶ Margaret Spellings, "The Perils of Trashing the Value of College," *The Chronicle of Higher Education*, February 22, 2018, https://www.chronicle.com/article/The-Perils-of-Trashing-the/242614.
⁵⁷ Ibid., para. 15.

economic choices for individuals...On the social side, they are weakening privacy, enabling and magnifying anti-social and malignant behaviour, and undermining democratic institutions and processes. Artificial intelligence offers many benefits, but also has dangerous unintended consequences that we are only beginning to discover...In other words, the ordinary individual and even national governments are losing control over the technology. [58]

Like the wildness of the wolf, we have lost control over technology, and technology is hard to spot. The economic, social, and political effects of technology are all-encompassing. Ellul's use of the word *technique* is probably better than the word *technology*.

> The term technique, as I use it, does not mean machines, technology, or this or that procedure for attaining an end. In our technological society, technique is the totality of methods rationally arrived at and having absolute efficiency (for a given stage of development) in every field of human activity. Its characteristics are new; the technique of the present has no common measure with that of the past [emphasis in the original].[59]

While the discourse of crisis rages, the real wolf comes and devours the sheep, destroys the community, and eats away at the reputation of anyone who questions the logic of technology. As Selwyn observes, any skepticism of educational technology risks being psychopathologized, and individuals may be tempted to blame themselves for technological failures without knowing why they are at fault.[60] It is simply impossible to argue that education serves any other function but to serve technology.

The technology forces in Ellul's definition of technique is akin to Postman's conception of *Technopoly*; a thought-world that destroys all other thought-

---

[58] Tony Bates, "The Coming Crisis in Canadian Post-Secondary Education: 1 – External Developments," Online Learning and Distance Education Resources (blog), paras. 9–13, accessed May 26, 2019, https://www.tonybates.ca/2019/05/26/the-coming-crisis-in-canadian-post-secondary-education-1-external-developments/.
[59] Jacques. Ellul, *The Technological Society* (New York: Vintage Books, 1964), xxv.
[60] Neil Selwyn, *Distrusting Educational Technology: Critical Questions for Changing Times* (New York: Routledge, 2014).

worlds.[61] Higher education must adapt to the demands of technology if it is to stay relevant. As Ellul (1964) forcefully puts it:

> The new pedagogical methods correspond exactly to the role assigned to education in modern technical society...[To] furnish administrators for the state and managers for the economy, in conformity with social needs and tendencies...education no longer has a humanist end or any value in itself; it has only one goals, to create technicians.[62]

Technology has created a crisis in society and in education, but it is a crisis that does not allow itself to be questioned, nor does it allow us to be in crisis—meaning pausing to consider if there is a better path forward for our culture and civilization. Liberal education's real crisis is that it will only be allowed to continue to exist to the extent that it supports the logic of technology. But it's best if we don't call it a crisis. There is a Buddhist saying that one should wash out their mouth every time they say the word Buddha. If there is any chance at all to avoid the irreparable harm looming to human beings and slow the irreversible impacts already well-documented in the larger biosphere, I encourage higher education writers to wash their mouths out every time they say crisis.

References

Abrams, Samuel J. "How Professors Contribute to the Democratic Deficit." *Inside Higher Ed*, 2018. https://www.insidehighered.com/views/2018/04/25/civic-engagement-and-social-change-not-priority-faculty-members-opinion.

American Association of Colleges and Universities. "Educating for Democracy: 2018-22 Stategic Plan." Washington, 2018. https://www.aacu.org/sites/default/files/files/about/AACU_StrategicPlan_2018-22.pdf.

Aoun, Joseph. *Robot-Proof: Higher Education in the Age of Artificial Intelligence*. Cambridge, MA: The MIT Press, 2018.

Arvindus. "Crisis: Etymological Considerations." Contemplationem, 2012. http://www.contemplationem.com/publications/20120325.html.

Bates, Tony. "The Coming Crisis in Canadian Post-Secondary Education: 1 – External Developments." Online Learning and Distance Education Resources (blog). Accessed May 26, 2019. https://www.tonybates.ca/2019/05/26/the-coming-crisis-in-canadian-post-secondary-education-1-external-developments/.

---

[61] Neil Postman, *Technopoly: The Surrender of Culture to Technology* (New York: Alfred A. Knopf, 1992).
[62] Ellul, *The Technological Society*, 348.

Bennett, Eric. "Dear Humanities Profs: We Are the Problem." *The Chronicle of Higher Education*, April 13, 2018. https://www.chronicle.com/article/Dear-Humanities-Profs-We-Are/243100.

Blumenstyk, Goldie. *American Higher Education in Crisis?: What Everyone Needs to Know* . What Everyone Needs to Know. Oxford; Oxford University Press, 2014.

Brookfield, Stephen. *The Power of Critical Theory: Liberating Adult Learning and Teaching*. 1st ed. San Francisco, Calif: Jossey-Bass, 2005.

Caplan, Bryan Douglas. The Case against Education: Why the Education System Is a Waste of Time and Money. Princeton: Princeton University Press, 2018.

Carnevale, Anthony, Nicole Smith, and Jeff Strohl. "Recovery: Job Growth and Eductional Requirements Through," 2016. https://cew.georgetown.edu/cew-reports/recovery-job-growth-and-education-requirements-through-2020/.

Drummond, Celia Deane. "Why Should Christians Care about Biodiversity? [Webinar]." Youtube, 2019. https://www.youtube.com/watch?v=4wIsGlf6498.

Ellul, Jacques. *The Technological Society*. New York: Vintage Books, 1964.

Felder, Ben. "How Colleges Are Adapting to the Decline in Liberal Arts Majors." *PBS News Hour*, November 30, 2018. https://www.pbs.org/newshour/education/how-colleges-are-adapting-to-the-decline-in-liberal-arts-majors.

Freeland, Richard. "Recovering Our Lost Public Esteem." *Inside Higher Ed*, January 22, 2018. https://www.insidehighered.com/views/2018/01/22/three-ways-higher-ed-leaders-can-respond-declining-public-confidence-opinion.

Friedman, Milton. *Capitalism and Freedom*. Chicago, Ill: University of Chicago Press, 1962.

Goodenough, Ursula. *The Sacred Depths of Nature*. New York: Oxford University Press, 1998.

Hawken, Paul. Blessed Unrest: How the Largest Movement in the World Came into Being and Why No One Saw It Coming. New York: Viking, 2007.

Hayashida, Marcelle. "The Crisis-Industrial Complex." *Inside Higher Ed*, January 31, 2019. https://www.insidehighered.com/views/2019/01/31/student-affairs-officers-should-avoid-always-operating-crisis-mode-opinion.

Hayot, Eric. "The Humanities as We Know Them Are Doomed. Now What?" *The Chronicle of Higher Review*, July 1, 2018. https://www.chronicle.com/article/The-Humanities-as-We-Know-Them/243769.

Hazelrigg, Nick. "Reorganizing Away the Liberal Arts." *Inside Higher Ed*, June 6, 2019. https://www.insidehighered.com/news/2019/06/06/cuts-leave-concerns-liberal-arts-tulsa.

Jaschik, Scott. "Shocker: Humanities Grads Gainfully Employed and Happy." *Inside Higher Ed*, February 7, 2018. https://www.insidehighered.com/news/2018/02/07/study-finds-humanities-majors-land-jobs-and-are-happy-them.

Lederman, Doug. "Is Higher Education Really Losing the Public?" *Inside Higher Ed*, December 15, 2017. https://www.insidehighered.com/news/2017/12/15/public-really-losing-faith-higher-education.

Macht, Josh. "Can Tech Save the Humanities?" *The*, April 6, 2018. https://www.bostonglobe.com/ideas/2018/04/06/can-tech-save-humanities/brxHDGlDgSUUAm4VRRzkuO/story.html.

Mayhew, Matthew J., Alyssa N Rockenbach, Benjamin Selznick, and Jay Zagorsky. "Does College Turn People into Liberals?" *The Conversation*, February 2, 2018. https://theconversation.com/does-college-turn-people-into-liberals-90905.

Meyer, Robinson. "The Unprecedented Surge in Fear about Climate Change." *The Atlantic*, 2019. https://www.theatlantic.com/science/archive/2019/01/do-most-americans-believe-climate-change-polls-say-yes/580957/.

Miles, Bart. "Discourse Analysis." In *Encyclopedia of Research Design*, edited by Neil J Salkind, 367–70. Los Angeles, [Calif.]; SAGE, 2010.

Mintz, Steven. "Is This Time Different?" *Inside Higher Ed*, April 8, 2019. https://www.insidehighered.com/blogs/higher-ed-gamma/time-different.

Myers, Ben, and Erica Lusk. "Rising Threat: As the Climate Changes and Seas Swell, Coastal Colleges Struggle to Prepare." *The Chronicle of Higher Education*, December 6, 2017. https://www.chronicle.com/interactives/rising-threat.

Postman, Neil. Technopoly: The Surrender of Culture to Technology. New York: Alfred A. Knopf, 1992.

Ramírez, Andrés, and Emery Hyslop-Margison. "Neoliberalism, Universities and the Discourse of Crisis." *L2 Journal* 7, no. 3 (2015): 167–83. https://doi.org/10.5070/L27323492.

Robinson, James Harvey. *The Mind in the Making: The Relation of Intelligence to Social Reform*. Harper & Brothers, 1921. https://doi.org/10.1037/10902-000.

Selwyn, Neil. Distrusting Educational Technology: Critical Questions for Changing Times. New York: Routledge, 2014.

Skeat, Walter. *An Etymological Dictionary of the English Language*. London: Oxford University Press, 1963.

Smith, Christian. "Higher Education Is Drowning in BS: And It's Mortally Corrosive to Society." *The Chronicle Review*, January 9, 2018. https://www.chronicle.com/article/Higher-Education-Is-Drowning/242195.

Spellings, Margaret. "The Perils of Trashing the Value of College." *The Chronicle of Higher Education*, February 22, 2018. https://www.chronicle.com/article/The-Perils-of-Trashing-the/242614.

Strauss, Valerie. "The Surprising Thing Google Learned about Its Employees – and What It Means for Today's Students." *The Washington Post*, December 20, 2017. https://www.washingtonpost.com/news/answer-sheet/wp/2017/12/20/the-surprising-thing-google-learned-about-its-employees-and-what-it-means-for-todays-students/?utm_term=.68b573bf1b93.

Sullivan, Kevin, and Mary Jordan. "Elitists, Crybabies and Junky Degrees: A Trump Supporter Explains Rising Conservative Anger at American Universities." *The Washington Post*, November 25, 2017. https://www.

washingtonpost.com/sf/national/2017/11/25/elitists-crybabies-and-junky-degrees/?utm_term=.f302491ae710.

Wall, Andrew F, David Hursh, and Joseph W Rodgers III. "Assessment for Whom: Repositioning Higher Education Assessment as an Ethical and Value-Focused Social Practice." *Research & Practice in Assessment* 9 (2014): 5.

Warner, John. "Disruptive Innovation? More like Destructive Innovation." *Inside Higher Ed*, November 20, 2017. https://www.insidehighered.com/blogs/just-visiting/disruptive-innovation-more-destructive-innovation.

Webster's Dictionary. Crisis. 1913.
https://www.webster-dictionary.org/definition/Crisis

Wright, Ronald. *A Short History of Progress.* Toronto: House of Anansi Press, Inc., 2004.

Chapter 4

Detecting Bullshit in a Culture of Fake News and Lies

David Ohreen
Mount Royal University

Abstract

The concept of "fake news" has been around for more than a century, but Trump's presidency has ushered in a post-truth society where the distinction lies and bullshit is increasingly hard to detect. This essay explores the differences between these concepts and why understanding them is important and necessary to discern the truth. Following the work of Harry Frankfurt, a lie is intended to intentionally deceive another by representing false information about some topic or issue, whereas bullshitters show an indifference towards truth or falsity itself. The rejection of truth and falsity makes bullshitters more dangerous than liars. What is needed is a bullshit detector, and liberal education can help. Liberal education can sharpen critical thinking skills in order to cast sceptical eyes towards "fake news" claims while, at the same time, cultivating a commitment to truth.

Keywords: fake news, bullshit, truth, liberal education

***

Introduction

Despite the concept of 'fake news' emerging at the end of the 19th century,[1,] Donald Trump's presidency has resurrected its use to the point where, according to researchers, he has used the term 'fake' more than 400 times since his inauguration—and the time of this article. His use of the terms 'fake news', 'fake polls', 'fake stories', and 'fake media' are now commonplace.[2] However,

---

[1] Joanna M Burkhardt, "Chapter 1: History of Fake News," *Library Technology Reports* 53, no. 8 (November 2017): 5–9.
[2] Margaret Sullivan, "'Fake News' Claims Are Untrue, and He Knows It," *Washington Post, The*, February 5, 2019, http://libproxy.mtroyal.ca/login?url=http://search.ebscohost.

what exactly does 'fake' mean and what is its intent? It appears Trump's use of the term is a dismissive gesture to what he perceives as being inaccurate, misleading, or untruthful news stories about him and his policies. In addition to his use of 'fake news', President Trump has publicly made 10,111 false or misleading claims (as of April 29, 2019)[3]. But Trump's statements are merely the epitome of a broader culture of lies and false claims going back to 1950 including alien experimentation in Area 51 and Bigfoot to the more recent Flat Earth and the QAnon conspiracy theories, the latter of which believes Democrats such as Hilary Clinton and George Soros are part of an underground child molestation ring.[4] Of these beliefs, some are outright lies and others, I hope to show, are *bullshit*. So, what is the difference between lying and bullshit? From a philosophical point of view, as Harry Frankfurt in his 2015 book, *On Bullshit*, argues lying is the intentional misrepresentation of information about some topic or issue in order to create a false belief in the listener. Bullshitters, in contrast, do not consciously deceive others but show an indifference towards truth or falsity. It is this apathy towards truth, according to Frankfurt, that makes bullshitters more dangerous than liars. Fake news claims are a kind of bullshit because its intent is to obfuscate the truth in order to confuse and dismay. In a culture and social media environment where bullshit is increasingly hard to detect, a bullshit detector is needed and a liberal education can provide a framework to enhance our understanding of what critical thinking is, while at the same time, cultivating a commitment to truth.

A Culture of Fake News and Lies

The rise of fake news on social media platforms has blurred the lines between what is real and made-up. For example, in a fake video created by BuzzFeed and comedian Jordan Peele, former President Obama insults Donald Trump by calling him a "complete dipshit." The video was made using software to illustrate how easy it is to create and distribute fake information.[5] In 2012, InfoWars host Alex Jones called the shooting at Sandy Hook Elementary School, where 20 six and seven-year-old children were killed, a conspiracy which, along

---

com/login.aspx?direct=true&AuthType=ip,url,cookie,uid&db=n5h&AN=wapo.b368b526-2881-11e9-984d-9b8fba003e81&site=ehost-live.

[3] Simon Houpt, "Why Are the Media So Reluctant to Call Politians Liars?," *The Globe and Mail*, May 8, 2019, A17.

[4] Kevin Roose, "What is QAnon, the Viral Pro-Trump Conspiracy Theory?" *New York Times*, September 1, 2020, https://www.nytimes.com/article/what-is-qanon.html.

[5] Stephen Maher, "Fake Video Is a Big Problem. In 2019, It Gets Worse.," *Maclean's (Online)*, December 28, 2018, http://libproxy.mtroyal.ca/login?url=https://search.proquest.com/docview/2161685117?accountid=1343.

other fake news claims, resulted in his ban from social media.[6] And when the fake news headline read 'Pope Francis Shocks World, Endorses Donald Trump for President'—shared by almost a million people on Facebook—it's rapid spread is deeply troubling.[7] A study published in 2018, using 10 years of tweets by 3 million users involving some 126,000 stories, revealed, "Falsehood diffused significantly farther, faster, deeper, and more broadly than the truth in all categories of information, and the effects were more pronounced for false political news than for false news about terrorism, natural disasters, science, urban legends, or financial information."[8] The authors report fake stories go viral more often than accurate stories reaching 1,500 people six times quicker because they tended to create the emotional reaction of surprise and disgust.

Perhaps fake news itself is not a problem if people can distinguish it with fact-based news. However, distinguishing fake from real news has become increasingly difficult especially when the President of the United States, Donald Trump, blatantly disregards the truth, either through ignorance or as a means of serving his own political ends. For example, his statement that President Obama tapped his phone during the presidential campaign had no evidential support. CNN reported the claim as being a lie.[9] Or consider Trump's statement, when campaigning in Ohio, that the US is the "highest taxed nation in the world."[10] Again, it's a lie motivated to drum up support for tax reform. He also claimed to win the electoral popular vote. Also, not true. These and many other claims by Trump are lies. *He is a liar.* Trump has used the term 'fake news' or 'fake media' in some 446 Tweets as a means of decrying a host of issues; he

---

[6] Dan Leger, "Online Hate Faces a Long-Overdue Reckoning," *Chronicle - Herald*, April 15, 2019, http://libproxy.mtroyal.ca/login?url=https://search.proquest.com/docview/2210020792?accountid=1343.

[7] Gillian Tett, "Facebook and the Fight against the Fakers: PARTING SHOT [Usa Region]," *Financial Times*, July 7, 2018, http://libproxy.mtroyal.ca/login?url=https://search.proquest.com/docview/2084120999?accountid=1343.

[8] Soroush Vosoughi, Deb Roy, and Sinan Aral, "The Spread of True and False News Online," *Science (New York, N.Y.)* 359, no. 6380 (March 9, 2018): 1146, https://doi.org/10.1126/science.aap9559.

[9] Jeremy Diamond, "Trump on Obama Wiretapping Claim: It Has 'Been Proven Very Strongly,'" *CNN Wire* (CNN Newsource Sales Inc., May 1, 2017), http://libproxy.mtroyal.ca/login?url=http://search.ebscohost.com/login.aspx?direct=true&AuthType=ip,url,cookie,uid&db=n5h&AN=BAQ41493648001&site=ehost-live.

[10] Jeanne Sahadi, "Trump Says the U.S. Is the Highest Taxed Country in the World. No, It's Not," *CNN Wire* (CNN Newsource Sales Inc., October 12, 2017), https://money.cnn.com/2017/10/12/news/economy/trump-us-highest-taxes/index.html.

has also made, according to the Washington Post, some 10,111 false or misleading claims since taking office.[11]

The fact Donald Trump lies should not be surprising; we all do it. On average, people tell two lies per day. Specifically, people mostly fib about their true feelings or opinions to spare others from the truth.[12] DePaulo and Kashy also found, unsurprisingly, that people tended to lie less to those they have close relationships with (friends, family members, and romantic partners) than strangers.[13] Moreover, when it comes to detecting lies, *we are bad it*. According to Bond and DePaulo, our ability to detect lies is no better than chance.[14] However, those who are more 'leery' or 'suspicious' of the truthfulness of other's statements may be more likely to regard others as being liars. Unfortunately, as the authors point out, there is no evidence to support such a claim. The largest determinant, says Bond and DePaulo, is not the ability to discern truth but the perceived credibility of the source of information.[15] In other words, if someone perceives the source as a reliable and honest bearer of knowledge, they are more likely to conclude the source is telling the truth. Similarly, if someone is perceived as being dishonest, the individual is more likely to believe the source is lying.

Determining the credibility and honesty of a source is more difficult than ever, especially with the explosion of social media technologies. Social media platforms, such as Facebook or Twitter, have changed the nature of lying by making it easier and more prevalent. Research shows that people are more likely to lie using instant messaging and email than face-to-face discussion. Computer-mediated communication has a deindividuating effect whereby the sender of the message is more psychologically and physically distant from the

---

[11] Glenn Kessler, Salvador Rizzo, and Meg Kelly, "Fallacy in Five Figures: Trump Blusters Past 10,000 False or Misleading Claims," *Washington Post, The* (Y, 4AD), http://libproxy.mtroyal.ca/login?url=http://search.ebscohost.com/login.aspx?direct=true&AuthType=ip,url,cookie,uid&db=n5h&AN=wapo.44abfb66-6a8f-11e9-be3a-33217240a539&site=ehost-live.

[12] Bella M DePaulo et al., "Lying in Everyday Life," *Journal of Personality and Social Psychology* 70, no. 5 (May 1996): 979–95, https://doi.org/10.1037/0022-3514.70.5.979; Bella M DePaulo, "The Many Faces of Lies," in *The Social Psychology of Good and Evil*, ed. A. G. Miller (New York: Guilford Press, 2004), 303–26.

[13] Bella M DePaulo, "The Many Faces of Lies," in *The Social Psychology of Good and Evil*, ed. A. G. Miller (New York: Guilford Press, 2004), 12.

[14] Charles F Jr. Bond and Bella M DePaulo, "Individual Differences in Judging Deception: Accuracy and Bias," *Psychological Bulletin* 134, no. 4 (July 2008): 477–92, https://doi.org/10.1037/0033-2909.134.4.477.

[15] Bella M DePaulo, "The Many Faces of Lies," 487.

receiver and thus more likely to engage in lying.[16] This deindividuation may account for expressed concerns over increased incivility across social networking sites.[17] Interestingly, during the last US Presidential election, Republican candidates made more lying accusations against Democrats than Democrats against Republicans, with Donald Trump leading the charge with his fake news rhetoric.[18]

At other times, Donald Trump does not lie; he bullshits. Trump claims to have invented the phrase, 'prime the pump.' He has said that millions of illegal voters cost him the popular vote. He touted the fact he only needed a very short time to understand everything about US healthcare.[19] And when Canadian Prime Minister, Justin Trudeau, correctly pointed out Canada does not have a trade deficit with the US, Trump insisted otherwise. Trump even bragged about not knowing or caring about the truth stating, "I didn't even know ... I had no idea." In other words, Trump admitted to making up an answer or bullshitting to cover up his own ignorance in regard to the evidence or facts related to the US/Canada trade deficit.[20]

Of course, Trump's *bullshitting* masks a deeper problem within society. As Frankfurt acknowledges, "[o]ne of the most salient features of our culture is that there is so much bullshit."[21] I am much more sanguine than Frankfurt. Yes, people bullshit but, unlike lying, its prevalence in society and its extent is uncertain and there is little psychological research to suggest otherwise. And even if such research existed, the reliability of its results might be questioned if bullshit's prevalence is as deep as Frankfurt argues. However, one study does show people are more willing to bullshit if they feel obligated to have an

---

[16] Mattitiyahu Zimbler and Robert Feldman, "Liar, Liar, Hard Drive on Fire: How Media Context Affects Lying Behavior.," *Journal of Applied Social Psychology* 41, no. 10 (October 2011): 2492–2507, http://10.0.4.87/j.1559-1816.2011.00827.x.
[17] Lee Rainie, Amanda Lenhart, and Aaron Smith, "The Tone of Life on Social Networking Sites," *Pew Research*, 2012, 30, http://pewinternet.org/Reports/2012/Social-networking-climate.aspx; Maeve Duggan, "Online Harrassment," Pew Research Center, 2014, http://www.pewinternet.org/2014/10/22/online-harassment/.
[18] Kate Kenski, Christine R Filer, and Bethany A Conway-Silva, "Lying, Liars, and Lies: Incivility in 2016 Presidential Candidate and Campaign Tweets During the Invisible Primary," *American Behavioral Scientist* 62, no. 3 (February 7, 2018): 286–99, https://doi.org/10.1177/0002764217724840.
[19] Matthew Yglesias, "The Bullshitter-in-Chief," *Vox Media*, May 30, 2017, https://www.vox.com/policy-and-politics/2017/5/30/15631710/trump-bullshit.
[20] Cristiano Lima and Megan Cassella, "Trump Repeats Canada Trade Deficit Claim After Bosting About Bluffing to Trudeau," *Politico*, March 15, 2018, https://www.politico.com/story/2018/03/15/trump-canada-trade-deficit-465464.
[21] Henry G Frankfurt, *On Bullshit* (Princeton, N.J: Princeton University Press, 2005), 1.

informed opinion about a topic that surpasses their current level of knowledge. In other words, the greater the social expectations to express an informed opinion, the greater the possibility of bullshit occurring.[22] The pressure to have an informed opinion might explain the bullshit spewed by Trump. He is the President of the United States, after all, and is expected to have a wide range of opinions on a host of economic, social, and political issues. Social media exasperates this pressure. Kitanya Harrison, a writer on the website Medium, states, "[t]here's something about the way social media is constructed that makes the people using it feel like we have to have an opinion on everything that comes across our feeds...Everything's designed to happen fast, before you can really think things through."[23] If Petrocelli is right and if others feel this way, especially when using social media platforms, it might lead to an increase in bullshit within society.

Protecting against lying and bullshit, thus, seems to be more important than ever. Liberal education, I will argue, can help us defend against both. However, the difference between lying and bullshit is not as clear-cut as it seems. To understand why, let us turn to a brief philosophical analysis of bullshit.

The Epistemic Difference Between Lying and Bullshit

Frankfurt argues the difference between lying and bullshit is based on the intention to deceive and awareness of truth. To lie is to deceive others by making a knowingly false claim. When Trump stated, in reference to the US immigration lottery program, it "randomly hands out green cards without any regard for skill, merit, or the safety of the American people," he is lying.[24] According to the US Citizenship and Immigration services, immigrant applicants must meet a number of criteria to enter the United States including high school education or equivalent, two years work experience, and a battery of security checks.[25] If we assume Trump knew (or should have known) the basic criteria for awarding green cards in the US, his claims were told in order to undermine the truth and deceive his audience into believing something

---

[22] John V. Petrocelli, "Antecedents of Bullshitting," *Journal of Experimental Social Psychology* 76 (May 1, 2018): 249–58, https://doi.org/10.1016/J.JESP.2018.03.004.

[23] Kitanya Harrison, "On the Pressure to Have an Opinion About Everything (and How It's Being Used Against You)," Medium, 2019, https://medium.com/@kitanyaharrison/on-the-pressure-to-have-an-opinion-about-everything-and-how-its-being-used-against-you-21451528d43c.

[24] Daniel Dale, "Donald Trump Made 12 False Claims in His State of the Union Address," *The Toronto Star (Online)* (Toronto: Torstar Syndication Services, a Division of Toronto Star Newspapers Limited, January 31, 2018), http://libproxy.mtroyal.ca/login?url=https://search.proquest.com/docview/1992713114?accountid=1343.

[25] Ibid.

which is false. Imagine another case where a student, who is struggling in the course, asks his professor for an extension on an assignment because he and his brother were in a car accident in which his brother died. The grieving student eventually completes the course and asks his professor for a letter of reference for medical school. The letter of reference is glowing, explaining how the student showed determination and perseverance in light of his brother's death. During the medical school interview, the interviewer asks about the student's brother. The student remarks his brother is doing fine and is an investment banker. When pressed about the contradiction regarding his brother, the student confesses he lied.[26] Clearly, the student's intent was to deceive the professor by stating something that was false. The liar's intent is to misrepresent the facts—to make a false claim—in order to deceive another person into believing it is true when it is not.[27]

Bullshit, on the other hand, has two important characteristics. First, bullshit is not about creating a false belief in the mind of others, but it is misrepresentative. As Frankfurt states, bullshit's "primary intention is…to give its audience a false impression concerning what is going on in the mind of the speaker."[28] The creation of such an impression, underlined by an attitude of pretentiousness, is the main point of bullshit. In espousing bullshit, the person does not need to lie but merely ensure the audience has a false impression of them—namely, the speaker knows something when they do not. Consider Trump's most egregious comments on abortion. At a rally in Wisconsin, he stated, "The baby is born. The mother meets with the doctor. They take care of the baby. They wrap the baby beautifully, and then the doctor and the mother determine whether or not they will execute the baby."[29] There is, of course, no evidence that doctors are killing babies, but Trump's comment is such an exaggeration, it cannot be assessed within the realm of truthfulness or falsity. By Frankfurt's lights, it is bullshit. Trump is attempting to bluff his way into the

---

[26] Karen W Arenson, "Columbia Lesson: No Lying to Professor," *New York Times* 149, no. 51357 (April 2000): B3.
[27] For additional reading on the philosophy of lying see Sissela Bok *Lying: Moral Choice in Public and Private Life* (New York: Pantheon Books, 1978). and David Nyberg *The Varnished Truth : Truth Telling and Deceiving in Ordinary Life* (Chicago, [Ill.] ; University of Chicago Press, 1993).
[28] Frankfurt, *On Bullshit*, 15.
[29] Mark Sommerhauser, "Leading Pediatrician Slams Donald Trump Claim That Doctors Are 'executing' Babies," *Wisconsin State Journal, The (Madison, WI)* (Wisconsin State Journal, The (Madison, WI), April 30, 2019), http://libproxy.mtroyal.ca/login?url= http://search.ebscohost.com/login.aspx?direct=true&AuthType=ip,url,cookie,uid&db= n5h&AN=2W63594461032&site=ehost-live.

hearts of the anti-abortion religious right and provide them with a misrepresentation of what is really going on.

The second characteristic, as mentioned above, concerns bullshit's lack of connection to truth. For Frankfurt, bullshit is "grounded neither in a belief that…is true, as a lie must be, in a belief that it is not true. It is just this lack of connection to a concern with truth—this indifference to how things really are—that I regard as of the essence of bullshit."[30] For the bullshitter, it is not a question of failing to get things right; it is a matter of not even trying. It is this lack of concern for the truth-value of their statements which entails they are not lying; they do not presume to know the truth but say things completely unconstrained by it. To tell a lie requires one to carefully construct a falsehood and set it within systems of beliefs that pushes truth out of the way. Bullshit, however, gives people the freedom to spew information that is not necessarily a falsehood and is thus not constrained by truth. Consider Frankfurt's original example, "a Fourth of July orator who goes on bombastically about 'our great and blessed country,' whose Founding Fathers under divine guidance created a new beginning for mankind.'" In this case, the bullshitter is not interested in whether the audience actually believes such truths about the Founding Fathers, God or new beginnings, the intent here is to create in the audience the impression they are a patriot through hyperbole. This freedom allows for improvisation. It is because the bullshitter ignores the demands of truth, writes Frankfurt, "bullshit is the greater enemy of the truth than lies."[31] Put differently, and if Frankfurt is right, for the liar there is still something true that is being lied about. For the bullshitter, the truth or, indeed, the falsity of a statement does not matter at all. The bullshitter is simply interested in the outcome of her or his interlocutor's actions subsequent to having been bullshitted to. And that is all; facts are swept aside to achieve particular ends.

Although Frankfurt thinks bullshit is more dangerous than lies, they both can have dire consequences when truth and facts are set aside. Hannah Arendt's work speaks to these dangers and, in particular, the use of bullshit and lies in aiding the rise of authoritarian political ideologies where freedom, democracy and truth are enemies. As Arendt points out in her essay, "Truth and Politics", facts are hated by tyrants because they are beyond consent and "possess an infuriating stubbornness that nothing can move except plain lies."[32] Hence, bullshit and propaganda are used to spread misinformation to attain or keep political power while, at the same time, suppressing reality and truth. Unfortunately, social media has only exacerbated the ability to spread

---

[30] Frankfurt, *On Bullshit*, 15.
[31] Ibid., 61.
[32] Hannah Arendt, "Truth and Politics," *The New Yorker*, February 25, 1967, 54.

misinformation because it provides platforms for anyone to express their point of view or share their opinions regardless of how uninformed, racist, misogynistic, or false they may be. When facts are transformed into opinion, truths disappear in a sea of personal or alternative points of view ('facts') and ultimately disappear itself. However, for lies to effect political and social change it requires organization, leadership and sympathizers, including the media, to spread them far and wide.[33] The deluge of lies and propaganda (bullshit) turn the average citizen, over time, into gullible and cynical supporters. As Hannah Arendt notes in her 1951 work the *Origins of Totalitarianism*:

> In an ever-changing, incomprehensible world the masses had reached the point where they would, at the same time, believe everything and nothing, think that everything was possible and nothing was true... The totalitarian mass leaders based their propaganda on the correct psychological assumption that, under such conditions, one could make people believe the most fantastic statements one day, and trust that if the next day they were given irrefutable proof of their falsehood, they would take refuge in cynicism; instead of deserting the leaders who had lied to them, they would protest that they had known all along that the statement was a lie and would admire the leaders for their superior tactical cleverness.[34]

Constant political lies often create cognitive dissonance in people, who recognize such lies, but become subordinate to cynical attitudes about political prowess and craftsmanship. Ultimately, says Arendt, in accepting and repeating such lies, supporters become increasingly complicit as a way of hiding their shame. Most importantly, lies undermine epistemological anchors to the point where foundational truths are threatened themselves. Arendt explains, "The result of a consistent and total substitution of lies for factual truth is not that the lie will now be accepted as truth and truth be defamed as a lie, but that the sense by which we take our bearings in the real world—and the category of truth versus falsehood is among the mental means to this end—is being destroyed."[35] The undermining of the bedrock of truth means reality itself becomes untethered; and unhinged. It's the deepest kind of cynicism whereby an individual "refus[es] to believe in the truth of anything, no matter how well this truth may be established."[36] But lies and bullshit, as a means to political power, cannot, says, Arendt, "produce a substitute for the secure

---

[33] Hannah Arendt, *The Origins of Totalitarianism* (Cleveland: Meridian Books, 1951), 383.
[34] Ibid.
[35] Ibid., 78.
[36] Ibid.

stability of factual reality, which, because it is past, has grown into a dimension beyond our reach."[37] In other words, truth and fact are stubborn and resilient; they are the hallmark of human action and cannot be manipulated out of this world.[38]

Regardless of the political consequences, Frankfurt's distinction between lies and bullshit needs to be more nuanced. Let me turn to this now.

Blurring the Lines between Lying and Bullshit

Frankfurt's distinction between bullshit and lying, I believe, is not as clear as he claims. The liar uses false statements as a way of trying to manipulate the beliefs and attitudes of others, whereas the bullshitter has no such intent and is indifferent to truth or falsity. However, this is not always the case. In some circumstances, the bullshitter is equally deceptive in trying to manipulate his audience's beliefs, opinions, and attitudes and equally misrepresents the truth. In this sense, like the liar, truth matters.[39] Imagine student X goes to Professor Y's office on the last day of class. Prof Y vaguely remembers X, as she only attended the first few classes then disappeared for the rest of the term. Checking his grade book, Prof Y finds X did not complete any assignments or exams. X tells Prof Y the following tale:

> 'My father came out as gay in early summer and separated from her mother, who I live with. Having come out as homosexual, my father decided to participate in the Gay Pride Parade. As he was riding on one of the floats, he fell off hitting his head on the pavement sending him to hospital in a coma, of which he remains. My mother, upon hearing the news, relapsed into drug and alcohol addiction and has been incapacitated for months. I am stressed at having to look after her and spend hours sitting by my father's side in the hospital. I did complete some of the assignments and had them ready to hand in but I recently got a therapy dog to cope with my stress and the dog, being young, got into my knapsack and ate my homework. Could I have an extension to complete my assignments?'

Confused, Prof Y doesn't know if this is a lie or bullshit. If the story is made up (bullshit), the student does not seem indifferent to truth but is trying desperately to create false beliefs in Prof Y about why they missed so much

---

[37] Ibid., 83.
[38] Ibid.
[39] Michael Wreen, "A P.S. on B.S.: Some Remarks on Humbug and Bullshit," *Metaphilosophy* (Oxford: Wiley Subscription Services, Inc, 2013), https://doi.org/ 10.1111/meta.12021.

school. In other words, the goal of bullshit, in many cases, is to manipulate opinions, attitudes and emotions, just like lying, in order to deceive their audience. In other words, bullshit can often consist of lies but not all cases of lies are bullshit.

Moreover, bullshit need not be indifferent to truth or misrepresentative of the speaker's mind. *The Secret*, written by Rhonda Bryne, is based on the idea that thoughts attract experiences by virtue of their specific frequencies. For example, thinking of an old friend and wanting to speak to her, will result in her phoning you, wanting and wishing to go to university will produce an acceptance letter. An individual's thoughts resonate with the universe in such a way that it creates their own reality. Unfortunately, there is no credible scientific support for the law of attraction but Bryne uses plenty of quotes from Gandhi, Thoreau, and St. Augustine to appeal to authority. *The Secret* also utilizes the illusion of potential which is based on the belief we can acquire skills, abilities, wealth, health, or respect with minimal effort. *The Secret* uses quantum mechanics to explain the power of thought on our experiences. But, as psychologists Christopher Chabris and Daniel Simons state, "whenever you hear someone appeal to impenetrable physics to explain the workings of the mind, run away."[40] In other words, appealing to the complex field of quantum physics to explain human thought is bullshit. For the sake of argument, let's assume the author of *The Secret*, who has made millions from her books and films, truly beliefs these ideas and is firmly committed to the scientific research she cites as evidence. She is not misrepresenting her own mind to audiences (she truly believes the connection between thought and experience); is not talking nonsense or bluffing her audience; there is nothing nefarious going on. If this is the case, contrary to Frankfurt, who argues the bullshitter is not concerned with the truth and falsity of their claims, *The Secret* seems to be a case in which non-deceptive bullshit is possible within the bounds of what she takes to be the truth. Moreover, and most importantly, Byrne's supposed scientific backed truths, gives the audience the false impression that Bryne knows what she is talking about when, in fact, she does not; it's bullshit. My point is that, whereas Frankfurt argues perspectival intent decides whether someone is bullshitting, I suggest intent is not a necessary criterion to call bullshit on claims.

Perhaps the problem with bullshit, at least in some cases, is not the lack of concern for truth but an obsession with truth. As Roberts-Miller states, the evidence to support birthers, anti-vaxers, homophobics, and climate change deniers, is "often incomprehensible, internally contradictory, and sometimes

---

[40] Christopher Chabris and Daniel Simons, "Fight 'The Power,'" *New York Times Sunday Book Review*, September 26, 2010, 27.

fabricated; the journals in which it is published are not as scientific as their names sound and rely heavily on cunning projection. But they do have evidence, and they do have people who claim expertise who support them."[41] And when it's pointed out there is no evidence to support their claims, they simply find alternative evidence. So long as the audience thinks the individual is speaking the truth, then the speaker is intentionally are trying to misrepresent their own thinking. Often the audience knows the evidence is faulty or problematic but feels justified because they want to believe social forces are conspiring against their conception of truth. Hence, like the bullshitter, those who believe in conspiracy theories or support bullshit claims might also show a kind of pretentiousness on their part to stand out from the crowd. In this sense, perhaps the fight is not against evidence as it relates to truth, but finding ways to prevent people from wanting to be part of fringe groups in the first place. But, if my previous arguments against Frankfurt are convincing, bullshit might be more connected to the truth than what he thinks. If so, then detecting bullshit is much more difficult but also much more important.

Although bullshit comes from many different sources, our current cultural and technological environment seems to spread it far and deep, especially when preferential algorithms skew information to feed and confirm pre-existing prejudices. Internet trolls demean, shame, and engage in *ad hominem* attacks and the US President denounces respectable news sources, like the *New York Times*, as fake news. Bullshit and lies work, as noted earlier, because people often trust the information source and, therefore, are less likely to engage in critical thinking. As Sperber et al. explains, "[o]ften, information spreads through a group from a single source, and is accepted by people along the chains of transmission because they trust the source rather than because of any evidence or arguments for the content."[42] Ideally, in cases where the source lies, falsifies evidence, or uses poor arguments, being skeptical of their trustworthiness should be paramount.

But being skeptical does not mean cynical. Skepticism, in its healthiest form, is an attitude or disposition of doubt towards specific claims or statements. In this sense, a person may be inclined to doubt or question a statement's veracity

---

[41] Patricia Roberts-Miller, "Conspiracy Bullshit ," *Rhetoric Society Quarterly* (Routledge , 2015), 466, https://doi.org/10.1080/02773945.2015.1088341.
[42] Dan Sperber et al., "Epistemic Vigilance," *Mind and Language* 25, no. 4 (September 2010): 380, https://doi.org/10.1111/j.1468-0017.2010.01394.x.

and not take it being true until proven otherwise.⁴³ In more extreme unhealthy forms of skepticism, such as the ancient Greek philosopher Pyrrho, nothing could be known with certainty and no truth could be ascertained. Unhealthy skepticism leads to a tendency to dismiss everything as being false, fake or untrue; it also slides into a cynical view about the human condition. The cynic, unlike healthy skepticism, is someone who finds faults with the world at every turn. It's a disposition to disbelieve in the sincerity and goodness in human actions; motives are suspect and held in contempt. Although both skepticism and cynicism both roughly mean the "questioning of facts or motives...one comes from the point of view of an open mind, and the other from a closed mind."⁴⁴ The skeptic is open to new ideas but may wait until sufficient evidence is provided; they may question the claims of others until it can be verified and confirmed. It is this kind of healthy skepticism that I espouse, not a cynical view of others or the world.

Unfortunately, taking a skeptical stance towards others is difficult because people are horribly gullible, often imputing truth to claims where there are none. The psychologist Dan Gilbert found people tend to accept propositions and claims from others as being true and, only in retrospect, do they assess the validity and truthfulness of such claims; this is especially important when statements are repeatedly made.⁴⁵ In other words, the more a statement is repeated, the more people will assess it as true. For example, Trump's repeated claim that immigrants are invading the US from Mexico bellies the facts, but because they are repeated so often it is perceived as having higher epistemic justification for some people.⁴⁶ This is known as the illusory of truth effect.⁴⁷ Moreover, simpler explanations about complex issues are also perceived as being more trustworthy because they are easier to process and understand.⁴⁸

---

⁴³ Merrill Perlman, "How Is Skepticism Different than Cynicism? Find the Answer in Acient Greece," *Columbia Journalism Review*, October 15, 2018, https://www.cjr.org/language_corner/skepticism-cynicism.php.
⁴⁴ Ibid.
⁴⁵ Daniel T. Gilbert, "How Mental Systems Believe," *American Psychologist* 46, no. 2 (1991): 107–19, https://doi.org/10.1037/0003-066X.46.2.107.
⁴⁶ John Cassidy, "A Weak and Rambling President Declares a Fake National Emergency," The New Yorker, 2019, https://www.newyorker.com/news/our-columnists/a-weak-and-rambling-president-declares-a-fake-national-emergency.
⁴⁷ Lynn Hasher, David Goldstein, and Thomas Toppino, "Frequency and the Conference of Referential Validity," *Journal of Verbal Learning and Verbal Behavior* 16, no. 1 (February 1977): 107–12, https://doi.org/10.1016/S0022-5371(77)80012-1.
⁴⁸ Christian Unkelbach, "Reversing the Truth Effect: Learning the Interpretation of Processing Fluency in Judgments of Truth," *Journal of Experimental Psychology. Learning, Memory, and Cognition* 33, no. 1 (January 2007): 219–30, https://doi.org/10.1037/0278-7393.33.1.219.

In addition, even when people know someone is lying, the lies can often be justified by imaging counterfactual situations in which the lies might be true and thus give the liar a moral pass.[49] All of these psychological processes lead to the acceptance or tolerance of lies and bullshit.

The most important factor influencing the acceptance of bullshit claims seems to be the lack of critical thinking. In order to determine participant receptivity to bullshit, Pennycook et al used a number of meaningless, yet profound, statements from the website New Age Bullshit Generator, quotes from the author Deepak Chopra, and several cognitive tests including a cognitive reflective test, ontological confusion scale, and religious belief questionnaire.[50] The authors found a positive correlation between bullshit receptivity and high levels of ontological confusions (e.g. prayers have healing powers), religious beliefs (e.g. angels exist), and paranormal beliefs (e.g. ghosts are real). They also found a positive correlation between those participants who have strong beliefs in conspiracy ideation, alternative medicine, and low levels of bullshit detectability. Individuals who are insensitive to bullshit tend to have an "uncritically open mind" which makes them increasingly gullible.[51] In other words, those who are more susceptible to bullshit claims tend to have a reflexive (uncritical) mindset which makes them more open to questionable information. The study suggests, as a way to guard against the acceptance of bullshit claims, increasing critical thinking skills and skeptical attitudes as key.

In another study, Sterling and Pennycook, found a modest correlation between neoliberal free-market ideological thinking and greater bullshit receptivity. Free market ideology tends to be more intuitive rather than analytic, heuristic rather than systemic, simple rather than complex and supporters tend to have lower verbal intelligence.[52] These results are consistent with other research which demonstrated a connection between bullshit receptivity and having favourable political views of Donald Trump, Ted Cruz

---

[49] Daniel A Effron, "Why Trump Supporters Don't Mind His Lies," *New York Times* 167, no. 57947 (April 29, 2018): 6–7, http://libproxy.mtroyal.ca/login?url=http://search.ebscohost.com/login.aspx?direct=true&AuthType=ip,url,cookie,uid&db=n5h&AN=129364312&site=ehost-live.
[50] Gordon Pennycook et al., "On the Reception and Detection of Pseudo-Profound Bullshit," *Judgment and Decision Making* 10, no. 6 (2015): 549–63.
[51] Ibid., 559.
[52] Joanna Sterling, John T Jost, and Gordon Pennycook, "Are Neoliberals More Susceptible to Bullshit?," *Judgment & Decision Making* 11, no. 4 (July 2016): 352–60, http://libproxy.mtroyal.ca/login?url=http://search.ebscohost.com/login.aspx?direct=true&AuthType=ip,url,cookie,uid&db=a9h&AN=117243485&site=ehost-live.

and Marco Rubio.[53] There was no significant relationship between bullshit and Hilary Clinton, Martin O'Malley, and Bernie Sanders. In other words, individuals with more conservative/Republican values have a greater tendency to see profoundness in bullshit than liberals/Democrat. Research also reveals individuals who are more susceptible to believe bullshit claims are also less likely to perceive fake news items because of skepticism and critical thinking.[54] In other words, those who are open to ideas or claims without critically assessing them and do not engage in analytic thinking are most susceptible to believe bullshit and fake news claims.

Using Liberal Education to Detect Bullshit

Bullshit is everywhere and we all contribute to the stench in our own way, says Frankfurt. The problem, he thinks, is coming to understand what bullshit is, not its detection. I think he's wrong. Liberal education can help detect and combat the acceptance of bullshit.

Ostensibly, the rhetoric on liberal education supports the notion that its study can make people better bullshit detectors. If liberal education can help people become better reflective critical thinkers and increase healthy skeptical approaches to information, then it should be an important preventative measure against the acceptance of bullshit. Optimistically, liberal education should aid the ability to "identify assumptions, draw inferences, distinguish facts from opinions, draw conclusions from data, and judge the authority of arguments and sources."[55] It is this kind of thinking that is essential to distinguishing between lies, bullshit and truth.

However, demonstrating a connection between liberal education and improvements in critical thinking is not supported by the academic literature because the research is usually isolated to specific courses, not to programmatic outcomes. For example, Mazer, Hunt and Kuznekoff assessed critical thinking using two communications courses, which are part of Illinois

---

[53] Stefan Pfattheicher and Simon Schindler, "Misperceiving Bullshit as Profound Is Associated with Favorable Views of Cruz, Rubio, Trump and Conservatism," *PloS One* (United States: Public Library of Science , 2016), https://doi.org/10.1371/journal.pone.0153419.

[54] Gordon Pennycook and David G Rand, "Who Falls for Fake News? The Roles of Bullshit Receptivity, Overclaiming, Familiarity, and Analytic Thinking," *Journal of Personality*, 2019, https://doi.org/10.1111/jopy.12476.

[55] Jefery Scheuer, "Critical Thinking and the Liberal Arts," *Academe* 101, no. 6 (November 2015): 38, http://libproxy.mtroyal.ca/login?url=http://search.ebscohost.com/login.aspx?direct=true&AuthType=ip,url,cookie,uid&db=ehh&AN=111164597&site=ehost-live.

State University's general education curriculum.[56] In the study, 324 participants were recruited and broken into two groups, one control and one experimental. Each student then took a basic communications course with critical thinking instruction. However, the experimental group had enhanced emphasis on argument analysis and used highly interactive techniques to cultivate learning such as actively applying learned reasoning, fallacies, and argumentative skills to specific examples and engaging in peer and self-evaluations of arguments. Results showed that students who took the enhanced training demonstrated significant improvement in critical thinking compared to those with basic exposure to key concepts. With regards to general education, it's unclear to what extent it played a role in these results, but it is clear course-specific emphasis on reasoning and argumentation can improve critical thinking.

Similar results were found when liberal arts and research-intensive institutions were compared. Using a sample of 920 students from 17 institutions in the United States, researchers assessed students in their first year using the critical thinking test called the College Assessment of Academic Proficiency (CAAP) to establish a benchmark and then followed up 4 years later as student's neared graduation.[57] When liberal arts institutions were compared with research-focused institutions, which tend to have larger classes and are less student-oriented, results initially revealed attending liberal arts institutions was associated with higher critical thinking skills. However, when classroom pedagogy was assessed at both types of institutions, specifically classroom instruction focusing on deep learning and immersion in critical thinking, no difference was found.[58] In other words, it's pedagogy, not liberal education, which is most important to develop critical thinkers.

Central to the deep learning and critical thinking pedagogy is exposure to diverse perspectives. Interestingly, Cole and Zhou found positive and frequent faculty-student interaction, inside or outside of class, to be the most important factor in cultivating critical thinking.[59] Professors who challenge student thinking encourage critical assessment. The authors also found students who took a greater diversity of courses (math, science, literature, humanities and

---

[56] Joseph P Mazer, Stephen K Hunt, and Jeffrey H Kuznekoff, "Revising General Education: Assessing a Critical Thinking Instructional Model in the Basic Communication Course," *JGE: The Journal of General Education* 56, no. 3–4 (July 2007): 173–99.

[57] Ernest Pascarella et al., "How the Instructional and Learning Environments of Liberal Arts Colleges Enhance Cognitive Development," *Higher Education (00181560)* 66, no. 5 (November 2013): 569–83, http://10.0.3.239/s10734-013-9622-z.

[58] Also see Abrami et al. 2008; Niu, Behar-Horenstein, and Garvan 2013.

[59] Darnell Cole and Ji Zhou, "Diversity and Collegiate Experiences Affecting Self-Perceived Gains in Critical Thinking," *The Journal of General Education* 63, no. 1 (2014): 15–34.

social sciences), opposed to those majoring in engineering or science fields or took a narrower range of courses, had lower critical thinking skills. The authors argue, because humanities and social sciences tend to focus on a broad range of diverse perspectives and ideas, it pushes students to cognitive disequilibrium which encourages them to transcend traditional thinking and encourage independent thought. However, reason dictates if this approach is broadened throughout the curriculum, including math, science, and literature, the effect on students can even be more pronounced. After all, science, math and literature can often challenge conventional thinking and can be used as an important antidote to the spread of bullshit in society. Unfortunately, many of the social media platforms, like Facebook and YouTube, often use algorithms to reinforce beliefs, not challenge them. This suggests a broad liberal education imbuing students with critical thinking skills is surely needed more than ever. As Tsui explains, it's important to build a curriculum which will allow students "to grapple with complex issues, consider multiple perspectives, question authoritative sources, and develop one's own nuanced interpretation."[60] Explicit emphasis on diverse perspectives can help uproot traditional or entrenched thinking by exposing students to alternative methodologies and assumptions.

These results suggest good critical thinking pedagogy is based on students coming to understanding diverse views within the context of specific disciplinary domains. In this sense, critical thinking is not a skill developed independently from the disciplinary knowledge in which it is used. As Willingham explains, "You can teach students maxims about how they ought to think, but without background knowledge and practice, they probably will not be able to implement the advice they memorize."[61] Critical thinking skills must be taught within a disciplinary context and thus students must have some background knowledge in order to understand how critical thinking applies. Without this knowledge base, the thin gruel of critical thinking cannot be digested in ways to produce intellectual nutrition. As individuals learn critical thinking skills and disciplinary content, it allows for great adaptability and transferability across disciplines.

Developing a healthy skepticism is also important for detecting bullshit. Bartz argues statements or claims by others should be scrutinized using the following process: students should describe the claim (C), determine the role of the claimant and their motives (R), look at the information backing the claim

---

[60] Lisa Tsui, "Cultivating Critical Thinking: Insights from an Elite Liberal Arts College," *The Journal of General Education* 56, no. 3/4 (2008): 206.
[61] Daniel T Willingham, "Critical Thinking: Why Is It So Hard to Teach?," *Reprinted from American Educator Summer 2007 Issue*, March 2008, 21.

(I), test to determine if the claim should be doubted (T), independently verify the claim is supported by evidence (I), and, finally, assess the claim based on logical consistency and reasonableness (C).[62] The CRITIC acronym can be applied to a host of disciplines and issues. For example, when a similar kind of skeptical approach was applied to accounting students engaged in auditing companies (i.e., being skeptical of managerial claims, evaluating audit evidence, taking an unbiased perspective, and assessing causal connections) the vast majority of students scored high on skepticism and also correctly assessed the level of management fraud risk.[63]

Given the cited research, liberal education can provide a beacon of hope against the darkness of bullshit and lies. Critical thinking within liberal education must be viewed programmatically grounded in a multidisciplinary framework where critical thinking is used ubiquitously throughout as a way of analyzing beliefs, ideas and concepts while, at the same time, imbuing student with a healthy dose of skepticism. Put more generally, liberal education can aid in developing what Sperber et al. calls *epistemic vigilance*.[64] Epistemic vigilance means using critical thinking skills and skepticism to adjust levels of trust depending on the source of the information and truth of the statements expressed. In other words, epistemic vigilance requires a labile view of trust whereby trust is tentative and should not automatically be affixed to statements. Liberal education, from a programmatic perspective, can play a pivotal role in developing such vigilance but further research is needed to validate such claims.

Conclusion

Frankfurt's analysis of bullshit has become increasingly important in our current cultural and political environment. Innovative deceptive video technology, algorithms reinforcing established beliefs, unprecedented presidential lies, and psychological factors, like the illusion of truth, all contribute to a culture of fake news, lies and bullshit. Even if the lines between lies and bullshit are increasingly blurred, liberal education can play a role in its detection and protection. Being epistemic vigilant requires critical thinking

---

[62] Wayne Bartz, "Teaching Skepticism via the CRITIC Acronym and the Skeptical Inquirer," *The Skeptical Inquirer* 26, no. 5 (2002): 42–44.
[63] Thomas Hayes, "Strategies for Teaching Professional Skepticism in the Classroom: Evidence from Senior-Level Auditing Students," *International Journal of Business, Accounting, & Finance* 10, no. 2 (2016): 110–21, http://libproxy.mtroyal.ca/login?url= http://search.ebscohost.com/login.aspx?direct=true&AuthType=ip,url,cookie,uid&db= bth&AN=122085990&site=ehost-live.
[64] Sperber et al., "Epistemic Vigilance."

and taking a skeptical eye towards the barrage of information hurled at us every day. A liberal education can provide the background knowledge necessary to understand and assess claims and beliefs, including the trustworthiness of its sources. In this sense, critical thinking should be seen as a case of epistemic virtue whereby individuals work towards broader truths about the world and not to achieve nefarious ends. Coherence between one's own beliefs and the source information is the foundation of epistemic vigilance. As new information is received from the source, an individual's background knowledge is activated as part of the comprehension process to ensure there is epistemic coherence between what they are hearing and what they know. At times coherence can be restored by distrusting the source or it can be restored by revising our beliefs; the latter requiring a meta-representational assessment of one's beliefs.[65] In short, liberal education should be seen as part of the epistemic vigilance process and thus an effective tool to detect bullshit.

References

Abrami, Philip C, Robert M Bernard, Evgueni Borokhovski, Anne Wade, Michael A Surkes, Rana Tamim, and Dai Zhang. "Instructional Interventions Affecting Critical Thinking Skills and Dispositions: A Stage 1 Meta-Analysis." *Review of Educational Research* 78, no. 4 (2008): 1102–34. https://doi.org/10.3102/0034654308326084.

Arendt, Hannah. "Truth and Politics." *The New Yorker*, February 25, 1967, https://hac.bard.edu/amor-mundi/truth-and-politics-hannah-arendt-2011-10-26.

———. *The Origins of Totalitarianism*. Cleveland: Meridian Books, 1951.

Arenson, Karen W. "Columbia Lesson: No Lying to Professor." *New York Times* 149, no. 51357 (April 2000): B3.

Bartz, Wayne. "Teaching Skepticism via the CRITIC Acronym and the Skeptical Inquirer." *The Skeptical Inquirer* 26, no. 5 (2002): 42–44.

Bok, Sissela. *Lying: Moral Choice in Public and Private Life*. New York: Pantheon Books, 1978.

Bond, Charles F Jr., and Bella M DePaulo. "Individual Differences in Judging Deception: Accuracy and Bias." *Psychological Bulletin* 134, no. 4 (July 2008): 477–92. https://doi.org/10.1037/0033-2909.134.4.477.

Burkhardt, Joanna M. "Chapter 1: History of Fake News." *Library Technology Reports* 53, no. 8 (November 2017): 5–9.

Cassidy, John. "A Weak and Rambling President Declares a Fake National Emergency." *The New Yorker*, 2019. https://www.newyorker.com/news/our-columnists/a-weak-and-rambling-president-declares-a-fake-national-emergency.

---

[65] Ibid.

Chabris, Christopher, and Daniel Simons. "Fight 'The Power.'" *New York Times Sunday Book Review*, September 26, 2010.

Cole, Darnell, and Ji Zhou. "Diversity and Collegiate Experiences Affecting Self-Perceived Gains in Critical Thinking." *The Journal of General Education* 63, no. 1 (2014): 15–34.

Dale, Daniel. "Donald Trump Made 12 False Claims in His State of the Union Address." *The Toronto Star (Online)*. Toronto: Torstar Syndication Services, a Division of Toronto Star Newspapers Limited, January 31, 2018. http://libproxy.mtroyal.ca/login?url=https://search.proquest.com/docview/1992713114?accountid=1343.

DePaulo, Bella M. "The Many Faces of Lies." In *The Social Psychology of Good and Evil*, edited by A. G. Miller, 303–26. New York: Guilford Press, 2004.

DePaulo, Bella M, Deborah A Kashy, Susan E Kirkendol, Melissa M Wyer, and Jennifer A Epstein. "Lying in Everyday Life." *Journal of Personality and Social Psychology* 70, no. 5 (May 1996): 979–95. https://doi.org/10.1037/0022-3514.70.5.979.

Diamond, Jeremy. "Trump on Obama Wiretapping Claim: It Has 'Been Proven Very Strongly.'" *CNN Wire*. CNN Newsource Sales Inc., May 1, 2017. http://libproxy.mtroyal.ca/login?url=http://search.ebscohost.com/login.aspx?direct=true&AuthType=ip,url,cookie,uid&db=n5h&AN=BAQ41493648001&site=ehost-live.

Duggan, Maeve. "Online Harrassment." Pew Research Center, 2014. http://www.pewinternet.org/2014/10/22/online-harassment/.

Effron, Daniel A. "Why Trump Supporters Don't Mind His Lies." *New York Times* 167, no. 57947 (April 29, 2018): 6–7. http://libproxy.mtroyal.ca/login?url=http://search.ebscohost.com/login.aspx?direct=true&AuthType=ip,url,cookie,uid&db=n5h&AN=129364312&site=ehost-live.

Frankfurt, Henry G. *On Bullshit*. Princeton, N.J: Princeton University Press, 2005.

Gilbert, Daniel T. "How Mental Systems Believe." *American Psychologist* 46, no. 2 (1991): 107–19. https://doi.org/10.1037/0003-066X.46.2.107.

Harrison, Kitanya. "On the Pressure to Have an Opinion About Everything (and How It's Being Used Against You)." *Medium*, 2019. https://medium.com/@kitanyaharrison/on-the-pressure-to-have-an-opinion-about-everything-and-how-its-being-used-against-you-21451528d43c.

Hasher, Lynn, David Goldstein, and Thomas Toppino. "Frequency and the Conference of Referential Validity." *Journal of Verbal Learning and Verbal Behavior* 16, no. 1 (February 1977): 107–12. https://doi.org/10.1016/S0022-5371(77)80012-1.

Hayes, Thomas. "Strategies for Teaching Professional Skepticism in the Classroom: Evidence from Senior-Level Auditing Students." *International Journal of Business, Accounting, & Finance* 10, no. 2 (2016): 110–21. http://libproxy.mtroyal.ca/login?url=http://search.ebscohost.com/login.aspx?direct=true&AuthType=ip,url,cookie,uid&db=bth&AN=122085990&site=ehost-live.

Houpt, Simon. "Why Are the Media So Reluctant to Call Politians Liars?" *The Globe and Mail*. May 8, 2019.

Kenski, Kate, Christine R Filer, and Bethany A Conway-Silva. "Lying, Liars, and Lies: Incivility in 2016 Presidential Candidate and Campaign Tweets During the Invisible Primary." *American Behavioral Scientist* 62, no. 3 (February 7, 2018): 286–99. https://doi.org/10.1177/0002764217724840.

Kessler, Glenn, Salvador Rizzo, and Meg Kelly. "Fallacy in Five Figures: Trump Blusters Past 10,000 False or Misleading Claims." *Washington Post, The*. Y, 4AD. http://libproxy.mtroyal.ca/login?url=http://search.ebscohost.com/login.aspx?direct=true&AuthType=ip,url,cookie,uid&db=n5h&AN=wapo.44abfb66-6a8f-11e9-be3a-33217240a539&site=ehost-live.

Leger, Dan. "Online Hate Faces a Long-Overdue Reckoning." *Chronicle - Herald*. April 15, 2019. http://libproxy.mtroyal.ca/login?url=https://search.proquest.com/docview/2210020792?accountid=1343.

Lima, Cristiano, and Megan Cassella. "Trump Repeats Canada Trade Deficit Claim After Bosting About Bluffing to Trudeau." *Politico*, March 15, 2018. https://www.politico.com/story/2018/03/15/trump-canada-trade-deficit-465464.

Maher, Stephen. "Fake Video Is a Big Problem. In 2019, It Gets Worse." *Maclean's (Online)*, December 28, 2018. http://libproxy.mtroyal.ca/login?url=https://search.proquest.com/docview/2161685117?accountid=1343.

Mazer, Joseph P, Stephen K Hunt, and Jeffrey H Kuznekoff. "Revising General Education: Assessing a Critical Thinking Instructional Model in the Basic Communication Course." *JGE: The Journal of General Education* 56, no. 3–4 (July 2007): 173–99.

Niu, Lian, Linda S. Behar-Horenstein, and Cyndi W. Garvan. "Do Instructional Interventions Influence College Students' Critical Thinking Skills? A Meta-Analysis." *Educational Research Review*, 2013. https://doi.org/10.1016/j.edurev.2012.12.002.

Nyberg, David. *The Varnished Truth: Truth Telling and Deceiving in Ordinary Life*. Chicago, [Ill.]; University of Chicago Press, 1993.

Pascarella, Ernest, Jui-Sheng Wang, Teniell Trolian, and Charles Blaich. "How the Instructional and Learning Environments of Liberal Arts Colleges Enhance Cognitive Development." *Higher Education (00181560)* 66, no. 5 (November 2013): 569–83. http://10.0.3.239/s10734-013-9622-z.

Pennycook, Gordon, James Allan Cheyne, Nathaniel Barr, Derek J Koehler, and Jonathan A Fugelsang. "On the Reception and Detection of Pseudo-Profound Bullshit." *Judgment and Decision Making* 10, no. 6 (2015): 549–63.

Pennycook, Gordon, and David G Rand. "Who Falls for Fake News? The Roles of Bullshit Receptivity, Overclaiming, Familiarity, and Analytic Thinking." *Journal of Personality*, 2019. https://doi.org/10.1111/jopy.12476.

Perlman, Merrill. "How Is Skepticism Different than Cynicism? Find the Answer in Acient Greece." *Columbia Journalism Review*, October 15, 2018. https://www.cjr.org/language_corner/skepticism-cynicism.php.

Petrocelli, John V. "Antecedents of Bullshitting." *Journal of Experimental Social Psychology* 76 (May 1, 2018): 249–58. https://doi.org/10.1016/J.JESP.2018.03.004.

Pfattheicher, Stefan, and Simon Schindler. "Misperceiving Bullshit as Profound Is Associated with Favorable Views of Cruz, Rubio, Trump and Conservatism."

PloS One. United States: Public Library of Science, 2016. https://doi.org/10.1371/journal.pone.0153419.

Rainie, Lee, Amanda Lenhart, and Aaron Smith. "The Tone of Life on Social Networking Sites." *Pew Research,* 2012, 30. http://pewinternet.org/Reports/2012/Social-networking-climate.aspx.

Roberts-Miller, Patricia. "Conspiracy Bullshit." *Rhetoric Society Quarterly.* Routledge, 2015. https://doi.org/10.1080/02773945.2015.1088341.

Roose, Kevin, "What Is QAnon, the Viral Pro-Trump Conspiracy Theory?" *The New York Times,* September 1, 2020. https://www.nytimes.com/article/what-is-qanon.html.

Sahadi, Jeanne. "Trump Says the U.S. Is the Highest Taxed Country in the World. No, It's Not." *CNN Wire.* CNN Newsource Sales Inc., October 12, 2017. https://money.cnn.com/2017/10/12/news/economy/trump-us-highest-taxes/index.html.

Scheuer, Jefery. "Critical Thinking and the Liberal Arts." *Academe* 101, no. 6 (November 2015): 35–39. http://libproxy.mtroyal.ca/login?url=http://search.ebscohost.com/login.aspx?direct=true&AuthType=ip,url,cookie,uid&db=ehh&AN=111164597&site=ehost-live.

Sommerhauser, Mark. "Leading Pediatrician Slams Donald Trump Claim That Doctors Are 'executing' Babies." *Wisconsin State Journal, The (Madison, WI).* Wisconsin State Journal, The (Madison, WI), April 30, 2019. http://libproxy.mtroyal.ca/login?url=http://search.ebscohost.com/login.aspx?direct=true&AuthType=ip,url,cookie,uid&db=n5h&AN=2W63594461032&site=ehost-live.

Sperber, Dan, Fabrice Clément, Christophe Heintz, Olivier Mascaro, Hugo Mercier, Gloria Origgi, and Deirdre Wilson. "Epistemic Vigilance." *Mind and Language* 25, no. 4 (September 2010): 359–93. https://doi.org/10.1111/j.1468-0017.2010.01394.x.

Sterling, Joanna, John T Jost, and Gordon Pennycook. "Are Neoliberals More Susceptible to Bullshit?" *Judgment & Decision Making* 11, no. 4 (July 2016): 352–60. http://libproxy.mtroyal.ca/login?url=http://search.ebscohost.com/login.aspx?direct=true&AuthType=ip,url,cookie,uid&db=a9h&AN=117243485&site=ehost-live.

Sullivan, Margaret. "'Fake News' Claims Are Untrue, and He Knows It." *Washington Post, The.* February 5, 2019. http://libproxy.mtroyal.ca/login?url=http://search.ebscohost.com/login.aspx?direct=true&AuthType=ip,url,cookie,uid&db=n5h&AN=wapo.b368b526-2881-11e9-984d-9b8fba003e81&site=ehost-live.

Tett, Gillian. "Facebook and the Fight against the Fakers: PARTING SHOT [Usa Region]." *Financial Times.* July 7, 2018. http://libproxy.mtroyal.ca/login?url=https://search.proquest.com/docview/2084120999?accountid=1343.

Tsui, Lisa. "Cultivating Critical Thinking: Insights from an Elite Liberal Arts College." *The Journal of General Education* 56, no. 3/4 (2008): 200–227.

Unkelbach, Christian. "Reversing the Truth Effect: Learning the Interpretation of Processing Fluency in Judgments of Truth." *Journal of Experimental Psychology. Learning, Memory, and Cognition* 33, no. 1 (January 2007): 219–30. https://doi.org/10.1037/0278-7393.33.1.219.

Vosoughi, Soroush, Deb Roy, and Sinan Aral. "The Spread of True and False News Online." *Science (New York, N.Y.)* 359, no. 6380 (March 9, 2018): 1146–51. https://doi.org/10.1126/science.aap9559.

Willingham, Daniel T. "Critical Thinking: Why Is It So Hard to Teach?" *Reprinted from American Educator Summer 2007 Issue*, March 2008.

Wreen, Michael. "A P.S. on B.S.: Some Remarks on Humbug and Bullshit." *Metaphilosophy*. Oxford: Wiley Subscription Services, Inc, 2013. https://doi.org/10.1111/meta.12021.

Yglesias, Matthew. "The Bullshitter-in-Chief." *Vox Media*, May 30, 2017. https://www.vox.com/policy-and-politics/2017/5/30/15631710/trump-bullshit.

Zimbler, Mattitiyahu, and Robert Feldman. "Liar, Liar, Hard Drive on Fire: How Media Context Affects Lying Behavior." *Journal of Applied Social Psychology* 41, no. 10 (October 2011): 2492–2507. http://10.0.4.87/j.1559-1816.2011.00827.x.

Chapter 5

Liberal Education and Truth in the Ages of Plato's Culture Industry

James Cunningham
Mount Royal University

Abstract

In *Republic*, the amplification of sound in public places is described as a tool of ancient mass culture. According to Plato, amplification allows Sophists to ride to power on a wave of public opinion so strong that even educated individuals cannot resist it. In *The Idea of the Good in Platonic-Aristotelian Philosophy*, Gadamer supports the view that Platonist philosophy must advocate for the removal of students from mass culture's influence. Only then can schools function as rational communities capable of aiding students in their attainment of a knowledge of the good. The good is that surety that allows scholars to stand fast in the truth against the force of mass culture. Without it, there is nothing to prevent even learned individuals from succumbing to activism that equates education with the promotion of their own prejudices on the big screen at the back of Plato's cave.

Keywords: Plato, Mass Culture, Education, Gadamer, Community

***

In this age of late modernity, where, at times, reality seems locked in a losing battle with the myriad virtual realities made possible by 'smart' communications technologies, are liberal arts education and its insistence on the educational value of truth out of date? Never before, say advocates of the democratizing value of social media, has it been possible for so many to tell their stories in a manner that affects common discourse for the better. As the example of the 'me too' movement is said to attest, these technologies, and the social media they support, allow ordinary individuals to have a positive effect on public affairs. In this brave new world, where anyone can garner mass followings and celebrity via social media, isn't liberal arts education simply one progressive voice amongst many? And really, how progressive is liberal education anyway? Many younger users of social media complain that liberal arts education does not speak to them or their interests because it resists meeting them on their platforms. How, they might ask, can liberal education be called progressive if it makes no progress with them?

But what if its social media that needs resisting? Presently, mainstream news buzzes with tales of how companies controlling social media are guilty of the most thorough invasion of privacy in history. Reports have it that social media (and the 'smart' web to which it is attached) is essentially a huge surveillance system: it captures each user's world view down to the minutest detail and mirrors it back as a vehicle for advertising tailored to the user's prejudices and presuppositions. If this sounds merely like an improvement on what commercial newsprint, magazines, radio, movies and television (what used to be called the culture industry) have being doing for the better part of a century, it is. And, as was the case with the old culture industry, fact checking is not proof against the effects of today's version.

The advice that critical distance from the promotional power of social media's claims can be achieved simply by googling them ignores the extent of surveillance in today's culture industry. For instance, if I, as a liberal academic, were to google 'Donald Trump,' Google would tailor its responses to my entire search history to produce a picture of the current POTUS very differently from that coming in response to searches by members of the so-called 'Alt-Right.' Likewise, even successful efforts by activists to replace 'non-progressive' images and expressions from main-stream entertainments (best seller novels and blockbuster movies and the like) with more 'progressive' content by more worthy artists amount simply to more of what the culture industry is doing already: saturating the market so that its target audience will get no exposure to the opposition. In turn, those who are not members of the target audience will migrate to more amicable corners of the web. Today's liberals complain that, for all their efforts, they can't seem to talk to conservatives, not realizing that, under the culture industry, everyone talks only to themselves. In the end, the present-day culture industry's aim is that of the twentieth century's culture industry: "the compulsive imitation by consumers of cultural commodities."[1] They differ only in that today's culture industry is more effective.

If there is no effective reality or 'truth' testing in today's culture industry, can liberal arts education provide and workable alternative? Further, is liberal arts education, which seems so irrelevant to many of today's culture industry consumers, even designed to remedy the illusions of the culture industry?

---

[1] Theodor Adorno, "The Culture Industry: Enlightenment as Mass Deception," in *Adorno, Max Horkheimer and Theodor. Dialectic of Enlightenment*, ed. Gunzelin Schmid Noerr and Trans. Edmond Jephcott (Stanford: Stanford University Press, 2002), 136.

While the theorists of the previous century's culture industry are many, most have little to say about the remedial nature of liberal arts education. For that, we have to look back some two millennia to a philosopher who theorized about how an education in aid of knowing the truth must function as a direct response to the confusion caused by the culture industry. I am speaking, of course, of Plato and of his greatest of educational work, *Republic*. In *Republic*, Plato argues that, for those who possess it, truth is the great corrective to the distortions of appearance, as well as to the confusion caused by the sophistic manipulation of those distortions under conditions of mass culture contemporary with Plato. That Plato is arguing, in *Republic*, for an education in truth as the remedy to mass culture, is an idea taken up by the philosopher, Hans-Georg Gadamer, in *The Idea of the Good in Platonic-Aristotelian Philosophy*.[2] An exponent of continentalist critical theory, Gadamer hails from one of the few traditions of twentieth-century philosophy to take seriously the ancient antecedents to contemporary social and intellectual trends.

With Gadamer's help, I intend to argue that, for Plato, in *Republic*:

- Amplification is the characteristic of mass culture which allows it to overpower human reason and will. In their exploitation of amplification as a mode of persuasion, the public sophists of Plato's time where like the purveyors of mass culture in any age.

- The capacity of mass culture to overpower will and reason requires a liberal education apart from mass culture.

- An education in philosophy must be liberal, in the sense that it liberates the student from the world of becoming and appearance over which the culture industry presides by way of a 'turning of the student's soul' from the sensible world towards its effective antidote in what Plato calls the intelligible world and the form of the good which rules over it.

- The student, as dialectician, sees his love of truth justified by truth's function within the form of the good. That is, to make all other forms beneficial and useful, as all good things should be, the form of the good illuminates them with truth and its partner,

---

[2] While Gadamer never names the culture industry in this work, his extensive discussion of Plato's views concerning the Sophists and their influence on the political life of the Greek Polis indicates that his concern is with those public sophists who Plato identified as the purveyors of what we would call the culture industry.

reality, so that the forms will become objects of knowledge. It is as objects of knowledge that the forms can be gathered under the good's orders of knowledge within which their usefulness and benefit to the arts, sciences, and good living generally becomes evident.

- The dialectician, now no longer a student, can discern truth's normative role in all its details only if he becomes virtuous. Being virtuous, the student can 'hold fast' to the truth and the good it serves against the pressures of the culture industry.

- Liberal education cannot be activism, but a preparation for activism. This is why Plato says of the dialectician that, being just, he must accept the justice of the imperative to return to the cave, exposing the things there to the light of truth and reordering them in terms of the good.

Most theorists of mass culture tend to treat the topic as one confined to modern society. But Plato knew of mass culture, which he describes in Book VI of *Republic* as the use, by public Sophists, of the acoustics in terrain where Athenians held their public meetings to amplify their voices with a view to giving them more sway over the crowd. Writes Plato:

> [the public Sophists] ... object very noisily to some of the things that are said or done, and approve others, in both cases to excess by shouting and clapping. Moreover, the rocks and the place of meeting re-echo and double the din of their blame or praise.[3]

Amplification of volume in aid of audience control is a standard technique of contemporary mass culture, as is evidenced in the ongoing tendency of the music recording industry to limit its volume range to a few levels at the loudest end. But, amplification is also achieved metaphorically by our contemporary culture industry in terms of its sounds and images being made ubiquitous and simultaneous: the impression to be conveyed is that, if cultural artifacts can be experienced everywhere and are available on demand, theirs is like a voice projecting so loudly that it reaches the end of the earth. To like effect, the public sophists of Plato's time took advantage of every type of public event: they were

---

[3] Plato, *Republic*, ed. G.M.A. Trans. Grube (Indianapolis, Ind: Hackett Publishing Company, 1974), sec. 492b-c.

always sure to turn up, always on message, "sitting together in assemblies, in courts, in camps, or in some other public gathering of the crowd."[4]

As we saw in the introduction, another way in which the culture industry achieves amplification metaphorically entails putting its audience under surveillance. In ancient Greece, this task fell to the private sophists, the teachers of public sophists.

> [the Sophistic teacher] studied the moods and desires [of the crowd as if it were] a mighty and powerful beast, how to approach it, how to handle it, how it becomes most difficult and most gentle and what makes it so, what sounds it utters on each occasion, and what sounds addressed to it soothe or anger it ... what it enjoys he calls good, and what angers it he calls bad.[5]

Having put mob under surveillance in order to learn its prejudices (shades of Google), the sophistic teacher instructs those who would be public sophists on how to reflect the crowd's prejudices back on it as the standards by which good and bad are judged. In this way, the Sophists use the biases of the mob to ensure its co-operation in 'drowning out' or shouting into silence all voices who would dare to advocate for other possible measures of morality. The effect is that the views voiced by the sophists are the only ones which the crowd hears. And, as the twentieth-century theorist of mass culture Theodor Adorno observed, utterances of the voice which has a monopoly on the public's attention always sound like commands.[6]

That the Sophist case seems so overwhelmingly loud and ubiquitous makes each member of the crowd feel as if everyone else is voicing the appeal in common and to the exclusion of any other sentiment; as if they too must join in lest they seem to be at odds with the crowd and thus the object of its censor. And this effect extends even to those young men who receive training in the art of reasoning and the virtues. Adorno writes:

> During this scene, what is the effect on [a] young man's psyche ... what private training can hold out against this and not be drowned by that kind of censure or approval, not be swept along by the current whithersoever it may carry it, and not declare the same things to be

---

[4] Ibid., sec. 492b.
[5] Ibid., sec. 493a-c.
[6] Adorno, "The Culture Industry: Enlightenment as Mass Deception," 129.

beautiful or ugly as the crowd does. [A] young man will follow the same pursuits as the crowd, and be the same kind of man.[7]

Plato concludes that no private training which leaves students free to experience the effects of mass culture is proof against the power of amplification. Everyone quails before the power of mass culture. Even the brilliance of the most gifted and virtuous students will not be proof against it: recognizing what the sophists have done, these finest of students will also see the power that it has brought them. In turn, the sophists will seduce such students with flattery and promises that they too can wield the same power, if only they conform.[8]

Writing on Plato's culture industry, Gadamer recognizes from Plato's description of mass culture that it trades ultimately on the leaders' "power want[ing] only itself."[9] Any education that can withstand the love of power, then, must make it self-evident to its student that there is something better to love. For this reason, argues Gadamer, Plato insists that if his liberal education must have as its ultimate goal, the knowledge of the good.[10] Only as it functions within the good can we see how truth is better than power.

Like many scholars, Gadamer is struck by Plato's "clumsy and circuitous demonstration of [the Kallipolis'] possibility, in Book VI of *Republic*."[11] While other scholars, however, have taken the argument's weakness as a sign that Plato is less interested in liberal education's implications for political activism free from mass culture's influence than he is in its theoretical aspects, Gadamer argues that Plato's defense of the possibility of the ideal city, structured and ruled by philosophers should be read as a series of "dialectical metaphors."[12] That is, its purpose is to contrast the philosophical ideal with the states we actually experience: first, "that [it]should make truly bad conditions and the dangers for the continued existence of the city visible e contrario"[13]; second, for "the positive insight that both aiming at the good and knowing reality pertain to the political actions of the true statesman."[14] For Gadamer, Plato's point is that, even if states cannot be ideal, they can be better. And, in bettering

---

[7] Plato, *Republic*, sec. 492c.
[8] Ibid., sec. 494b-c.
[9] Hans Georg Gadamer, "The Polis and Knowledge of the Good," in *The Idea of the Good in Platonic-Aristotelian Philosophy*, ed. Christopher P. Trans. Smith (New Haven and London: Yale University Press, 1986), 72.
[10] Ibid., 76.
[11] Ibid., 70.
[12] Ibid., 71.
[13] Ibid.
[14] Ibid., 71.

themselves, they should look to the ideal for their guide. Since, for Plato, the chief evil of existent cities seems to reside in the confusion Sophists sow, the guidance they should seek from the ideal city is "the distinction [it uncovers] between the ideal and reality of power."[15]

Quite the opposite of being an escape into theory from political life, says Gadamer, Plato's education must concern "how the existence devoted to theoria must see itself in this world of appearances, the world of social power structures."[16] Under this preparation, the student learns to pursue politics successfully as it should be pursued: that is, "to remain steadfast as they are pulled this way and that"[17] by the distractions accompanying political life as it is actually pursued. Under Gadamer's interpretation, then, Plato is not saying that the student must leave the political life behind. He is saying, rather, that the student will cease to frequent meetings of the mob and the company of the many who practice politics as it should not be practiced, who "are continually abusing each other and being quarrelsome; they always talk in personalities which is quite unsuited to philosophy."[18] In their stead, the student seeks out those people capable of "fine and free discussions which eagerly seek in every way to find the truth for the sake of knowledge."[19] With their help, "as [the student] looks upon and contemplates things that are ordered and ever the same, that do no wrong to, and are not wronged by, each other, being all in a rational order, he imitates them and tries to become as like them as he can."[20]

Gadamer concludes that, for the truly philosophical student, even theoretical knowledge is pursued within the context of its practical, that is, its political/moral application. He writes that the student's studies are presented, "not [as] theoretical treatises but as imitations of real discussions played out between partners and drawing them all into a game in which they all have something at stake."[21] Even the study of mathematical abstractions, says Gadamer, with which Plato would start the student of philosophy, *Republic* Book VII, is practical inasmuch as it is part and parcel with "preparing us for the idea of the good."[22] That is to say, Plato does not see these studies as primarily in aid of acquiring specialized academic knowledge. Rather, says Gadamer,

---

[15] Ibid., 72.
[16] Ibid., 68.
[17] Plato, *Republic*, sec. 539e.
[18] Ibid., 500b.
[19] Ibid., 499a.
[20] Plato, *Republic*, sec. 500c.
[21] Gadamer, "The Polis and Knowledge of the Good," 97.
[22] Ibid.," 83.

Plato sees studies in abstract mathematics as concerned primarily with "turning the whole soul around."[23]

Plato's philosophy has been criticized repeatedly for finding reality in abstractions. But, in line with Gadamer's view of Plato, we must conclude that the critics have Plato all wrong. Plato has the student seek realities distinct from sensible appearances because it is sensible appearances that are themselves unreal. According to the metaphysical thrust behind Plato's pedagogy, it is the world of sensible experience that is a pale abstraction from reality; and, by virtue of its ever-changing nature, one that is full of confusion. What Plato seeks in the study of mathematics is the turning of the soul from its dependence on the senses and the copies of numbers and other mathematical figures that are visible to them, towards real numbers and figures which the soul perceives directly through the 'eye of the soul' (by which Plato means reason and understanding).[24] As such, mathematics is the first stage in preparing the student for the ideal political life. That is, it prepares him to provide justifications for both his thoughts and actions based on the direct mental perception of things as they really are and not what their poor copies from sensible appearance make them seem.

Plato continues that the student, having mastered studies that allow him to perceive real things directly, is now ready to embark on the journey of the dialectic.[25] Gadamer interprets Plato's use of the term, dialectic, to mean the art of making distinctions.[26] In light of this definition, the dialectician is seen as "guiding [a] discussion (with his students) through all its episodes and gathering and holding together what is sought and really meant through all the unsteadiness and errancy that pervade any discussion."[27] The dialectical discussion is said to be successful when an understanding is reached by the dialectician and his students about the meaning of things. Understanding is reached when the distinction between aspects essential and aspects non-essential to the things meant is made. For Gadamer, it is through the practice of the dialectic that the student learns to resolve confusion, not concerning the essence of numbers only but of all things that are (that is, the forms), by way of logical argumentation alone: in other words, to become a dialectician, himself. The goal is the student's ability to hold every form before his mind's eye clearly and with no recourse to the distortions of sensible experience.

---

[23] Ibid.
[24] Plato, *Republic*, 508d.
[25] Ibid., sec. 532b.
[26] Gadamer, "The Polis and Knowledge of the Good," 67.
[27] Ibid., 97.

The last and most important thing, for Plato, that the student must distinguish from other forms, in all its reality, is the good. Plato argues, however, that the student has not fully distinguished the good as that form that makes all good things beneficial and useful unless he also apprehends the good as the source of truth and reality, and truth and reality as media (analogous to light) capable of illuminating the things on which they fall as objects of knowledge.[28]

Plato is arguing, therefore, that to be apprehended at all, the good must be recognized as having a noetic as well as a normative aspect. Since Plato alludes to good's possession of noetic as well as normative aspects in almost mystical terms, whether or not there is a connection between these aspects remains unclear. I think, however, that the relationship can be clarified with reference to Plato's argument from the knowledge of health and disease, Book IV, *Republic*.[29]

According to the argument from health and disease, knowledge of disease is no more diseased than is knowledge of health healthy. This is to say, that while health is good and disease bad, when regarded strictly as objects of knowledge, neither health nor disease are good or bad. Likewise, knowledge of disease is just as capable as that of the health of coming under the category (the order) of medical knowledge.[30] If disease can be the object of medical knowledge, I take it to follow that knowledge of disease must inform the medical arts in the same manner as all other medical knowledge: that is, in a manner that is both useful and beneficial to the art. In so far as it is an object of medical knowledge, then, the knowledge of disease is, like all beneficial and useful things, a good. By radiating truth, which illuminates its objects as objects of knowledge, then, the good renders its objects fit to be included under its orders of knowledge where they can function as goods.

Gadamer, however, raises another problem of clarity regarding the nature of the good. He has it that, for Plato, the student finds the unity of the arête (virtues) in knowledge of the good and that, in some manner, the sciences function as a 'propaedeutic' (that is, a preparatory training for) "the [student's] attaining this knowledge" of what it is in the good that binds the virtues.[31] It is "more or less obscure" says Gadamer, what exactly the connection is between the training of the student in the sciences and his attaining insight into how the

---

[28] Plato, *Republic*, sec. 508d.
[29] Ibid., secs. 438e-439. I use this argument as I have knowing full well that Plato used it for another purpose: in aid of his conclusion that 'self-control' is a misnomer for the proper ordering of the soul's parts 442 a-b.
[30] Ibid., sec. 438e.
[31] Gadamer, "The Polis and Knowledge of the Good," 67.

good finds its unity of the arête.³² As it did for the connection between the good's noetic and normative aspects, I think that the above-mentioned argument, from Book IV sheds light also on the connection between scientific knowledge and the student's apprehension of the unity of the arête in the good.

The study of the sciences, especially when it progresses to the point where the dialectic is deployed to move beyond their founding hypotheses towards their supporting first principle (the good), reveals each science to constitute one of the orders of knowledge possessed by the good (for instance, medical knowledge, biological knowledge, and knowledge of physics). Further, the recognition that an object of knowledge belongs under a scientific order makes the usefulness and benefit of the object evident. In these orders of knowledge, therefore, the student sees an important content of the good with the eye of his soul.

There is, however, more to see. This is because it is also true that objects capable of being known need not be ordered in a manner that renders them useful and beneficial. That is, these objects can be ordered in accordance with the love of power, in which case they can be the cause of harm and hindrance for those against whom they are used. The student will see the good in its totality, then, when the eye of his soul beholds the manner in which the good brings the arête together that they may co-operate to ensure that objects of knowledge are shielded from abuse by power.

And, here's the kicker. Since to arête are conditions of soul, the student cannot apprehend the good's bringing together of the arête in aid of its objects unless he imitates the arête so that his soul, being virtuous, is willing to pursue and apprehend them wherever they lead. It follows that the student cannot know what it is about the good that ensures objects of knowledge will serve the sciences unless he comes to embody the unity of the arête at work in the good.

Neither can the student be sure to recognize the truth in all its clarity, unless he is virtuous. For, as we have already seen, truth is a medium of noetic illumination radiating from the good itself. The virtuous man cannot ignore the contradiction inherent in saying that the truth, in itself, could illuminate its objects as knowledge to any end other than their virtuous use: neither could he fail to recognize that any malevolent illumination is mixed with the 'darkness' of becoming and vice and is thus reduced to producing mere doxa (opinion).³³

If I have clarified what Gadamer found obscure, the eye of a virtuous soul *must* apprehend in the truth's illumination of knowledge as the good's preparation of its objects for their transformation into goods. To reach the

---

³² Ibid.
³³ Plato, *Republic*, sec. 508d.

knowledge of the good, the student's pursuit of the dialectic must constitute not only a turning of the eye of the soul from the appearance but also, a transformation of the soul, itself, into something akin to its objects of study. Of course, the project of psychic transformation must be a long one. The student who pursues it, Plato says, will be, "an older man ... who is willing to converse in order to discover the truth rather than one who is merely playing and contradicting for play; he will be more measured [than young men] and will bring honour rather than discredit to the pursuit of philosophy."[34] Of the project itself, Plato says, "it will be enough to stay with the study of the dialectic continuously, intensely, doing nothing else, in a similar way to the time spent in physical training, but for twice the number of years. ...I ...make it five [years]."[35] For Gadamer, Plato's notion of the total transition of soul required for the practice of the dialectic and the length and intensity of the training involved are both entailed in "opposing the true dialectic to the art of confounding someone" practiced by the sophists in their management of the culture industry.[36]

When Gadamer discusses Plato's analogy of the divided line, end of Book VI, *Republic*, he is at pains to point out that, for Plato, the upper part of the line represents not only an ascent to the good, but also a returning descent from the good.[37] After all, for Plato, it is by way of this returning descent that the dialectician, having grasped the good as a source of scientific ordering, is capable of using his knowledge of the forms to prove all of the hypotheses on which the different sciences 'so-called' are founded.[38] Since proof of the scientific hypotheses must involve the employment of the forms by the dialectic, the understanding derived from these proofs must result from an act of distinguishing. That is, by proving the hypotheses by way of logical demonstrations from and through the forms, the dialectician distinguishes

---

[34] Plato, *Republic*, sec. 539c.
[35] Ibid., sec. 539d-e.
[36] Gadamer, "The Polis and Knowledge of the Good," 103. Indeed, now that we are faced with a modern culture industry, training in academic disciplines as rigorous as that prescribed by Plato for the dialectic are more necessary than ever. This is because the contemporary individual has internalized the conventions of the culture industry in the way he thinks, speaks and moves. Says Adorno: "The way in which the young girl accepts the obligatory date, the tone of voice used on the telephone and the most intimate situations, the choice of words in conversation, indeed, the whole inner life is compartmentalized according to ... an apparatus which, even in its unconscious impulses, conforms to the model presented by the culture industry. Adorno, "The Culture Industry," 136.
[37] Gadamer, "The Polis and Knowledge of the Good," 92.
[38] Plato, *Republic*, sec. 511b-c.

between the hypotheses and the visible symbols and physical objects which helped the student formulate them in the first place. In so doing, the dialectician reaches an understanding liberating them and those who grasp their meaning from the tendency to confuse the appearance of the symbols with the authority of the forms. Gadamer's insistence on emphasizing the downward path of the dialectic is in aid of showing how the Platonist concept of truth, by turning mathematical hypotheses into forms of knowledge, secures their usefulness to the mathematical sciences. It shows also how truth can be of use in clearing up confusions deriving from the sensible world as well as those in the noetic world.

But, Gadamer does not stop his discussion of the dialectic's descent with the proof of scientific hypotheses. For Gadamer, sciences such as ethics are practical and this means that practice of the dialectic is not complete until the dialectician has solved the confusion that underlies the ordering of human affairs.[39] That is, the student, now a trained dialectician, must bring the power of the dialectic into the fray of political life as it is. And, of course, even Plato questions why the dialectician would want to do this.

For Gadamer, it is no surprise that the Myth of the Cave should come at the beginning of Book VII of *Republic*, immediately after the analogy of the divided line at the end of the previous book. Plato's great allegory, which places political life under conditions of mass culture in a cave and envisions the philosophical education as the long tortuous path out of the cave and into the world of actual things, poses the question with which Gadamer is left in his discussion of the divided line. Why, having turned his soul towards the noetic realm so that he has come to know it in all its goodness and love it, would the student, now a dialectician in the true sense of the world, want to return to the world of men? Plato answers that, being just, the dialectician will feel the justice of the demand that they return.[40] Gadamer, echoing Plato at other points in *Republic*, says philosophers will not be concerned with personal happiness, only that of the whole state.[41] Neither of these responses really answers the question, however. They explain why the philosopher would go, not why he would want to.

---

[39] For Gadamer, the dialectic seeks even to make clear *logoi* about sensible objects. Under the dialectic the "individual thing which participates in the *eidos* 'counts' in an argument only in regard to the *eidos* in which it participates, that is, only in regard to its essential eidic content. Thus, does the dialectic resolve all logical confusion [concerning particulars, which] has its origin in not keeping the *eidos* separate from what participates in it" Gadamer, "The Polis and Knowledge of the Good," 102.
[40] Plato, *Republic*, sec. 520e.
[41] Gadamer, "The Polis and Knowledge of the Good," 68.

Gadamer does seem to provide another answer, however: one more nuanced. For Gadamer, the proper activity of the dialectic, that of distinguishing between things that are confused, applies to everything and therefore takes in the world of appearances as well as that of reality. Further, as Plato avers, the good renders the dialectic of use in allowing its practitioners to "look upon the good itself and taking it as their model ... [to] put in order the city and its citizens as well as themselves for the remainder of their life."[42]

The good will not allow the dialectic to rest, therefore, until it has dragged the dialectician into the ways of humans. And, though they will take no pleasure in human's ways, the dialectician will be motivated to meet them by their love for the dialectic, for the people who helped them embody it and, above all, for the form of the good, for reality and for truth, all of which the dialectic has placed before the eye of their soul. Finally, the desire to be as like the dialectic in character as they can be will cause the dialectician to constantly test themselves against "the Sophistry [that] is always threatening danger – something that can always happen to the *logoi* (assertions) in us,"[43] that by withstanding the test, they might, "as [they are] pulled this way and that" by sophistic confusion, remain steadfast in living the life they love so passionately.[44]

For Gadamer, as for Plato, it is upon entry into political life as it is practiced that the dialectician is faced immediately with the greatest danger. In the myth of the cave, Plato describes this danger as the temporary blindness which the dialectician faces upon entering darkness from the light.[45] For Gadamer, the dialectician's blindness is a metaphor for their unfamiliarity with the game that is being played by the culture industry. What the dialectician meets, says Gadamer, is the 'proximity' of the Sophist's art to his own.[46] That is, like the dialectician himself, the Sophist is a master at sniffing out inconsistencies and, beyond that, seems adept at making clever distinctions. Unlike the dialectician, the sophist also put their greatest stock in the "dazzling art of the forceful answer."[47] As indicated in the last paragraph, there is every reason to believe that the dialectician can be tripped up by the Sophist.

Gadamer says, however, that what the sophist knows nothing of and cares less about is the good which informs all knowledge, and truth, the medium which

---

[42] Plato, *Republic*, sec. 540a-b.
[43] Gadamer, "The Polis and Knowledge of the Good," 99.
[44] Plato, *Republic*, sec. 539e.
[45] Ibid., sec. 517d-e.
[46] Gadamer, "The Polis and Knowledge of the Good," 99.
[47] Ibid.

illuminates its objects as knowledge in of service to the good.[48] To the Sophist, then, knowledge is not really available—only bastardized versions of the same subsumed to the acquisition of power for its own sake. These bastardized versions of knowledge "lack ... the art of differentiating"[49] and, therefore, see distinctions and realities where none exist. It is the sophist's lack of knowledge of the good and of truth which serves the dialectician's refutations of sophistry and the dialectician's possession of good and truth which sees them 'holding fast' against the force of sophist's answers, even when they are amplified by the culture industry.[50] As a result, the dialectician has immunity against mass culture that is proof against its changing, distracting, and turning them from opposition to it.

In Plato's description of the dialectician turned activist, we see implied the wisdom that the point of activism is not only to change the world but, equally, to keep the world from changing you. For activists from every age, who would object that Plato sets the bar too low, I reply that we should guard against underestimating the influence commanded by the example of a life lived well. A good life must nurture the lives around it. As such, it has a multiplying effect, like the circular waves extending out from the impact of a pebble dropped in a pond. On this model, the greatness of an individual's activism is measured not in terms only of its results during his lifetime but also in terms of those lives influenced, in succeeding generations, by the example of their virtue. Thus, in Plato's account of Socrates' address to his jury, Socrates castigates the jurors who voted for his death for having failed to still the influence of his arguments stating, "There will be more who will refute you, whom I have now been d holding back; you did not perceive them. And they will be harsher, inasmuch as they are younger, and you will be more indignant."[51] For any activism, its progress is due in part to the fact that its activists, today, stand on the shoulders of those who came before, even after they castigate their predecessors for not having done enough or lionize them for having done far more than they did. The true greatness of their predecessors must be measured more in terms of their capacity for courage, temperance, wisdom and justice than of their apparent success in the short term.

What must it have been about Plato's academy that its influence on liberal arts education is felt to this day? I think Plato has told us already. It must have striven to be a community like the one described in Book VI, *Republic*, in which

---

[48] Ibid., 94.
[49] Ibid., 95.
[50] Gadamer, "The Polis and Knowledge of the Good," 97.
[51] Thomas G. West, *Plato's Apology of Socrates: An Interpretation, With a New Translation* (Ithaca, NY: Cornell University Press, 1979), 39d.

members were constrained from "abusing each other and being quarrelsome ... [and] always talking in personalities, which is quite unsuited to philosophy."⁵² In this way the community might be part of "fine and free discussions which eagerly seek in every way to find the truth for the sake of knowledge, and which keep away from [the sophistry] of clever debating points that aim only at opinion and disputation."⁵³

In this sense, Plato's liberal education is not a flight from the culture industry so much as it is a banishing of the culture industry and its influences from education. Notice, however, that the banishing is not of people; instead it is of the 'forceful answer' characteristic of the culture industry. This banishing of the culture industry from the academy is characterized in the scene from Book I, *Republic*, when Thrasymachus, having delivered a sophistic tirade, seeks to leave the company before Socrates can make his reply, "Having said this and poured this mass of close-packed words into our ears as a bath man might a flood of water, Thrasymachus intended to leave, but those present did not let him, and made him stay for a discussion of his views."⁵⁴ Without the discipline of the dialectic, even the most dedicated activism is prone to becoming like Thrasymachus: shocking, confusing and intimidating its audience so that they can think of naught to say and of leaving them with no venue in which to speak. There is troubling evidence of this tendency today in what purports to be progressive activism, as my updated version of the myth of Plato's cave will illustrate.

To accommodate for contemporary sensibilities, I have amended the cave analogy by adding to the cave's description an underclass of laborers working on their knees to clear up the detritus dropped by Plato's constrained prisoners.⁵⁵ Because they are ever kneeling, these laborers do not see their shadows reflected on the cave wall as do the prisoners, neither do they think that the giant shadows cast by the puppets resemble them so much as they do the shadows of the prisoners. The laborers rail in their hearts at the falseness of the spectacle from which they are excluded. Should some of these laborers, tiring of their misery and invisibility, stand and make their way to the front of the cave, they will take the puppeteers for their oppressors and drive them from behind the wall where they have played puppet master. Seeing the philosopher,

---

⁵² Plato, *Republic*, sec. 500b.
⁵³ Ibid., sec. 498.
⁵⁴ Thomas West, *Plato's Apology of Socrates*, 39d.
⁵⁵ Plato, *Republic*, secs. 514-515b. On Plato's account, the cave is filled with prisoners whose bodies have been so constrained that they can look only at the shadows on the back of the cave. In turn, the shadows are of puppets made to dance between the prisoners and a fire at the front of the cave.

pointing to the exit passage behind the puppeteers, the laborers will take him for a puppeteer and drive him away, as well. Then they will replace the puppeteers, fashioning puppets in their own likeness and, when these puppets cast their giant shadows, all the laborers will feel liberated because they think they are no longer invisible, even though still, no one looks at them, only at shadows on the back of the cave.

When activists, today, declare that women have progressed because a woman has the marquee role in the cinematic rip off of a superhero comic which, in all other respects, is like one where the marquee role is played by a man, then activism is cheering for shadows on the wall of a cave. When activists, today, accuse authors, actors or artists, talented and able, of cultural appropriation for daring to tell stories about ethnic or gendered groups to which they do not belong, activism is hissing at the shadows on the wall of a cave. When activism, today, cheers authors, actors or artists, talented and able, from ethnic and gender groupings outside the dominant ethnic and gendered groups so-called, simply for playing roles previously played only by members of the dominant ethnic and gendered groups so-called, activism is cheering for shadows on a cave wall. When progressive activists, today, fight with their conservative opponents over the types of body that should be allowed in the images of mass culture, they are fighting over images on the cave wall. For, in every case, they are fighting over who gets to make an appearance in what is otherwise the same kind of commercial spectacle that we are always given. Such spectacles are the business of the culture industry in all its ages.

References

Adorno, Theodor. "The Culture Industry: Enlightenment as Mass Deception." In *Adorno, Max Horkheimer and Theodor. Dialectic of Enlightenment*, edited by Gunzelin Schmid Noerr and Trans. Edmond Jephcott, 94–136. Stanford: Stanford University Press, 2002.

Gadamer, Hans Georg. "The Polis and Knowledge of the Good." In *The Idea of the Good in Platonic-Aristotelian Philosophy*, edited by Christopher P. Trans. Smith, 63.103. New Haven and London: Yale University Press, 1986.

Plato. *Republic*. Edited by G.M.A. Trans. Grube. Indianapolis, Ind: Hackett Publishing Company, 1974.

West, Thomas. Plato's Apology of Socrates: An Interpretation, With a New Translation. Ithaca, NY: Cornell University Press, 1979.

Chapter 6

How to 'Handle' the Truth from a Liberal Arts Perspective

Ronald Peter Glasberg
University of Calgary

Abstract

Identifying problems associated with handing the truth, the essay presents some liberal arts strategies designed to facilitate a more constructive discourse as well as a pedagogy that allow truth seekers to accomplish two things: (1) identify those places where debate about ultimate questions breaks down; and (2) explore the nature of truth with respect to both its repulsive (ugly truth) and attractive (beautiful truth) qualities. Specifically, the interpretation of classic texts is emphasized as a way of handling the ongoing cultural conversations that constitute the liberal arts. It is by way of such conversations that truth can emerge, disappear, re-emerge and perhaps ultimately merge with the foundational reality it is forever approaching.

Keywords: truth, liberal arts, interpretation, cultural assumptions, classic texts

***

Introduction

When the marine colonel played by Jack Nicholson bellows at his courtroom adversary (played by Tom Cruise in *A Few Good Men*) that he cannot handle the truth, the words have a chilling resonance. What does it mean to be incapable of handling the truth? What does it mean to be able to handle it? What, finally, is truth?

In an age when science appears to be the touchstone of truth, what role do the humanities or liberal arts play in the struggle to determine and present what is true in the context of human affairs—a context that is currently in a kind of 'truth crisis' when certain politicians regularly call their opponents liars while the latter sadly return the 'compliment'? To make matters worse, a flood of information from the Internet threatens to drown us in a sea of unverifiable claims as to what is really going on, what is true and what is false. Finally, there is the age-old problem of human disagreement—something that obviously predates the rise of science and, in fact, exists within it. That is, even if all humans were honest and the Internet were not inundating us, truth seekers of good will would still clash and thus give occasion for a skepticism that makes the very idea of truth problematic.

How then can the liberal arts be of assistance in dealing with these problems? In order to answer the foregoing question, the present discussion aims to accomplish the following: (1) develop a working definition of truth and explore some of the implications of that definition; (2) examine what causes conversations pertaining to truth-seeking to break down by way of one or both parties becoming entrenched in their respective positions; (3) illustrate some of the challenges in handling truths that are deemed 'ugly' or even 'terrible'; (4) contrast the foregoing with an examination of what might be called 'beautiful' truths and how these might figure in truth-seeking; and (5) conclude this discussion with recommendations for educational reform geared to facilitating the pursuit of truth at a pedagogical level. Also, to be considered throughout the course of this essay is how the liberal arts might be utilized effectively to bring truth into the world—a world that may be becoming ever more inhospitable to the latter if not the former as well.

Toward a Definition of the Truth

Just what is the truth and why might it be hard to 'handle'? The problem of difficulty in handling the truth may be related to two of its inherent qualities: (a) its ultimate value as a guide to life in general; and (b) its apparent depth, which is something that makes it an object of dispute among those who seek to discover and articulate it. Obviously, I am not here referring to what might be called trivial truths pertaining to the mundane aspects of the world. I am referring to the foundations that may be said to underlie all things and constitute reality at its deepest levels. Because one would want to order one's life in such a way as to be in some kind of harmonious relationship with reality, truth as an articulation of that foundation must be of the utmost importance and disagreement must be the occasion for much concern—a concern that makes truth hard to handle.

Does reality's apparent depth have to be the occasion for dispute over truth—a dispute fraught with an intensity so great that many would rather avoid the struggle altogether? Why cannot people of good will who are engaged in the search for truth simply admit that they do not grasp what I would call the truth of reality? Perhaps there is a hidden vanity at play in this game—a vanity in which we take our speculations to be some kind of absolute and those of our opponents to be wrong. Perhaps there is also a fear that we are loathed to face—a fear that we live in a world that we do not understand at a fundamental level but that we must live in, nonetheless. Whatever the case, we can frame a tentative definition of truth as a contested discourse with respect to making sense of a significant level of reality, where significant level pertains to the meaning, organization, and purpose of life. Because humans live together in groups, major differences with respect to what is taken to be foundational truth could seriously undermine the social solidarity that makes human life possible.

With respect to the liberal arts, one would think that it is their function to mediate if not resolve such conflict. But it often appears that they exacerbate the disputes and even take a kind of pride in the richness of the debate and the free flow of ideas. The idea of resolution of disputes might even be viewed with suspicion as if the resolution were bound to be some kind of hegemonic suppression of unique perspectives. Moreover, when the matter of freedom is not at issue, the liberal art known as philosophy stands out as the discipline that at one and the same time tackles foundational reality head-on while manifesting an endless refinement of the conflict over the nature of being. When philosophy is confined to the 'academy' or university, this ongoing flurry of conflicting interpretations of the real may do little harm; but as it leaches out into the world of political economy, what might be called hermeneutic wars can become deadly. Truth accordingly becomes hard to handle when reality is interpreted from the perspective of personal or class interests or even cultural agendas. Even when academic philosophers appreciate the nature of this dynamic, their expertise does not necessarily move in the direction of finding inclusive overviews, but instead can turn toward developing a stronger justification for one particular interpretation and/or a critique of an oppositional one.

Of course, truth would be easier to handle if parties to the dispute (about the underlying nature of reality) agreed to work within a common framework that served to guide their investigations. Some might take the scientific method to be such a common framework—one that is a vital aspect of the liberal arts. However, while mathematical modeling might be applied to economics in some contexts, experimenting on a large 'economic body' is not suitable for determining a truth that transcends what might be called the problem of conflicting class interests. Moreover, to the extent that the locus of the conflict goes beyond that of political-economic struggles and settles instead in the area of spiritual concerns (e.g. one's eternal relation to God), we enter into the sphere of religious wars where the possibilities of conflict resolution are often submerged in seas of blood. While the liberal arts, particularly in the discipline of religious studies, can look at spiritual traditions in a sociological and/or psychological manner, it is no position to mediate the conflicting truths of spirit, which from some scientific perspectives are deemed to be delusional.

Given the foregoing outline, one can see why truth is hard to handle: it is an object of contestation; there is no clear way of resolving the conflict; and conflict is often seen to be a positive thing to the extent that it is identified with a kind of freedom of discourse. Yet given the suffering to which conflict can give rise, let alone the sheer waste of intellectual energy, one cannot help but ask if the conflict can somehow be muted—not with a view to silencing a salutary opposition, but with a view to reaching some kind of agreement.

The Problem of Entrenchment

Here the liberal arts could turn its arsenal toward clarifying a set of factors that serve to entrench oppositional truth-seekers in their respective positions. The point here is a subtle one. Assuming that there is a truth to reality (and reality is not inherently chaotic), then mutual opposition can only be based on some flaw on the one or both parties to the conflict. If that flaw can be isolated and overcome, the path is open to reaching agreement. In other words, if opposition becomes entrenched on the basis of attributing some flaw to the position or person of one's opponent—a flaw that accordingly 'explains' why a contrary view is held—then the opposition between conflicted truth seekers might be weakened on two complementary counts: (a) the flaw might be overcome by some kind of analysis of the flaw in question; and (b) if the flaw is shown to be unavoidable, the heat of the argument can be subject to a certain cooling and an openness to new perspectives accordingly encouraged.

Before considering how the liberal arts might be of help here, let us examine the nature of these flaws that oppositional speakers attribute to each other in order to justify their respective viewpoints. While awareness of these flaws is meant to weaken oppositional entrenchment, it can also strengthen it if a given flaw is taken as a way of justifying one's own view while 'de-justifying' the view of the other. However, if one moves beyond a quasi-conscious attribution of flaws and begins to explore these in greater depth, the contest over truth might move from a sterile rigidity to a fertile flexibility whereby parties to a dispute might see each other in a new light.

The question then is what negative qualities do truth seekers attribute to their opponents in order to justify their outlooks? I believe there are four, and I have derived them from Erasmus's *Praise of Folly*. The latter is an irony-laden 'praise' of folly for blinding people to their own foolish behavior; and although the varieties of folly identified by Erasmus are not directly correlated with a struggle over truth, one cannot help but see that the foolish behaviors in question are viewed negatively. Whether or not this is fair is beside the point. What is of importance is how the negative attribution of folly in any argument can end the discussion by de-legitimizing the outlook of the other. Is not the position of one's opponent illegitimate if at bottom that opponent is thinking in a foolish manner? Worse, might not the opponent be some kind of fool? When individuals in their search for truth reach some kind of impasse, they can be lazy about it and simply 'agree to disagree' or they can attempt to make some kind of sense of the impasse by attributing some kind of fault to their opponents. Even then, they can bring the fault into the discourse by openly examining its nature or they can be silent about it and thereby entrench themselves into a position that is not subject to the possibility of revision.

In any case, Erasmus's 'fool-osophy' can bring these potentially self-entrenching strategies to light and at least in principle open the door to a greater self-reflection on the part of each side in the dispute. Furthermore, what progress in handling the truth could be made if some negative attribute that consigns an opponent's argument to folly were somehow reversed in such a way that progress toward truth was accordingly abetted? Such a possibility of reversal might well be the work of the liberal arts, but at this point one must rise above the Erasmian blindness to folly and accept the pain that comes from facing it. If in the course of an impasse over truth, one side or even both sides are guilty of adopting a position that is the occasion for an argument-ending attribution of folly, it is no laughing matter—Erasmus' consummate wit notwithstanding.

The first of the four negative attributions directed to an opponent is that of simple ignorance or innocence.[1] Those who share this defect are perhaps too young (or, if senile, too old) to grasp the requisite knowledge deemed necessary for resolving some dispute over truth. Ignorance can also come from a lack of education or from a failure to explore, study, or conduct experiments with respect to a certain area of knowledge. Paul Johnson, in his monograph, *Darwin – Portrait of a Genius*, quotes Erasmus Darwin, Charles' paternal grandfather, as saying, "Any man who does not conduct an experiment is a fool."[2] The fact that Charles' grandfather bears the name of the man who wrote *Praise of Folly* is not without irony in this context.) In any case, once it is identified as a reason for the breakdown of discourse pertaining to truth-seeking and parties to the dispute are ready to acknowledge their ignorance, then progress toward resolution may be possible by making efforts to overcome the ignorance.

The second of the negative attributions is more subtle and harder to deal with. Although Erasmus does not name the quality as much as he illustrates it, I would call this occasion for discursive breakdown nothing less than stupidity, albeit of a willful kind rather than arising from some mental defect. What is

---

[1] Erasmus, Desiderius. *The Praise of Folly, trans.* John Wilson (1668) (Ann Arbor: University of Michigan Press, 1958), 18-19.
[2] Paul Johnson, *Darwin: Portrait of a Genius,* (New York: Penguin Publishing Group, 2012), 4.

going on here is more a matter of taking an inappropriate 'short-cut' in order to reach a certain goal rather than acknowledge the necessity of taking a harder path so that the goal is reached in a more appropriate and ultimately effective manner. For example, if instead of utilizing the short-cut of paying off a priest as a way to escape the full consequences of his/her sin, an individual chooses to take the longer, harder and more appropriate road of changing his/her life, then the person otherwise tempted to take short-cuts would avoid the obvious stupidity of trying to 'trick' God, who presumably knows what is going on anyway, "… the best way to get quit of sin is to add to the money you give the hatred of sin, tears, watchings, prayers, fastings, and amendment of life; such or such a saint will favor you if you imitate his life."[3]

Stupidity, based on inappropriate trickery, can also be connected with the actions of the trickster archetype—an archetype associated with a figure who is also a kind of cultural hero celebrated for bestowing some technological benefit upon humanity. The link is subtle but is worth elaborating upon because of its connection to discursive breakdown. Any invention that moves a culture forward is a kind of short-cut with respect to how individuals interact with reality. For example, writing circumvents memory; and while many would think that is a good thing, it has its costs, one of which is the weakening of human memory and all that such a weakening entails. Insofar as some of the practices developed by the Catholic Church are a kind of spiritual technology, they also offer short-cuts to salvation; but as Erasmus points out, the cost is a kind of short-term gain of feeling good, but a long-term (i.e., infinite) loss with respect to salvation. God is not to be duped. In the context of searching for truth, awareness of stupidity is not an occasion for name-calling, but an opportunity for assessing openly the costs of adopting short-cuts that can negatively affect our engagement with the real.

Beyond tricksterish stupidity there exists another occasion for discursive breakdown—one to which Erasmus does not give a specific name, but I would call linguistic insularity. Here we enter the world of professional jargon that proliferates among scientists[4], grammarians[5], lawyers[6], etc. As an example of what might be termed a private world, the figure of Folly offers this critique of scientific discourse: "These [the scientists], though they have not the least degree of knowledge, profess yet that they have mastered all; nay, though they neither know themselves, nor perceive a ditch or block that lies in their way, …

---

[3] Johnson, Paul. 2012. *Darwin: Portrait of a Genius*, (New York: Penguin Publishing Group, 2012), 84-85.
[4] Ibid., 92.
[5] Ibid., 84-85.
[6] Ibid., 92.

yet give out that they have discovered ideas, universalities, separated forms, first matters, quiddities, haecceities, formalities, and the like stuff; things so thin and bodiless that I believe even Lynceus was not able to perceive them."[7] At a more extreme level one cannot help but wonder if the exclusivist language of the professional can be associated with the quasi-private language of the mad person. In any case, the search for truth is hampered when language starts to become overly complex and hyper-fragmented in a disciplinary sense.

The last obstacle to handling the truth from an Erasmian perspective is that associated with spiritual penetration of the real. Those who have transcended the limitations of the body and therefore have direct contact with the spiritual foundations of reality appear crazy to those whose spirituality is more conventional: "And when they come to themselves, tell you they know not where they have been, whether in the body or out of the body, or sleeping; nor do they remember what they have heard, seen, spoken, or done, and only know this as it were in a dream, that they were most happy while they were out of their wits."[8] Erasmus knows that not many have experienced such spiritual 'ecstasy, but from the perspective of truth handling this obstacle is perhaps the most crucial because it challenges the entire sphere of conventional discourse, which is geared to a sense of truth that is controllable, rational, and/or clear. The deepest levels of truth might not be and calling those who have experiences of the mystical 'out of their minds' is dangerously presumptuous.

To sum up, Erasmus provides us with at least four ways of accounting for discursive impasse with respect to determining the truth. There can be attributions of ignorance with respect to one or two contending parties. Tricksterish stupidity could also play a role inasmuch as one or both parties are involved with taking short-cuts that blind them to the consequences of such a strategy. Linguistic insularity could cause a breakdown in understanding with respect to those on the outside of a particular sphere of discourse. Finally, discourse can falter when one party is possessed of a mystical insight into the reality that more conventionally minded individuals do not share. The point is that knowing or understanding or working with these points of impasse could weaken the forces of entrenchment based on a devaluing of one's opponent. Why should one truth seeker work with someone deemed ignorant, stupid, insulated in a private world, or in a state of mystical ecstasy (or conventional superficiality)? Yet awareness of these devaluative attributions can lessen their power and provide the liberals arts with strategies that allow for a more productive handling of the truth.

---

[7] Johnson, *Darwin: Portrait of a Genius*, 92.
[8] Ibid., 84-85.

What strategies? With respect to ignorance, the obvious antidote is an acknowledgement of that state and a resolve to acquire a measure of knowledge that might resolve the dispute. A key liberal art that may be brought to bear is that of science (which I take to be an important liberal art), where repeatable experiments framed in the context of mathematical models are utilized to gain insight into the external world. But what is it that makes science so compelling with respect to the problem of ignorance? Here we must conduct a kind of phenomenology of scientific knowing and broaden our perspective so to speak. If ignorance can be correlated with an early state of awareness, knowledge as a diminution of ignorance can be correlated with a kind of cumulative growth of the person. Science then figures strongly in this growth dynamic insofar as the knowledge it gains (and this does not have to be mathematical although, as we shall see, that can help) tends to be more cumulative than that afforded by the probing into reality of other liberal arts. In other words, it would be hard to argue that such liberal arts as those associated with painting, philosophy, or religion are characterized by an inherently cumulative nature. In contrast, science as a way of truth handling appears most cumulative; and when it comes to an impasse with respect to truth-seeking—an impasse characterized by the negative attribution of ignorance—any discipline geared to building a cumulative body of knowledge is implicitly addressed to the growth dynamic shared by individuals, groups, and cultures. Thus, instead of having discourse grind to a halt by attributing ignorance to one's opponent, the liberal arts can study differing growth patterns and apply the most appropriate to the joint construction of what I would term 'knowledge cumulation projects.'

By way of elaborating on cumulativeness with respect to mathematics, I hesitate to include the following personal anecdote instead of a scholarly article or monograph, but extensive interviews with many mathematicians would be required to place my anecdotal account on solid ground. The point I am putting forward is that because mathematical truth requires a cumulative understanding that many liberal arts disciplines do not, the Erasmian problem of ignorance is set in a revealing light with respect to discursive breakdown.

To unpack the foregoing, I must disclose my disciplinary background as that of history, albeit the history of ideas. In a conversation I had with a mathematician—a conversation wherein I admitted my lack of understanding of his current research project—I asked him why I was having such trouble grasping his ideas since, to my way of thinking, mathematics was essentially rational and I fancied that I was capable of reasoning. His answer to my query surprised me because I was not expecting it. He essentially attributed my difficulty in comprehension to the fact that math was so old. Now as a long-standing student of history, I thought I could 'do old'; but upon reflection I realized that I could not because my subject was far too diffuse while his was much more focused on an extensive trajectory that stretched into a distant past and ostensibly into a distant future. I built my historical understanding—and this may apply to other liberal arts disciplines—on the basis of contextualizing a given object of inquiry and necessarily 'forgetting' what did not apply because it lacked 'contextualization value.' As such, my historical understanding is anything but cumulative, and I accordingly bring a significant measure of ignorance into any truth-directed discourse. Contrariwise, my mathematical colleague has to know to a much greater degree the history of mathematical thinking lest gaps make his quest for truth problematic. Understanding, for him, means that one cannot be ignorant of any link in the chain (let alone take it on faith). In that sense, mathematics provides a kind of model for cumulative knowing—a model that mutes ignorance insofar as cumulative knowing is a kind of systematic and necessary growth in understanding. Whether this model can be applied to other liberal arts disciplines is, of course, an open question that is outside the scope of the current discussion.

As for tricksterish stupidity, let us recall that this involved taking short-cuts without consideration of the costs. An antidote would be a liberal art that took the long-way-around and brought truth-seekers closer to the reality that would otherwise be ignored. What is the long-way-around? From a liberal arts perspective, I would suggest that aesthetic investigation is the appropriate antidote to the impasses characterized by the penchant for taking short-cuts. This is because art in general has the capacity to take us closer to reality in a personal sense than is the case with a more detached approach. For example, a painting or a novel engages us in what it is attempting to represent. Moreover, the engagement can be emotional and not just physical. To the extent that the truth of reality emerges from such an experience of intimacy, truth-seekers at an impasse can look to or even create aesthetic representations of what they are seeking to understand. Contemptuous denigration of one's opponent for appearing as a stupid trickster might be replaced by a more constructive approach associated with aesthetically sensitizing oneself to the position of one's opponent in the debate over truth.

When it comes to linguistic insularity as an obstacle to handling the truth, the liberal arts could diffuse the situation by mounting a kind of linguistic critique of the jargon that stands between truth seekers. Clearly, we are in the world of philosophy, where linguistic analysis can be used to clarify meaning while the creation of integrative overviews and popularizations can serve to extend the range of participation in otherwise forbiddingly narrow areas of specialization. Truth can only be handled to greater advantage when our very words do not function as barriers to understanding.

The last of the Erasmian occasions for discursive impasse is that of mystical ecstasy in opposition to conventional superficiality. In our own day, when the scientific approach to reality is paramount, the truths associated with mystical ecstasy are easily given short shrift, but there are ways of facilitating discourse. First, there a vast array of first-hand accounts (e.g. William James, *Varieties of Religious Experience*) that might give sceptics a sense of what is going one. Secondly, there is also the ever-growing literature (e.g. Edward Kelly et al. *Irreducible Mind – Toward A Psychology For The 21st Century*) pertaining to the paranormal—a science that can explore the mystical (and other associated states) without taking on religious baggage. Thirdly, there is the possibility of making a direct experience of the mystical a major pillar of the liberal arts. Why should students not explore prayer, meditation, sweat-lodge experiences, and even supervised drug-taking as a way of gaining direct experiences of the mystical state, with which Erasmus concluded his *Praise of Folly*? Are we so afraid to live in a world where conventional superficiality is challenged? If we are afraid of truth in its depth, access to that depth via the foregoing liberal arts strategies might free us from that fear.

The Ugly Truth

The previous section put forward some ideas of how the liberal arts could be used to dis-entrench individuals from rigid positions, where that rigidity stands in the way of resolving conflicts over the truth. However, each age probably has its unique set of challenges with respect to the struggle over truth, and it would be wise to address these now. For the present time has, in certain ways, made truth 'ugly' and that ugliness needs to be explicated before a countervailing sense of its beauty can be rekindled in the hearts of human beings. It is no doubt harder to handle the truth if it has somehow been made repulsive to human seekers. If its inherent beauty can be resurrected by liberal arts strategies that go beyond dis-entrenchment with respect to mutually hostile positions, then the attractiveness of truth will draw us to it. Perhaps then it is a matter of letting truth handle us in a gentle manner.

But what is the 'ugly truth' that we would like to avoid in our own day? Indeed, the ugly truth pertains to the very nature of truth, which at one level refers to its ever-growing inaccessibility to most of us. For example, how many can do the math that underlies our technology, science, economics, etc.? If access to the truth now requires a level of intellectual prowess that few can muster, then an ugly truth of growing inequality is coming to the fore. Worse yet, if a significant part of the new technology is devoted to keep us distracted by playing computer games, then our very interest in pursuing deeper truths may be undermined. (See Nicholas Cadrr's *The Shallows—What the Internet Is Doing to Our Brains.*) In short, the ignorance of a large proportion of our population with respect to the knowledge base of contemporary culture may be growing.

Returning to the theme of tricksterish stupidity, the short-cuts criticized by Erasmus are minimal compared to the short-cuts of our 'cyber-culture'. No doubt some of these have value, but the ugly truth may be that we are not aware of some of the more onerous costs. For example, while most would find Wikipedia worthwhile, there may be a hidden cost in the way it cheapens knowledge. If we had to search harder for what is now available with a mere click, we might value what we found and might not skim it in the cursory manner that comes with the speed of delivery. In short, has the short-cut culture of the Internet come with the cost of cheapening the value of the truth?

More telling perhaps is the manner in which short-cuts truncate our relationship to the real. If aboriginal cultures were aware of this issue and limited their technology accordingly, a hyper-technologized cyber-culture, such as our own, has begun to 'virtualize' our relationship to the real; and if the truth is an authentic relationship to the real, a virtual-reality technology may be pushing us toward a virtual sense of the truth. How 'virtual'? In the manner of prisoners in Plato's cave—prisoners who engage in endless discourse about shadows projected on a wall—prisoners of the cyber-culture are endlessly discoursing about the truth of what is on their 'screens' (e.g. desktop computers, iPads, smartphones, etc.). Thus, truth becomes ugly to the extent that it cannot be distinguished from illusion and uglier still if the illusion is more appealing and convincing than the reality which is unmediated by screens. Finally, should the screen-mediated reality become unsatisfying but still hold us in thrall, because of its omnipresent convenience and our inherent laziness, we might very well become addicted to it, where addiction is associated with a compulsive repetition that grows out of an excessive attachment to some substitute (i.e. 'virtual' in this case) reality.

Moving beyond how cyber-culture provides us with short-cuts to the truth and may truncate our relationship to the real, there is another level of ugliness; namely, the conflict over privacy. To the extent that we are at the mercy of programmers, hackers, internet trolls, to that extent we may be driven to adopt defensive strategies that can serve to insulate us from each other. This is not the insulation that comes from the private or professional language insularity criticized by Erasmus as contributing to the isolating entrenchment of truth-seekers, but an atmosphere of suspicion about truth can make it hard to handle especially when that suspicion is reinforced by a pervading sense of uncertainty regarding sources and an inability to check them out. The sheer vastness of the Internet can turn it in what I would term a 'lie-byrinth', within which a seeker of truth can easily get lost. As the myth of the labyrinth suggests, what lies within its many passageways is a monster that will devour truth-seekers with doubt.

There is yet a more subtle disfiguring of truth that may be associated with another aspect of cyber-culture. This is what I would call a tendency to 'cyber-ficiality'—a play on superficiality that may be associated with a loss of depth in communication. Twitter, along with similar venues that keep messages confined to a certain limit, sacrifice depth for speed, and I would suggest that the consequences of that sacrifice are not fully understood. However, in the context of linguistic insularity as an obstacle to truth, there is something ominous about being directed away from the depth of one's self and moved toward what can only be expressed in a few words and images. Would such 'cyber-ficiality' subtly trap us in our private worlds; not that of professionalized knowledge, but of a 'cyber-persona' that estranges others, not to mention ourselves, from the deeper parts of our being? These are parts through which more authentic connections could be made and a more meaningful search for truth undertaken.

In a sense cyber-culture is only the latest of trends that have contributed to making truth ugly. Indeed, one may think of it as an off-shoot of Western civilization in its pursuit of power over the external world—a pursuit that goes back at least as far as the Scientific Revolution (17th Century) and, before that, the ventures of imperial expansion associated with voyages of exploration (15th Century). The ugliness here may be associated with a fundamental imbalance with respect to the West's fundamental relation to reality and the sense of truth that follows from what I would call that 'flawed' relationship. The essence of the imbalance that skews our sense of truth is an excessive focus on the external at the expense of the internal. It is based on a fundamental cultural assumption that the external is somehow more real than the internal; and while the evolution of that world view has been gradual, it has evolved in some circles to the point that the internal does not even exist and that at best it is some kind of epiphenomenon of the human brain, which is essentially material, that is, external in nature.

What then is the internal and what role would it play in a more balanced search for truth? Returning briefly to Erasmus, the internal may be associated with the joy-engendering realm of the mystical. Those who espouse or experience an authentic as opposed to a more superficial (if not false) relationship to God seem to be indifferent to the external world and its survivalist emphasis. To such spiritually inclined individuals the kingdom of God truly is 'within', that is, internal. But that internal is not some space within the body such as the brain. It is a non-physical space akin to that of consciousness (i.e., a mind-like space wherein thought in and of itself exists) understood as something that has a measure of independence from such material structures as that of the physical brain. Correlations between mind and brain obviously exist. However, while some might take these correlations as the locus of a balance between mind and body, the body (in contemporary Western Civilization) is more often than not clearly taken as fundamental and the underlying project is to increase our physical power over the mind by a thorough understanding of the functioning of the brain. The problem of imbalance here and its attendant ugliness is that of silencing those who hold to an internalist view. It is not that debate is entirely absent, but the relative dearth of those holding internalist views within a contemporary Western university would suggest an uncritical, if not dogmatic, emphasis on the truth of an externalist way of looking at the world. If this were not the case, paranormal studies, which explore the world of the internal, would exist in most universities rather than just a handful. When evidence of the existence of the internal is roundly ignored or inappropriately criticized, the cause of truth has been slighted. (See references to Chris Carter's trilogy in the bibliography.)

While 'ugly truth' may be associated with such barriers to discourse as imbalance, 'cyberficiality', truncation, and inaccessibility, there is a more telling obstacle to discourse that may be said to make truth even harder to handle. I am referring here to what might be called a terrible truth—that is, a truth that may be too horrible to contemplate, but may nonetheless lie at the 'heart of darkness' that lies within individuals, groups, cultures, and entire civilizations. While this is not the place for a full-fledged exposition, light may be shed on terrible truth by way of a list of open-ended questions: Do sadistic serial killers know the truth of their compulsion to do evil even if they know the difference between right and wrong? Did the most abusive colonists of the New World know that they were savagely objectifying their victims? Given that a few of the colonizers were aware that genocidal atrocities were taking place, what kept the majority from grasping the deeper truths of their actions?[9] Even if apologies are issued to aboriginal peoples for past abominations (e.g. residential schools), does that gesture mask a deeper and more unpalatable truth; namely, that the current socio-economic system is still rooted in the same predatory instincts that led to past acts of abuse? Worse, do we hide from a hidden (i.e. suppressed) truth that the costs of our current socio-economic system are destructively high and do we maintain this self-deception by continuing to affirm the superiority of corporate capitalism over such discredited 'rivals' as Stalinist or Maoist communism?

---

[9] Bartolomé de las Casas, "The Devastation of the Indies," in *World Literature and Thought, Vol. III –The Modern. World to 1900*, ed. Donald S. Gochberg (Orlando: Harcourt), 2001, 745-748.

As one can see, this list of questions can go on; and it is not good enough to acknowledge[10] that the line between good and evil cuts through every individual if we do not confront in a more direct fashion the dark side associated with a terrible truth. Moreover, it may be the case that this darkness of soul may only exist at a depth that is not amenable to direct or even indirect elucidation and that such terrible truth may never become completely clear because of the inherent limits of human memory. To explain this, let us consider human growth from a generalized Freudian perspective. Even though what follows is admittedly speculative, much pertaining to terrible truth may be explained thereby.

Before the emergence of language an event perceived as traumatic by an evolving personality might have engendered what I would term a 'fatal choice'—fatal in the sense that it sets up a behavioral pattern that controls subsequent actions as fate may be said to control the actions of individuals in the context of myth (e.g. the story of Oedipus being controlled by a pre-given fate, which he cannot escape). What would make this unconscious or quasi-conscious response a 'terrible truth' is that it defines subsequent behavior in terms of a traumatic (i.e. terrifying) event that has a strong emotional charge, but which cannot be directly known because of the subject's pre-linguistic level of development. Disturbing experiences may be laid down in the creative soil of consciousness, and, as seeds, they may later produce 'flowers of evil' that are imperfectly understood by a growing individual.

I am obviously treading on unsolid ground in a murky forest, and the terrible truth to which I am referring may also be disturbing not so much because of its possibly traumatic origin, but also on account of its inherent unknowability. We all come from a deep place; a place from which the emergence of our consciousness bears the mark of a troubling discontinuity as if the secret of the self is its inescapable secrecy. Once (before we were born?) we were not conscious or so we surmise. Now, in our respective journeys through life, we are. But from where did that consciousness come? We are not even sure when it appeared. In other words, the terrible truth is that our very mode of awareness, that to which we are closest and in a way defines our very identity, may be something from which we are deeply alienated—perhaps to a degree so extreme that we can hardly bear to face that alienation. Surely that is so terrible a truth that we do not even wish to know that we cannot handle it.

---

[10] Alexsandr Solzhenitsyn, "The Gulag Archipelago," in *Classics Of Western Thought, Vol. IV – The Twentieth Century*, ed. Donald S. Gochberg (Fort Worth: Harcourt Brace Jovanovich, 1980), 94.

Yet we probably do engage in truth-handling strategies, but only in what I would call acts of mythic projection. That is, we create stories of alarming but fascinating depth that allow us to handle the dark truths, but at the same time afford us the opportunity of distancing ourselves from them by configuring them in fantastic and strange narratives that make them difficult to understand no matter how powerfully they may resonate with our emotional sensitivities. Perhaps certain myths may be thought of as a pre-historic form of psychology; a psychology that allowed humans to have a controlled access to terrible truths without having to live with the draining energy expenditure that we associate with repression. What we at the present time do not find particularly frightening because of a familiarity gained over the course of centuries may have been much more disturbing during earlier epochs. For example, as Curtis Hoffmann points out in his study of myth (*The Seven Story Tower – A Mythic Journey Through Space and Time*), the newly concentrated powers of kingship that emerged in ancient Sumer had associated with them certain myths wherein kings were made to suffer for acts of pride (*hybris*)[11] —something that touches on what I would interpret as a terrible truth, which is that of a great power disparity between ruling figures in society and those who were vulnerable to their ever-increasing authority. The Sumerian myths identified by Hoffman may not resonate with us to the extent that the truth of power may no longer be so unusual. In any case, traumas may be personal and/or cultural, and the truths of these traumas may require some kind of mythic construction that both hides at the same time that it expresses what we do not wish to face directly.

Up to this point I have been speaking of a terrible truth in terms of a hidden trauma, and handling these requires a liberal arts strategy, wherein the objectivity of a detached analysis is replaced by a painful recognition that truth is emotionally situated. Whether the locus of a painful truth is personal or cultural, bringing it to the surface entails a kind of suffering on the part of the individual or society and, in the wake of that suffering, a possible restructuring of fundamental behavioral patterns in a way that draws the liberal arts away from the stance of scientific objectivity. In other words, ugly or painful truth can only be handled in the context of a painful self- or cultural transformation.

Even then we must consider what may be thought of as a more extreme possibility; namely, that some terrible truths might not be subject to handling at all and that the liberal arts might have a role to play in acknowledging that possibility. What I am referring to is a lie that is disguised as hate-inspiring truth. It is a lie that has many variants: racism, sexism, classism, etc., but it

---

[11] Curtiss Hoffman, *Seven Story Tower: A Mythic Journey Through Space And Time*, (New York: Basic Books, 2008), 111.

reaches the status of an ultra-terrible truth when it calls for the destruction of some group. For those who hold such destructive 'truths', what comes to be deemed terrible (at least from the perspective of putative victims) is the attribution of evil to some enemy and also the inescapable conclusion that extermination is in order if the society wherein the holder of this truth lives is to survive. However, when a monstrous lie evolves into a terrible truth, there is yet a more terrible truth lurking beneath it; namely, that an individual or an entire culture has adopted a lie and made it a principle of life. In such a manner that facing the truth of one's lie would entail personal or cultural disintegration. Thus, if handling the real truth that one's life is based on a destructive lie entails the risk of disintegration, then the handling means very little because the self that should grow from an encounter with the truth has in large measure dissolved. The only counter to this negative possibility would be for one who does grasp the real truth to direct love and compassion toward the hate-crazed and by-now fragmented individual. Even if the liberal arts can muster a stance of subjective engagement with respect to facing the trauma of terrible truths, can one expect even the most empathy-based humanities (rooted in a cultivation of spirituality) to put forward the love and compassion that may be required to handle the holders of such a destructive truth and keep them from enduring a fatal disintegration?

The Beautiful Truth

If ugly and/or terrible truth can be handled by facing up to its darkest aspects in the context of myth, we are led to consider the opposite, which I would call beautiful truth. What kind of truth is that which is associated with beauty and how might it be handled? The famous line from Keats' *Ode on a Grecian Urn* is more than apt with respect to introducing this dimension of truth: "Beauty is truth, truth beauty."[12] Truth here is portrayed as a kind of 'friend' that proclaims to humanity something of its essential nature (that is, beauty) and gives us thereby the means to cope with 'other woe'. The other woe presumably lies in the future; and whatever it might be, the urn and Keats' beautiful description of its beauty suggest that the truth embodied in aesthetic expression supports us.

But in what way is truth both attractive and supportive? Is the attractiveness inherently supportive? If the urn is meant to hold the ashes of the dead, we are reminded of the ugly truth of death and decay, wherein the order of the human body is reduced to a chaotic dissolution. Not only does the urn and what it

---

[12] John Keats's "Ode on a Grecian Urn," in *Classics of Western Thought*, ed. Edgar E. Knoebel (Belmont, CA: Wadsworth, 1998), p. 270.

portrays not decay (except perhaps on a timescale beyond that of most human lives), it points to a quality of truth, which is its inherent incorruptibility. If something is true, it is true forever. It is not a thing of the moment. Even truths pertaining to the patterns of time (e.g. *The I Ching or The Book of Change*) are valued because the flow of time has been shown to manifest an eternal structure within the ambit of 64 hexagrams that are synchronously correlated with the life of some seeker. The eternalistic quality of truth is thus part of its attractiveness, and it supports us in the context of facing an impending dissolution. Moreover, are we not in a better position to handle the truth to the extent that we realize its supportive nature—a nature to which we are drawn by its underlying attractiveness?

From the perspective of the liberal arts we can draw critical attention to those venues of truth that are neither attractive nor emotionally supportive. I am here referring to what are commonly called textbooks, and before considering truth's other attractive qualities we should say a few words about this more mundane approach to the truth. In contrast to the liberal arts emphasis on classic texts (e.g. Keats' poetry), wherein the beauty of truth makes its natural home, textbooks (e.g. explaining or situating Keats' poetry) present truth in a pre-digested manner which is served up to students as a set of facts or principles. The living quality that characterizes classic texts is thereby lost, and students who are fed on such a diet become bored even though the textbook fare might be considered easier to handle. What I would call 'textbook truth' may be thought of as a kind of tentative summary of what intrepid explorers have found after much effort. The question that comes to mind is whether students would be more engaged if some aspects of that struggle were presented to them and/or their teachers found ways to directly engage them in the quest for truth. Of course, the students also need to be reminded that the summary to which the textbooks are exposing them is only tentative because the quest for truth is as endless as is the truth itself.

Turning then to other attractive qualities of truth, classic texts remind us of what I would call its inexhaustibility. For example, a classic text such as Dante's *The Divine Comedy* can be read again and again without ever exhausting its rich vein of meaning and insight. To put it another way, it has a depth that is infinite. Indeed, such a text seems to be alive since it grows with the engagement of readers from different times and cultures. Other readers can even be nurtured when they read of how certain significant writers responded to the original text. For example, Primo Levi has arguably produced a classic, *Survival in Auschwitz*, in the recounting of his concentration camp experiences. But within that text Chapter 11 is, perhaps, especially moving wherein he describes how he is trying to explain Dante's "Canto of Ulysses" to another prisoner, Jean. Ulysses (also known as Odysseus) is in the Inferno (Canto XXVI) for his 'evil counsel,' but Dante has elaborated on the original myth where Ulysses engineered the fall of Troy, with his famous horse, by describing how a lust to experience the far-flung world[13] drove Ulysses onto the open sea, past the pillars of Hercules, where a violent squall ended his life and those of his fellow explorers (*truth seekers?*). However, in the midst of their degradation in the camp, Levi experiences a profound need to explain this passage to Jean. He finds new and perhaps unexpected inspiration in Ulysses' admonition to his fellow Greek adventurers and struggles to recite the passage despite his weakened memory:

> 'Think of your breed; for brutish ignorance
> Your mettle was not made; you were made men,
> To follow after knowledge and excellence.'[14]

Levi goes on to state, "As if I was also hearing it for the first time: like the blast of a trumpet, like the voice of God. For a moment I forget who I am and where I am."[15] When Jean (also known as Pikolo) asks Levi to repeat the passage, he (Levi) has a powerful realization, "… perhaps, despite the wan translation and the pedestrian, rushed commentary, he has felt that it has to do with him, that it has to do with all men who toil, and with us in particular, and that it has to do with us two, who dare to reason of these things with the poles for the soup on our shoulders."[16]

The foregoing does not end with Levi commenting on Dante. It does not end at all. When I, as a teacher, recite the Levi passage to my students, I am passing it on to them as they may pass it on to others. I might add that Dante is himself building on Virgil, who built on Homer, who built on a complex structure of myths, which themselves may be derived from a set of archetypes rooted in what Jung called the collective unconscious. In any case, what I have tried to demonstrate by way of this example is the inexhaustibility of truth in the context of classic texts; and, as Levi pointed out, this inexhaustibility sustained him even in the hell of Auschwitz. If truth manifests itself in that inexhaustible richness, it makes life itself easier to handle. Moreover, we become more

---

[13] Dante Alighieri, and John Ciardi, The Divine Comedy: *The Inferno, the Purgatorio, and the Paradiso* (New York: New American Library, 2003).
[14] Primo Levi, *Survival in Auschwitz: The Nazi Assault on Humanity* (New York: Touchstone Books, 1996), p. 113.
[15] Ibid.
[16] Ibid., p. 114.

attracted to the truth, the more we appreciate its quality of putting us in touch with the infinite.

As might be expected, inexhaustibility is not just a quality of classic texts, but of myths as well. Indeed, the inexhaustibility level of myth might be higher than that of classic texts insofar as myths seem to be interconnected with each other in a multitude of ways; and while classic texts share this quality of interconnectivity to some degree (as we have just seen with the Levi-Dante passage), Hoffman, in his *Seven Story Tower*, has demonstrated an inter-connectivity that encompasses myths from cultures which are widely separate in time and space. Secondly, to the extent that myths are made by many speakers (if not truth-seekers), their meanings are broader and more diverse in scope than what can be created by one classic text creator. In that sense, the inexhaustibility level of these attractive truths can only be raised. Finally, mythic truth manifests another dimension of inexhaustibility by virtue of its ability to address a broader audience than do some classic texts. By this I mean that those who have not been educated to understand the subtleties of erudite classic texts can nonetheless respond to the truths embedded in popular myths that are designed to reach out to the collective unconscious of a vast audience—an audience that might include the entire world. Thus, with respect to the theme of truth being inherently attractive within the context of myth and folklore, its inexhaustibility seems to go beyond that of classic texts.

While the liberal arts have a long history of myth interpretation, what could be expanded with a view to enhancing our perception of truth's inexhaustibility is a kind of mythic exploration of cultural artefacts that are not normally viewed as mythic in nature. In other words, to see the surrounding culture as possessing mythic traits or revealing mythic themes opens up possibilities of truth's attractively inexhaustible nature to be found outside the sphere of more traditional myths and within comics, games, advertisements, sports, etc. One can thus envision liberal arts hybrid disciplines such as 'mytho-sociology', 'mytho-economics' and the like. Imagine a world where truth in all its richness and fecundity is brought forward by a kind of mytho-analysis of everyday life!

Beyond inexhaustibility, truth has other attractive qualities, one of which is perhaps central to beauty. The quality of symmetry figures strongly in beauty and, by extension, truth as well. It plays a role in the scientific understanding of nature in addition to its aesthetic portrayal —a portrayal which engages the viewer/listener via the power of beauty. Symmetry is easily recognized as a kind of repetitive pattern—repetitive in space (e.g. mirror-like reflection) as well as time (i.e. a pattern that stays constant over time).[17] It thus goes beyond the attractive quality of truth associated with eternality and instead draws our attention to what stays the same in a process of transformation. In the case of Keats's 'Ode' the story portrayed on the urn is preserved over time while the geometrically regular shape of the urn presents a constant outline from a variety of spatial perspectives. At a deeper level what is preserved is a sense of impending consummation ever delayed, "Bold lover, never, never canst thou kiss, Though winning near the goal…"[18] What is painted or carved on the urn is a lover about to kiss his beloved, but the act is frozen in time. How is this pattern of delayed consummation symmetrically repeated and what does it say about truth in its attractive aspect?

To the extent that truth does not exhaust reality but is always approaching it, there is a psychological sense of impending gratification that can never be realized. We can see this when reading classic texts or pondering great myths. They are the same in the sense that they exist as unchanging artefacts of culture (if not consciousness), but that sameness is preserved in the context of different times and even different cultures. Seekers of truth who are engaged with these artefacts return to them again and again, not just because they are inexhaustible, but also because they manifest a sense of truth being near yet never to be completely or thoroughly appropriated. It is a symmetry that Keats tries to capture by expressing the constancy of impending but never to be realized consummation. It is as if he were trying to articulate a kind of meta-symmetry, where the image on the urn is an image of how symmetry actually functions in a psychological sense. To put it another way, truth is attractive because it excites with a promise that, while unrealizable, is everywhere recognizable when we see patterns repeated in radically different contexts. Thus, to see the world as a work of art, is to get a sense of truth that is captured and inspired by an awareness of symmetry. Cultivating such awareness, then, might be a strategy of the liberal arts with respect to being able to handle the truth in its symmetrical aspect.

Just as we are drawn to inexhaustibility and symmetry, we are also drawn to a quality of truth that I would call containment, where beauty manifests itself in a kind of topological hierarchy wherein one aspect of the real is contained within another although these aspects are ultimately centered on the locus of the self with respect to the truth. To clarify, is the truth ultimately outside of us or is it inside of us? Outside of us means external whereas inside of us is associated with internality. On the one hand, if truth is exclusively external,

---

[17] Leon Lederman and Christopher T. Hill, *Symmetry and the Beautiful Universe* (Amherst, N.Y.: Prometheus, 2008).
[18] Keats, "*Ode on a Grecian Urn,*" 278.

then it might be too hard to handle especially if that externality places it too far away from our all-too-human conceptual apparatus. On the other hand, if truth is essentially internal to ourselves, then it loses some of its allure by the danger of succumbing to excessive subjectivity. Thus, if internal and external are dissociated with respect to our personal relationship (or that of some culture) to the truth, a subtle sense of beauty is lost. Contrariwise, the beauty of truth is accordingly enhanced if the topological hierarchy of internal and external is refined in a balanced manner.

To give an example, Shakespeare's *Hamlet* features a play within a play, where the former is set up by the protagonist to unmask Hamlet's uncle as the murderer of Hamlet's father. The details here are not as important as the nested structure of play being internal to a play—a situation wherein the characters of Shakespeare's play are external to the play they are watching, which takes on a kind of internality with respect to a space external to it. By that token, Shakespeare's play takes on an internal quality with respect to the audience currently viewing Shakespeare's play, and that audience now may view itself as an internal or shared common space with respect to an 'audience' that is perceiving it from some external venue; a situation that could be repeated endlessly.

This topological aspect to the truth need not be confined to plays within plays or stories within stories (e.g. *The Thousand and One Nights*). In Keats' 'Ode' the urn itself is a container, that is itself 'contained' in the poem as an object being written about, but as a container itself it might hold the ashes of a deceased person, whose remains are a kind of symbolic container for a life that once contained many experiences. Similarly, the reader may contain, by emotional identification, the lives depicted on the urn, but may also feel contained by the possibility of an impending death that the urn ultimately represents. As one can see, this topological structure of internality and externality exfoliates in a multitude of directions; and one may develop a sense that truth can be touched at a deeper level as its internal and external aspects reveal themselves in a kind of multi-dimensional hierarchy. The sense of beauty arises from a balance between internal and external, but also (I suspect) from the truth seeker's feeling that encountering the hierarchy gives one a kind of access to the infinite—an infinite that has a double direction defined by ever-larger spheres of containment as well as ever-smaller ones. In any case, this topological aesthetic can be exploited by the liberal arts insofar as it seeks to creatively arrange its many disciplines in an internal-external hierarchy beyond the one traditionally adopted by the hard sciences, where math contains physics, which contains chemistry, which contains biology, etc. Thus, in some circumstances, history could contain sociology which could act as a container for psychology with respect to representing some aspect of reality within an inter-disciplinary context, but it could just as easily be arranged in the reverse direction. The point is that truth can be handled in a more effective manner if different aspects of its beauty are brought to the surface by various topological strategies that I can hardly outline within the confines of a brief discussion.

There is one more aspect of truth's beauty that I would like to discuss, and that is its quality of embodying or pointing to a kind of oneness or unity that underlies all things and which I would describe as a kind of creative energy. That underlying unity has an attractive aspect, which can be seen in the quest for a theory of everything in the sciences, but it can also be seen in a way in which monotheism attempts to eliminate discord by having one law, one faith, and a religious framework that seeks to bring people together. Creativity figures in both of these areas of knowing inasmuch as God is viewed as a creator of all things while, from the perspective of science, the big bang is indicative of structured development that emerges from a singular or unified point. The emergence of a richly diverse and complex universe from such a singularity can be considered an embodiment of creative power even if the force behind it is deemed not to be a higher form of consciousness—i.e. a god. Why may this unifying creative power be considered attractive or, in the case of divinity, an object of love? Creativity is attractive in the sense of its association with life and procreation and the way it stands against the force of dissolution, entropy and death. In Keats' poem it may be represented by the erotic undertone of happy love. Unity is attractive by way of its association with integration, intimacy and what I would call dis-alienation from a world of radical otherness. Again, in the poem the radical otherness of death is not just contained in the physical space of the urn, the very beauty of the urn is brought to the fore by and in a sense unified with the beauty of Keats' poetic description of it. By implication, other manifestations of beauty can be unified with each other to the extent that they engender a common sense of attraction in the ones who perceive them.

If truth is easier to handle by way of its association with a unifying creative power, the liberal arts can seek to harness this attractive aspect by adopting some appropriate strategies. First, they could take as objects of study the great works of unification that already lie within its arsenal (e.g. Aristotle, Aquinas, Hegel, A.M. Young, K. Wilber; to take only a few Western exemplars). Secondly, inter-disciplinary studies, that seek to solve specific problems, by mobilizing the insights of several disciplines, could be supplemented by what I would call integral-disciplinary studies. The goal here would be to develop strategies for unifying knowledge by studying how different disciplines can be united or integrated with a view to overcoming narrow and mutually exclusive disciplinary turf-wars. Thirdly, cultural barriers could be overcome by developing a comparative analysis and synthesis of differing fundamental cultural assumptions as these evolve over time.

In any case, the foregoing hardly exhausts what can be done to make the pursuit of truth in its beauty more attractive to seekers. By the same token, awareness of what makes the pursuit of truth a fearful proposition is not exhausted by our description of those features of truth that are ugly or terrifying. However, even the elements which have been identified give seekers a deeper understanding that can be used to develop the appropriate liberal-arts strategies to enhance possibilities or counter obstacles. With these in hand, who knows how far and how fast the world of knowing may advance.

Pedagogical Conclusions on How to Handle the Truth

While we have looked at truth from the perspective of liberal-arts strategies, these have been largely set in the framework of scholarly endeavor. But research is not the only task of the liberal arts. Pedagogy in the context of teaching the truth should also be considered.

When it comes to truth's inexhaustibility with respect to myths, teachers would do well not just to talk about myths from the outside as it were, but to express them in a manner that they would have originally been communicated. This is because inexhaustibility is better appreciated if it is directly experienced by an appeal to the student's collective unconscious. Otherwise, the inexhaustibility of truth will be more of an abstract concept than a living reality. As mythic truth in a pedagogical setting can be expressed by one who has studied the art of myth recounting, it can also be absorbed by one who has been taught at an early age to hear these tales with the ear of imagination.

Turning to the issue of classroom dynamics, teachers often have to put up with the antics of students acting like 'stupid tricksters'. This occurs when students, given the pressures that are besetting them, desperately look for short-cuts to get through a course with minimal work. 'School' is taken by no small number as a boring burden that must be endured to enhance usually slim employment prospects, and many teachers take that negative attitude on the part of students to be par for the course; whatever the course may be. And yet, if truth is inherently attractive, a viable pedagogical strategy would be to expose students to its beauty—perhaps in a manner that allowed them to discover that beauty for themselves. Performances of great plays could be supplemented by exposure to paintings, music, and literature that emerged at the same time. A classroom that has become the occasion for an explosion of culture is a place where truth is exposing itself in a way that draws students into the heart of the symmetry experience where they can directly experience that mysterious repetition of pattern in a mode of transformation. Should such pedagogical aspirations appear unrealistic, that might because refining symmetrical sensitivities should begin at the earliest years of education. We, as humans, are natural lovers of beauty, and an educational environment that fosters such love at formative stages of development might reduce the tricksterish game-playing that makes learning a tiresome chore for teachers and students alike.

Experiencing the inexhaustibility of truth and exposing students to its inherent attractiveness are only part of a pedagogy of truth. Let us recall that truth has a topological depth wherein it contains us as we contain it. The question is how to teach this. The teacher has to probe what is within the student as well as what is outside. What is within is the self that is focused on an ancient question: who am I in terms of my hopes, fears, and even 'fate' or destiny; but also who am I in terms of the deepest questions that press upon my soul? At the same time, this topology of truth is developed by encouraging the student to ask a complementary question, which is: what is the world that contains me and how does it influence me at the same that I might be influencing it? One's engagement with the truth is enhanced when the internal and external questions are inter-connected: how is my inner self connected to the external environment? In other words, truth can be effectively taught by setting an agenda for the student to explore its internal-external topological depth, and that requires a certain work on the part of the teacher—the work of helping the student articulate the questions that define her/his life.

But a pedagogy of teaching truth cannot stop with posing questions that situate the student within a topological structure of internality and externality. There is a final and perhaps ultimate step, and that pertains to truth's unity. Here I am not content with talking about truth's unity in the form of a foundational creative energy although that could be a start. Instead, I would want students to have a direct experience of truth's inherent unity. How? There are only two ways that I can see. The first is by exposure to a mystic who can channel this unity to those who are open to experiencing it. The second is by teaching the student to be such a channeler and create thereby a classroom where each student can function as a channel for the other. The techniques for developing such abilities are not unknown: prayer, meditation, and perhaps the taking of certain drugs under the careful supervision of those trained in the art of conducting vision quests.

I do not expect readers of this essay to follow me on this last point, and I daresay I would be more than a little hesitant to develop such a radical pedagogy. And yet the truth, as a way of expressing an authentic relationship to reality, always beckons and ultimately cannot compromise with what Erasmus would have called a conventional relationship with the real—a relationship that is unfortunately the touchstone of education in most venues.

I suppose teachers can always leave their students on the threshold of the truth and encourage them to go forward by themselves while these same teachers stay comfortably and fearfully behind. But that is not real education because real education is leading others into that unknown country from which no traveler returns: not because that country is a place of death (as intimated by Hamlet in his famous soliloquy, Act III, i, ln79, p. 94), but because it is a place of life as higher or enlightened consciousness; and from there no seeker wants to go back to a place of lesser truth.

References

Alighieri, Dante. *The Divine Comedy.* New York: New American Library, 1954, 1961, 1970.

Carr, Nicholas. *The Shallows – What the Internet Is Doing to Our Brains.* New York: W.W. Norton & Company, 2011.

Carter, Chris. *Science and Psychic Phenomena – The Fall of the House of Skeptics.* Rochester, VT: Inner Traditions, 2007, 2012.

_____ . *Science and the Near-Death Experience – How Consciousness Survives Death.* Rochester, VT: Inner Traditions, 2010.

_____ . *Science and the Afterlife Experience – Evidence for the Immortality of Consciousness.* Rochester, VT: Inner Traditions, 2012.

de las Casas, Bartolomé. "The Devastation of the Indies." In *World Literature and Thought, Vol. III –The Modern World to 1900*, edited by Donald S. Gochberg, 745-748. Orlando: Harcourt, 2001.

Erasmus, Desiderius. *The Praise of Folly.* Translated by John Wilson (1668). Ann Arbor: University of Michigan Press, 1958.

Hoffmann, Curtis. *The Seven Story Tower – A Mythic Journey Through Space and Time.* Cambridge, Mass.: Perseus Publishing, 2001.

James, William. *The Varieties of Religious Experience – A Study in Human Nature.* Oxford: Oxford University Press, 2012.

Johnson, Paul. *Darwin – Portrait of a Genius.* New York: Penguin, 2012.

Keats, John. "Ode on a Grecian Urn." In *Classics of Western Thought, Vol. III – The Modern World.* 4th ed., edited by Edgar E. Knoebel, 268-270. Belmont, CA: Wadsworth, 1998.

Kelly, Edward, Emily Kelly, Adam Crabtree, Alan Gauld, Michael Grosso and Bruce Greyson. *Irreducible Mind – Toward A Psychology For The 21st Century.* Lanham, MD.: Rowan & Littlefield, 2010.

Lederman, L. and C.T. Hill. *Symmetry and the Beautiful Universe.* Amherst, NY: Prometheus Books, 2008.

Levi, Primo. *Survival in Auschwitz – The Nazi Assault on Humanity.* Translated by Stuart Woolf. New York: Collier Books, 1958, 1960.

Shakespeare, William. *The Tragedy of Hamlet Prince of Denmark.* New York: New American Library, 1963.

Solzhenitsyn, Alexander. "The Gulag Archipelago." In *Classics Of Western Thought, Vol. IV – The Twentieth Century*, edited by Donald S. Gochberg, 75-116. Fort Worth: Harcourt Brace Jovanovich, 1980.

Wilhelm, Richard, ed. *I Ching or Book of Changes.* Princeton: Princeton University Press, 1977.

Chapter 7

Black Criminality:
A Matter of 'Truth' and our Acquiescence

Navneet Kumar
Medicine Hat College

Abstract

The dominant mainstream media representation of the black body as a repository of decadence and criminality has been played out over and over again to the extent that it has normalized our acceptance of violence and dehumanization against it. The systematic state violence against minorities and the black body in particular finds a legitimizing ground in the essentially propagandist images and terminology deployed by the state and mainstream media, and all this further justifies increased surveillance and militarization of black neighborhoods.

Even as social scientists rejected biological racism, they created a new statistical discourse around black criminality and heredity that went on to have a far more direct impact on subsequent law enforcement policies and served as the intellectual foundation of mass incarceration. I wish to deploy Andrew Kushnir's argument of humanizing the classroom space as a possibility of counteracting the propaganda.

Keywords: propaganda, dehumanization, humanizing, criminalblackman, mass incarceration.

***

Introduction

The dominant mainstream media representation of the black body, as a repository of decadence and criminality, has been played out over and over again to the extent that it has normalized our acceptance of violence and dehumanization against it. Additionally, the systematic state violence against minorities and the black body in particular finds a legitimizing ground in the essentially propagandist images and terminology deployed by the state and mainstream media and all this has further justified increased surveillance and militarization of black neighborhoods in the US. Although racial oppression has been a persistent theme in Black history, the belief is that the civil rights movement has overturned the legacies of slavery, segregation and subordination and made racism a thing of the past. Following from this logic, it has been further argued that African Americans have been given a fair chance with the removal of segregation and discrimination and the overwhelming success of a few African Americans is pointed to vindicate this position. Michelle Alexander writes how she believed that "the problems plaguing poor communities of color, to be a function of poverty and lack of access to quality education—the continuing legacy of slavery and Jim Crow."[1] Alexander argues that because we live in the age of colorblindness, the basic structure of our unequal society has not changed; rather than rely on race to justify discrimination, systematic exclusion and social contempt, we deploy the criminal justice system to label people of color as criminals. [2] In other words, we have legalized discrimination against people of color and the African American population in particular, and therefore taken them out of the fold of all rights, respect, and dignity. We have not ended racism in America; we have merely refashioned and redesigned it using propaganda.

This paper traces the development of this big lie, presented as the truth of our times through tracking the war on crime under Lyndon Johnson, the war on drugs under Ronald Reagan and the use of propaganda to justify both initiatives and finally some ruminations on how to discern the truth. Through the deployment of race theory and propaganda, black criminality has been presented as a matter of truth, and this has led to a natural vilification of African Americans and people of color, while at the same time maintaining that our criminal justice system is largely fair and nondiscriminatory. Scientific experts have packaged racial bias as an objective truth. Elizabeth Hinton in *From the War on Poverty to the War on Crime* points out how "considered an objective truth and a statistically irrefutable fact, notions of black criminality have justified both structural and everyday racism."[3] Even as social scientists rejected biological racism, they created a new statistical discourse around black criminality and heredity that went on to have a far more direct impact on subsequent law enforcement policies in the US and served as the intellectual foundation of mass incarceration. Likewise, Michelle Alexander in her book

---

[1] Michelle Alexander, *The New Jim Crow: Mass Incarceration in the Age of Colorblindness*, (New York: The New Press, 2012), 3.
[2] Alexander, *The New Jim Crow*, 2.
[3] Elizabeth Hinton, *From the War on Poverty to the War on Crime: The Making of Mass Incarceration in America* (Cambridge, Massachusetts: Harvard University Press, 2016), 19.

The New Jim Crow (2010) argues that the criminal justice system in the US discriminates against the black body and the history of slavery and its legacy have morphed that body into something criminal today and led to mass incarceration of young black people. Thus, Alexander argues that the mass incarceration of the black body may be termed as the new Jim Crow, since the black body is essentially discriminated against, vilified, and ultimately seen as readily disposable. This paper argues that black criminality has been presented as a matter of truth and thus the state-sanctioned violence and incarceration against the community have led to the creation of one of the greatest fallacies of modern times. Systematic propaganda or political rhetoric realized in its variance through demagogic speech has been craftily deployed to foster flawed ideologies. In the second part of my paper I argue that a liberal education curriculum can nurture debate and discussion, encourage civic rhetoric and rational will and lead us to a demystification of authority and political rhetoric among other pursuits.

Use of Propaganda to construct the black criminal

It is not an accident that propaganda has posed a problem for a democracy since the times of the Greeks. Even though Aristotle chose democracy to be the least bad of the various forms of government in his *Politics*, he recognized that democracy's flaw came from demagogues whose flawed ideology stirred up the people. In other words, propaganda is characteristically part of the apparatus by which people are tricked about how best to realize their goals and perceive what is in their own best interests. In this paper the focus is on propaganda and its deployment in liberal democracies to mask the truth and bypass reason and rationality. According to Jason Stanley, in *How Propaganda Works*, he writes that "Propaganda is the manipulation of the rational will to close off debate."[4] He writes further that "in so far as ...propaganda is a kind of manipulation of rational beings towards an end without engaging their rational will, it is a kind of deception."[5] In other words, propaganda makes the nation congregate on one central idea, stirred by emotions, that far surpass the evidence for their intensity. Since public reason is essential for a liberal democracy to function effectively, undermining reason becomes one of the problematic results of demagoguery. Civic rhetoric, on the other hand, promotes democratic values of freedom, equality and reasonableness. For example, using rhetoric to extend rights enjoyed by white folks to blacks falls under necessary civic rhetoric because it promotes democracy and it is clearly reasonable. The danger,

---

[4] Jason Stanley, *How Propaganda Works* (Princeton and Oxford: Princeton University Press, 2015), 48.
[5] Ibid., 58.

however, is that such speech only appears to be reasonable and offers reasonable proposals, but in fact erodes reasonableness. In fact, the liberties allowed by democracy too easily permit the demagogues to seize power and thereby pose a threat to freedom and equality; ideas that sound familiar in our modern day and age. One of the problems for a liberal democracy invaded by propaganda is that the demagogue uses the vocabulary of liberal democracy to mask an undemocratic reality. People can be deceived from seeing and comprehending what is in their best interest. Stanley writes of how the "failure of democracy could be hidden by the propagandistic use of the very vocabulary of liberalism."[6] The question then becomes, how do we activate this rational will back into action. Can liberal education have a role to play so that it remains strengthened against demagoguery? How has this flawed ideology worked in the case of African Americans?

The 'Problem' of Black youth

The explicit association between welfare programs in the US and their recipients, primarily the black people, have been seen as the problem by the state. The confluence of the supposed laziness with criminality was achieved and amplified after the gains of the civil rights movement, when such improvements were seen as a threat to the established race hierarchy. Stanley writes that the "belief that Blacks are excessively prone to criminality and inherently lazy is a central feature of white American ideology dating back at least two hundred years."[7] After the Watts riot in August 1965, a growing consensus of policymakers, federal administrators, law enforcement officials, and journalist came to understand crime as specific to black urban youth and argued that "only intensified enforcement of the law in black urban neighborhoods, where contempt for authority seemed widespread, would quell the anarchy and chaos on the nation's streets."[8] The Johnson administration believed that African American youth, swayed by civil rights activists and advocating for self-determination and community engagement, were primarily responsible for the unrest. The African American youth became the target of not only the Johnson administration but subsequent administrations as well, who spurred arguments and support for an intensified crackdown against the black urban youth.[9] The specified targeting of black

---

[6] Stanley, *How Propaganda Works*. 51.
[7] Ibid., 152.
[8] Hinton, *From the War on Poverty to the War on Crime*, 12.
[9] Nicholas deB. Katzenbacj, et al. *The Challenge of Crime in a Free Society: A Report by the President's Commission on Law Enforcement and Administration of Justice*, (Washington, DC: US Government Printing Office, 1967), 5, 35, 44.

youth, or *the problem* as it was specified by President Richard Nixon's chief of staff, H.R. Haldeman who wrote in his diary, that the "President emphasized that you have to face that the whole [welfare] problem is really the blacks. The key is to devise a system that recognizes this, while not appearing to…"[10] One can argue that subsequent governments have been successful to a large extent in this exercise of devising a system that has recognized blacks, especially the black youth, to be the problem without appearing to explicitly say so.

War on Crime

The Johnson administration had identified black youth to be the problem in US society and through successive legislations they were able to produce a carceral state involved in confining an entire group of citizens. Since President Johnson's call for 'War on Crime' and the passage of the Safe Streets Act of 1968, large federal sums of money were diverted to the Law Enforcement Assistance Administration (LEAA) that came to be housed within the Department of Justice. The punitive legislation offered a response to the threat of future disorder by establishing a direct role for the federal government in local police operations, court systems and state prisons for the first time in American history.[11] It became the fastest-growing federal agency in the 1960s and 1970s with a mandate to supervise and control low-income communities. Federal policymakers jumped in too to share a set of assumptions about African Americans, poverty and crime to offer interpretations of black urban poverty as pathological—a product of individual and cultural deficiencies. Hinton comments on how this seemingly neutral statistical thinking and sociological 'truth' of black criminality concealed the racist thinking that guided the strategies federal policymakers developed for the War on Crime. Daniel Moynihan's *The Negro Family: A Case for National Action* (1965) was circulated as an internal document in the Department of Labor which argued that the combined impact of a long history of racial discrimination and cultural deprivation had produced a 'tangle of pathology' in urban black families and communities, evidenced by high rates of illiteracy, single-parent households and delinquency.[12] Thus, pathology as the root cause of poverty and poverty as the root cause of crime was officially accepted by the Johnson administration. Not surprisingly then the Johnson administration militarized its law enforcement agencies by providing military-grade weapons and surveillance technologies to police officers in the streets of the US. The constant twinning

---

[10] Tali Mendelberg, *The Race Card*. (Princeton: Princeton University Press, 2001), 194.
[11] Hinton, *From the War on Poverty to the War on Crime*, 1.
[12] Daniel Moynihan, *The Negro Family: The Case for National Action*. US Department of Labor. (Office of Policy Planning and Research. University of Michigan Library, 1965).

of receding social welfare programs with the ever-expanding social control programs led to the establishment of the modern carceral state.[13] The two systems had worked in tandem as they shared similar beliefs about the socioeconomically disadvantaged and racially marginalized Americans as a criminal class. Thus, the image of the poor black man as criminal gained ground, further justifying the punitive legislations and increased militarization of such neighborhoods.

High arrest rates and increased incarceration of black youth served to create a statistical discourse about black crime in the popular and the political imagination and these data became the subject matter of policy concerns. The data cemented the 'truth' of black youth crime, deemed them to be a problem demographic and justified racial legislation and intensified incarceration and surveillance. It is this statistical discourse that became the 'truth' about an entire race and rationalized "the expansion of the American prison system, sustained harsh sentencing practices, informed decisions surrounding capital punishment, and endorsed racial profiling in general."[14] Black teenage arrests, even if they were for petty crimes made it into the national measurement of crime and their database, thus influencing subsequent policy decisions. While Frederick Hoffman's work, *Race Traits and Tendencies of the American Negro* argued for how cultural and behavioral traits of African Americans made them predisposed to crime and criminal activity, W.E.B. Du Bois, in *The Philadelphia Negro: A Social Study* emphasized on the socioeconomic factors, questioning the credibility of genetics and culture to arrive at a pathology of crime. Hinton argues that notions of such black cultural pathology concealed policymakers' own racism and justified the punitive turn in domestic policy. Even as urban civil disorder intensified, the focus of domestic policy shifted from fighting poverty to controlling its inhabitants.

Since control of the black population has been at the centre of the intensification of government policy, a few years later the justification for the War on Crime against the black criminal was further strengthened by the *Report on the Governability of Democracies* to the Trilateral Commission (1975) which was titled, "The Crisis of Democracy" and was coauthored by Samuel Huntington. Huntington worries about the democratic surge after the Civil Rights movement and the weakening of democracy stemming ironically from

---

[13] Julilly Kohler-Hausmann, "Guns and Butter: The Welfare State, the Carceral State, and the Politics of Exclusion in the Postwar United States," *Journal of American History,* 102 (June 2015), 87-99.
[14] Hinton, *From the War on Poverty to the War on Crime*, 19.

"an excess of democracy."[15] He recommends installing obedience to authority in negatively privileged groups and making them feel unqualified in the face of self-proclaimed experts. Huntington advocates the need to restore "prestige and authority of central government institutions."[16] Needless to say, Huntington's arguments and work along racial lines created divisions between the 'unqualified' and upstart blacks and the white experts. Since the report focused on the problem of governability of populations, it ended up suggesting a remedy through an increase in government authority. One can argue that such control was affected through devising a legal system of discrimination that was bound to have a lasting impact on the American policymakers.

Michelle Alexander, in her thought-provoking monograph *The New Jim Crow*, argues how we use our criminal justice system to label people of color 'criminals' and make it perfectly legal to discriminate against them in nearly all ways that it was once legal to discriminate against African Americans. Once labeled a felon—housing discrimination, denial of right to vote, denial of educational opportunities, denial of food stamps, and numerous other exclusions from social benefits—the person has no more rights and respect than a black man living in Alabama at the height of Jim Crow. Throughout the 60s and 70s, flawed statistical data overstated the problem of crime in African American communities and produced a distorted picture of American crime as imbued with a black hue. If police arrested a group of black teenagers for stealing a car, even if they were released without charges, this encounter with the criminal justice system factored into the national measurement of crime which influenced future policy decisions. Thus, the figures federal policymakers referenced as they developed a national law enforcement program reflected the crimes committed by low-income and unemployed African Americans. The flawed statistical data deepened the federal policymakers' racialized perception of the problem.

The War on Crime changes to the War on Drugs under President Reagan in 1982 and his media campaign becomes a huge success as the public space is seen inundated with images of black crack whores, black crack dealers and black crack babies—images that seemed to confirm the worst negative racial stereotypes about impoverished inner-city residents with specific skin color. One of his favorite and most often repeated anecdotes was the story of a Chicago welfare queen with 80 names, 30 addresses, and 12 Social Security cards. Reagan's repeated citing of this 'welfare queen' became a not-so-subtle

---

[15] Samuel Huntington, Michael Crozier and Joji Watanuki. "The Crisis of Democracy." *Report on the Governability of Democracies to the Trilateral Commission*. (New York University Press, 1975), 113.
[16] Ibid., 170.

code for the "lazy greedy, black ghetto mother; someone who wishes to live off state welfare."[17] Reagan's appeal can be considered propaganda and demagoguery at its best. Stanley argues that propaganda need not be necessarily a false claim or even an insincere claim; in fact it can be a true claim and uttered with sincerity. In the above case, Reagan's assertion is both true and uttered with sincerity as well; however, what makes this claim a piece of propaganda is that it communicates something false. It communicates that blacks are by nature lazy and invariably dependent on the welfare state, thus leading us to believe that true claims but uttered with a malicious intent or to reveal only a part of the truth can be considered propaganda. Stanley argues how everyday discourse involves using apparently "innocent words that have the feature of slurs, namely, that whenever the words occur in a sentence, they convey the problematic content."[18] Stanley identifies the use of the word, 'welfare' in the American context to suggest how this primes racial bias against Blacks.[19]

Since I argue that propaganda is political rhetoric, one can see that language as a mechanism of control is central to the dissemination of ideas. When the news media connects negative images with certain groups of people: of urban blacks repeatedly with drug crime, immigrants to be criminals, Muslims to be inherently violent or Mexicans as drug dealers and rapists, then this can lead to an erosion of empathy for that group. Language and word choices can prejudice not only political debate but also everyday comprehension of relations and cultural meanings. A comprehension of differentiation between at-issue content and not-at-issue content is crucial at this distinction can play an important role in a liberal education classroom. A claim that there are Jews or Muslims among us expresses a perfectly ordinary at-issue content, one that is true, but it equally and clearly conveys the not-at-issue content that Jews and Muslims are the enemy, and distinct from us. According to Stanley, this blending of the reasonable, the true, needs to be teased out from the evocative and the unreasonable to have a clear and critical understanding of political rhetoric.

Even as propaganda and negative images of black criminals dominated the American landscape, average citizens were being convinced of security, safety and law and order. Mass incarceration of this deviant population was justified in the name of curbing the threat to the safety and security of the nation.

---

[17] Michelle Alexander, *The New Jim Crow: Mass Incarceration in the Age of Colorblindness*, (New York: The New Press, 2012), 49.
[18] Jason Stanley, *How Propaganda Works* (Princeton and Oxford: Princeton University Press, 2015), 151.
[19] Ibid., 154.

Further, this mass incarceration served to create a 'statistical discourse' about black crime in the popular and political imagination and such data has continued to and still informs debates about racial differences and attendant behavior attributes. Interestingly, biology explained black behavior the way it has never offered an explanation for crime in poor white neighborhoods. And yet, as Alexander reveals how this war on drugs can be seen as the new Jim Crow: a backlash against a particular race to overturn the concessions of the Civil Rights movement. She writes, "Although the majority of illegal drug users and dealers nationwide [US] are white, three-fourths of all people imprisoned for drug offenses have been black or Latino."[20] According to a study published in 2000 by the National Institute on Drug Abuse, white students use cocaine at seven times the rate of black students, use crack cocaine at eight times the rate of black students and use heroin at seven times the rate of black students and yet blacks were more likely to be incarcerated than whites. Any notion that drug use among blacks is more severe or dangerous is belied by the data. The question then is: if the data is out there then what is stopping us from looking at the data and making our own conclusions? The problem is that such data is overshadowed by populist appeals to black criminality and police and criminal justice system practices which further perpetuates the myth of black criminality. The system of mass incarceration operates with stunning efficiency to sweep people of color off the streets, lock them in prisons and then release them into an inferior second-class status. The process occurs in two stages: The first step grants law enforcement officials extraordinary discretion regarding where to look for drugs, whom to stop, search, arrest and charge, thus ensuring that conscious and unconscious racial beliefs and stereotypes are given free rein. The second is to demand that anyone who wants to challenge racial bias in the system, offer in advance, clear proof that racial disparities are the product of intentional racial discrimination. This simple design, according to Alexander, has ensured the perpetuation of the big lie and produced one of the most extraordinary systems of racialized social control the world has ever seen. For more than six decades now, news stories regarding virtually all street crimes have disproportionately featured African American offenders thus perpetuating the myth. One study suggests that the standard news script is so prevalent and so thoroughly racialized that viewers imagine a black perpetrator even when none exists. In this study 60% of viewers who saw a story with no

---

[20] Alexander, *The New Jim Crow*, 98.

image falsely recalled seeing one and 70% of those viewers believed the perpetrator to be African American.[21]

Decades of cognitive bias research suggests that both unconscious and conscious biases lead to discriminatory actions even when an individual does not want to discriminate. Once blackness and crime became conflated in the public consciousness, Kathryn Russel-Brown writes the 'criminalblackman' inevitably becomes the primary target of law enforcement.[22] The differential access to private spaces makes it easier for police to detect illegal drugs in open and public spaces than in white gated neighborhoods. Concentrating such efforts in locations where drugs are easier to find is viewed as a race-neutral organizational necessity. Secondly, in many cities the focus on drugs more likely to be sold by African Americans has skewed the debate and perception against them. For instance, in Seattle, the focus on crack cocaine has made the illegal drug seller to be invariably black. This racialized cultural script about who and what constitutes the drug problem renders illegal drug activity in white neighborhoods to be invisible. Years and years of propaganda constituting the black man as criminal bears fruit when any arrests are made and the person 'happens' to be black. The script is reinforced once again.

Can Liberal education help?

A general acquiescence to the dominant media images and metaphors of black criminality pervades and hence it becomes crucial to disrupting the pattern of this compliance. Educational institutions play a vital role in any nation's democracy and citizen building and if they end up withholding crucial information, they can become vehicles of propaganda. A school that produces partially informed citizens who believe they are fully informed is a vehicle of propaganda, even if it has never produced any actual propaganda.[23] Demystification, incredulity towards received information, joining the dots to create a full historical perspective of issues, and differentiating an emotional/charismatic appeal from one of reason are some of the things that a liberal education classroom can offer. In addition to all of the above I wish to propose Andrew Kushnir's argument of humanizing the classroom space to be a possible reflection on the idea of a solution. Even though Kushnir makes his

---

[21] Iyanger Gilliam, "Prime Suspects: The Influence Local Television News on the Viewing Public," *American Journal of Political Science*, 44, no. 3 (July 2000): 560–73. https://doi.org/10.2307/2669264.

[22] Katheryn Russel-Brown, *The Color of Crime: Racial Hoaxes, White Fear, Black Protectionism, Police Harassment, and Other Microaggressions* (New York: New York University Press, 1998), 71.

[23] Stanley, *How Propaganda Works*, 55.

argument vis-a-vis theatre, the imperative of his argumentation can lend credibility to the sphere outside of theatre as well. He writes that "To humanize is to necessarily deepen our understanding of something and to complicate or challenge preconceptions...It is to put a human face to statistics or conjecture."[24] Kushnir continues, "what certain individuals and groups lack are not voices, but listeners."[25] In other words, the playhouse can provide a theatrical encounter that can keep listeners engaged on questions of social justice and prejudice. He says theatre can humanize because unlike other forms of engagement it can slow time; the act of sitting still with that particular focus in communion with others, can be revivifying as it requires a patient engagement with characters on stage, but for us it could be a careful and slow reading and unravelling of the meanings of texts in the classroom. Theatre for Kushnir is replete with metaphors; metaphors allow for the possibility of multiple truths at once. It forces students to see these multiple viewpoints and question the linearity of historical truths. The social and the simultaneously introspective nature of theatrical activity/close reading of texts in a liberal education classroom is something that is needed to activate the imagination and conscience simultaneously. With an emphasis on civic responsibility and opportunities for community engagement, a liberal education classroom can prepare students to deal with the reality of the world around them. Sensitization to racial, gender, linguistic, and class others provides them with the opportunities to ponder about cohabitation and humanizing others in nuanced ways.

References

Alexander, Michelle. *The New Jim Crow: Mass Incarceration in the Age of Colorblindness*. New York: The New Press, 2012.

Du Bois, W.E.B. *The Philadelphia Negro: A Social Study*. Philadelphia: University of Pennsylvania Press, 1899.

Gilliam, Franklin and Shanto Iyengar, "Prime Suspects: The Influence of Local Television News on the Viewing Public. *American Journal of Political Science*, 44.3 (July 2000), 560-573.

Hinton, Elizabeth. *From the War on Poverty to the War on Crime: The Making of Mass Incarceration in America*. Cambridge, Massachusetts: Harvard University Press, 2016.

---

[24] Andrew Kushnir, "If You Mingle: Thoughts on How Theatre Humanizes the Audience," In *Defence of Theatre: Aesthetic Practices and Social Interventions*, ed. Kathleen Gallagher and Barry Freeman, (Toronto: University of Toronto Press, 2016), 85.

[25] Kushnir, "If You Mingle: Thoughts on How Theatre Humanizes the Audience,." 86.

Hoffman, Frederick. *Race Traits and Tendencies of the American Negro*. New York: Macmillan Co. 1896.

Huntington, Samuel, Michael Crozier and Joji Watanuki. "The Crisis of Democracy." *Report on the Governability of Democracies to the Trilateral Commission*. New York University Press, 1975.

Katzenbacj, Nicholas deB. et al. *The Challenge of Crime in a Free Society: A Report by the President's Commission on Law Enforcement and Administration of Justice*, Washington, DC: US Government Printing Office, 1967.

Kohler-Hausmann, Julilly. "Guns and Butter: The Welfare State, the Carceral State, and the Politics of Exclusion in the Postwar United States," *Journal of American History* 102 (June 2015): 87-99.

Kushnir, Andrew. "If You Mingle: Thoughts on How Theatre Humanizes the Audience." In *Defence of Theatre: Aesthetic Practices and Social Interventions*, *edited by* Kathleen Gallagher and Barry Freeman, 83-98. Toronto: University of Toronto Press, 2016.

Mendelberg, Tali. *The Race Card*. Princeton: Princeton University Press, 2001.

Moynihan, Daniel. *The Negro Family: The Case for National Action*. US Department of Labor. Office of Policy Planning and Research. University of Michigan Library, 1965.

Russel-Brown, Katheryn. *The Color of Crime: Racial Hoaxes, White Fear, Black Protectionism, Police Harassment, and Other Microaggressions*. New York: New York University Press, 1998.

Stanley, Jason. *How Propaganda Works*. Princeton and Oxford: Princeton University Press, 2015.

Chapter 8

Complexity, Chaos, Collaboration: Untangling Strands of Truth; Teaching/Learning/Teaching in the 21st Century

Deborah Forbes
Medicine Hat College

Abstract

Collaboration, chaos, and complexity are deeply interrelated in the art of teaching and learning, as a dynamical, creative system that can move toward important, if messy, truths. The 'problem' of truth is a tangled web; linear processes that rely on mechanistic proving or disproving, sometimes miss essential elements that allow for untangling dense webs. The liberal arts can draw from chaos and complexity theories and use these in the collaborative context of the post-secondary classroom to move into uncharted, unanticipated, and emergent learning, the importance of which is sometimes ignored." Complexity theory, initially developed in the field of physics, has attracted many educators as a means to illuminate and value the many uncertainties and simultaneities that do not fit comfortably into more conventional theories of learning. This paper explores complexity theory at work in a critical theory class.

Keywords: truth, chaos, complexity, collaboration

***

Introduction

The edge of chaos is the balance point where the components of a system never quite lock into place, and yet never quite dissolve into turbulence, either... The edge of chaos is the constantly shifting battle zone between stagnation and anarchy, the one place where a complex system can be spontaneous, adaptive and alive.[1]

Spontaneous, *adaptive*, and *alive* are words that describe the interconnected strands of meaning, interpretation, and understanding which shape various interrelationships in teaching and learning a dynamical, creative system of collaboration that can move toward important, if messy, truths. The 'problem' of truth is a tangled web; linear processes that rely on mechanistic proving or disproving, sometimes miss essential elements that allow for untangling a dense web of notions. The liberal arts can draw from chaos and complexity theories and use these in the collaborative context of the post-secondary classroom to move into uncharted, unanticipated and emergent learning, the importance of which can sometimes be ignored. To examine this tangled web, complexity theory, which derives from chaos theory, seems a reasonable fit. Initially developed in the field of physics to supply insights into how "complicated, dynamical systems rapidly cease to be predictable even if their initial states are known in detail," various educators have been attracted to complexity theory as a means to illuminate the many uncertainties and simultaneities that do not fit comfortably into more conventional theories of learning.[2] Mason emphasizes the importance of complexity theory on interpretive perspectives that are "trans-phenomenal, transdisciplinary, trans-discursive, that invite and tolerate ambiguity."[3] Emergent phenomena derived from relationships may be valued differently when viewed from the perspective of complexity and reveal truths about the world.

The following discussion begins to explore relationships from the perspective of complexity and within the context of creative, cognitive, affective, and physical learning. I draw from my experiences as an instructor of critical theory, as it applies to contemporary art, to discuss complex, active learning as a process of collaborative inquiry as a pedagogical strategy to aid students derive truths about themselves and the world. Sullivan states that it is a "useful assumption to consider the complexity of contemporary art in a similar way to the stance taken by qualitative researchers who seek to understand multi-

---

[1] M Mitchell Waldrop, *Complexity: The Emerging Science at the Edge of Order and Chaos* (Toronto; Simon and Schuster, 1992), 12.
[2] Philip Ball, *Critical Mass: How One Thing Leads to Another*, 1st Americ (New York: Farrar, Straus and Giroux, 2004), 5.
[3] Mark Mason, "Complexity Theory and the Philosophy of Education," *Educational Philosophy and Theory* 40, no. 1 (2008): 4, https://doi.org/10.1111/j.1469-5812.2007.00412.x.

faceted realities such as life in communities or classrooms."[4] The parallels and intertwinings of critical theory and how it is reflected in collaborative human relationships will be the focus of the stories from experience. And it is from these experiences we can surmise various forms of truth.

Relationships and Complexity

A complex system has three interrelated hallmarks: "Growth, mutual influence and nonlinear connectedness."[5] For example, one could think about a messy ball of yarn composed of many different types, lengths, colours, weights, and textures, as similar to the types of relationships belonging to each of thirty adults and one instructor which make-up many post-secondary classes. Each adult has at least five different kinds of relationships (with oneself, with others in the class, with the course material, with one's instructor, with the universe). If these factors are multiplied by the number of persons in the class, the result is one hundred and fifty-five (155). The product of the multiplication of these interactions with each other is twenty-four thousand and twenty-five (24,025). Each group of thirty-one students comprises a different set of thousands of relationships; therefore, as a whole, each group will operate as a distinct 'organism.' Complex systems grow organically; "they are not assembled piece-by-piece and cannot be viewed as such."[6] Just as wetness is an index of water, unpredictability is a mark of a complex system of relationships. Growth in a complex system is "the result of a series of highly contingent events that would not happen again if we could rewind the tape."[7] As a result, when viewed through the lens of complexity, the relationships in a class (a community of learners) will experience growth, will change in ways that cannot be predicted or replicated, and their progression will be non-linear in nature. These characteristics are neutral (neither positive nor negative). The role of the instructor is to be highly vigilant and intuitive in facilitating toward meaningful learning within the context of a dense web of relationships. Bennett and

---

[4] Graeme Sullivan, "Critical Interpretive Inquiry: A Qualitative Study of Five Contemporary Artists' Ways of Seeing," *Studies in Art Education* 37, no. 4 (1996): 10, https://doi.org/10.1080/00393541.1996.11650456.
[5] Bernard Ricca, "Beyond Teaching Methods: A Complexity Approach," *Complicity: An International Journal of Complexity in Education* 9, no. 2 (2012): 10, https://doi.org/10.29173/cmplct17985.
[6] Bernard Ricca, "Beyond Teaching Methods: A Complexity Approach," *Complicity: An International Journal of Complexity in Education* 9, no. 2 (2012): 10, https://doi.org/10.29173/cmplct17985., 31.
[7] Brian Rosenberg, "Gould Promotes the Entity Theory of Evolution," *The Tech*, December 7, 1990, http://tech.mit.edu/V110/PDF/V110-N56.pdf.%0A%0A.

Rollheiser discuss, "knowing the learner through multiple lenses."[8] These multiple lenses could be extended to 'inter-viewing' amongst all the relationships, including the relationships that are constructed with the content of the course. As Waldrop writes, "In every case, moreover, the very richness of these interactions allows the system as a whole to undergo spontaneous self-organization."[9] A self-organizing system is one that "spontaneously generates order that is complex and adaptive."[10]

In the post-secondary context, the relationships between teaching, learning, and content, for both instructors and students, seem to move into authentic learning when complexity is embraced. There is discomfort and risk on the parts of instructors and students; nothing is clear; ambiguities rage; if there is willingness to struggle through the storm, the sky often clears and there rises up new truths that are complex and adaptive. A leap of faith, on everyone's part, is required to get there. To meaningfully construct concepts and relationships, in contexts that involve real-world problems, and projects that are relevant to the learner, it is not an easy business. Making room for sustained lateral thinking about divergent notions requires both trust and practice.

Chaos, Complexity and Creative Learning

However, lateral thinking about complex issues is often difficult because, as Mason discusses, Western education tends to think in terms of discontinuities around such matters as theory and practice, knowers and knowledge, self and other, mind and body, art and science.[11] These dyads are often presented as necessarily distinct and opposed or on a linear continuum. Complexity challenges these modes of interpretation and, in the process, offers useful insights into education by viewing the dyads as simultaneities. Creativity, at the apex of Bloom's Revised Taxonomy, demands that one must embrace simultaneities; it cannot be understood or developed without associating phenomena, blending disciplinary perspectives, and, risking the use of authentic voice.[12] Doll posits that the aim of complexity is a process of, "cross-

---

[8] Barrie Brent Bennett and Carol Rolheiser, *Beyond Monet: The Artful Science of Instructural Integration* (Toronto: Bookation, 2001), 26.
[9] Waldrop, *Complexity: The Emerging Science at the Edge of Order and Chaos*, 11.
[10] Glenda Holladay Eoyang, "Conditions for Self-Organizing in Human Systems," (The Union Institute and University, 2001), https://capitalrevolution.typepad.com/a_free_enterprise/files/conditions_for_selforganizing_in_human_systems.pdf.
[11] Mason, "Complexity Theory and the Philosophy of Education," 5.
[12] David R Krathwohl, "A Revision of Bloom's Taxonomy: An Overview," *Theory Into Practice* 41, no. 4 (2002): 212–18, https://doi.org/10.1207/s15430421tip4104_2.

fertilization, pollination, crystallization of ideas."[13] Trygestad considers chaos theory as revealing conditions in learning that are constructive, dynamic, and holistic, that enhance learning by reinforcing systemic approaches to human interactions. These, in turn, encourage cultural diversity as beneficial, and reaffirm theoretical notions of intelligence as multidimensional and "without linear progression."[14] As Mason states, "Complexity therefore suggests a shift from our preoccupation with causes to a focus on effects."[15] It the effects that are most important. It is through chaos and complexity that truths can emerge if students are allowed the freedom to document their intellectual progress by non-standard means (i.e. no research papers).

Effects of Stamping the Doc-thing or 'Feelings in the Air'

My interest in complexity theory and collaborative inquiry in action has grown out of the needs and patterns I have observed in a course on critical theory, which I taught for several years. In this course, most of the students are in the second or third years of a program leading to a Bachelor of Applied Arts in Visual Communications. I would have had these students for a course in each of the three previous terms before I see them in critical theory class, so we all know each other well. There are usually thirty to thirty-five students in the class. There are opportunities for both individual and group inquiry in each three-hour class, with time for reflection at the end. Students are required to come to every class with the required readings completed and their understandings and questions documented in; what we have come to call, the *'documentation thing.'* The *'documentation thing,'* or *'doc-thing,'* for short, can take any form that makes sense to the student. For some it is a binder with notes; for others it is sketchbook with colour-coded maps; for others it is a cut and paste system of images that acts as a symbols system for concepts. For one student the *doc-thing* grew into a graphic novel, with a character named Spando who interacted with his coffee cup by discussing and wrestling with 'really hard things' (this one was hilarious and probably publishable). Another student used a small suitcase of objects that each represented a theory; main theorists were duct-taped onto the main object. She performed tape reconfigurations with great facility. All that is required of the *doc-thing* is that it be a reasonable method for

---

[13] William E Doll Jr, "Complexity and the Culture of Curriculum," *Complicity: An International Journal of Complexity and Education* 9, no. 1 (2012), https://doi.org/10.29173/cmplct16530.

[14] JoAnn Trygestad, "Chaos in the Classroom: An Application of Chaos Theory," in *Annual Meeting of the American Educational Research Association* (Chicago, Ill, 1997), https://files.eric.ed.gov/fulltext/ED413289.pdf.

[15] Mason, "Complexity Theory and the Philosophy of Education," 12.

advancing and demonstrating an individual student's engagement with the content of the course.

Because the doc-thing invites messy, lateral thinking, and opens channels to divergence, more complex relationships start to reveal themselves in ways that do not seem as available when using more linear, conventional methods for exploration. Connections amongst various kinds of content start to emerge that could not easily be accessed in less loose, individualized, and quirky methods. Life is messy, human constructs are messy, and by using methods that invite stages of 'messiness,' the mind can become freer of constraints, biases, and prejudices that stand in the way of access to truth.

At the beginning of every class, everyone puts her/his doc-thing out on the table. I come around with a date stamp (like an old-fashioned library stamp) and I stamp the relevant area of each doc-thing with the date. We chat as I go around; students get excited about something they have found or express confusion and frustration with the articles they are required to read. Students mill around looking at each other's doc-things and get ideas for their own. For some reason, everyone is always excited about the stamp. Maybe it is about the opportunity for a chat, the tangible, physical engagement with their work, or maybe the stamp itself looks 'official,' but stamping, with its cluster of undefined signifiers, has become a tangible relationship builder.

This phase also acts as a greeting time during which I get an opportunity to 'read' the emotional tone of the room ("I am so tired," "I didn't get any of this," "Too many words to read—do we get to watch a movie today?"). If the engine of worry is whirring ("I don't know where I'm going to scrounge up rent this month," "My student loan is maxed out and it's only October," "I am so worried about court on Tuesday—I am so afraid of losing my kids.") the day will require considerable reassuring humour and camaraderie. This brief phase is revelatory of students' relationships with themselves as inner and outer voices are revealed in the doc-thing; of peer relationships as they are strengthened by the curiosity shown in each other's work; of student/instructor relationships as these are strengthened by a few words with each one; of each student's inchoate relationship with the course content. Each student's relationship to learning starts to emerge when depth and means of engagement become visible to the student, to other students, and to the instructor. The doc-thing grows and morphs over time. Students become emboldened to risk to give their doc-thing a stronger individual and externally communicative voice in relationship. Areas of interest emerge out of this process; if a certain concept or particular theorist starts to leap out in several doc-things or if a particular quality of question is emerging, an idea starts to bubble to the surface about focus for that day's class. It is never the same or predictable. I have a skeleton of concepts to be explored that day, a bag of useful tricks and some idea of how/when they could be used, a selection of readings and videos, and then there is *Ba*.

Ba

Ba is that, "constantly shifting place, that edge of chaos, spontaneous, adaptive and alive."[16] Bennett and Rollheiser write about complexity theory and education in terms of, "the idea that when certain forces come together, patterns will emerge. Patterns emerge in the moment; the teacher must respond to that moment."[17] *Ba* has become a useful code to describe the time/space when we will focus, reflect, and share findings and experiences. I have never discussed *Ba* with students. I hand out cards to groups of students with Shimizu's definition the first time we prepare to enter *Ba*. After that, *Ba* exists as part of our shared vocabulary. Everyone knows where we are going. Shimizu defines *Ba* as:

> A context in which knowledge is shared, created, and utilized in recognition of the fact that knowledge needs a context in order to exist. The most important part of Ba is interaction. The power to create knowledge is embedded, not just within an individual, but also within the interactions with other individuals or with the environment. Ba is a space where interactions take place.[18]

Yorks discusses *Ba* as a "generative space that intentionally changes relationships in the way it renders repetitive cycles of action and reflection, supported by data and experience."[19] When *Ba* is called for, students inevitably call out things like, "Baa-baa black sheep, Ba humbug, ba-ba-da ding!" The room lightens and the focus moves from individual life to the collaborative work of the day. Patterns in relationships shift to new configurations where the strengths of individuals in a group are recognized and used to explore course content as a collective. *Ba* is the fancy handshake, the secret shared code. By integrating *ba* as part of the routine of every class, by opening non-judgemental spaces for interacting thoughts, students and instructors can risk constructing perhaps, unlikely webs, which in the working, start to reveal obvious but

---

[16] Waldrop, *Complexity: The Emerging Science at the Edge of Order and Chaos*, 14.

[17] Bennett and Rolheiser, *Beyond Monet: The Artful Science of Instructural Integration*.

[18] Hiroshi Shimizu, "Ba-Principle: New Logic for the Real-Time Emergence of Information," *Holonics* 1 (1995): 67–69.

[19] Lyle Yorks, "Adult Learning and the Generation of New Knowledge and Meaning: Creating Liberating Spaces for Fostering Adult Learning Through Practitioner-Based Collaborative Action Inquiry," *Teachers College Record* 107, no. 6 (2005): 1221, https://doi.org/10.1111/j.1467-9620.2005.00511.x.

unexposed truths. Like the 'murder boards,' so popular in detective television, truths reveal themselves as the webbed, disconnected information on the board, starts to emerge in new coherence.

Drops in the Pond or Complexity in Action

I see my role as an instructor as one who drops pebbles into the pond. As a pebble drops into a pond, fish respond as a self-organizing system. Sometimes they move in one direction as a group; sometimes they disperse into several groups; sometimes the dispersal is seemingly random; however, the five aspects of complex relationship all reconfigure in response to the nature of the dropped pebble. Mason (2008) writes:

> Over time…a network of connections and interconnections becomes more and more webbed. Learning now occurs, not through direct transmission from expert to novice…but in a non-linear manner through all in a class exploring a problem together…In other words, the curriculum is now an emerging one within an ongoing process that actually catalyzes itself via interactions within the system.[20]

In this description, Mason raises an additional factor that is key to working in complex, learning relationships: time.[21] "Without *having* the time and *taking* the time, exploration will be superficial at best and confusing at the very least."[22] Kelly notes time constraints as a major factoring in limiting creative development, which is essential for learning in complexity.[23] The learning processes are heuristic for both instructor and students.

The instructor can act to stimulate interest (drop a pebble) as a means to further investigation. The stimulation could be to ask the question that leads to the formulation of other questions so that the students can then proceed to develop means, as individuals and in groups, to move through trials and errors as they work toward understanding. Because critical theory studies involve theories and theorists, who have established various lenses with which to look at issues of power, race, class, ethnicities, religion, and gender, there is seldom a clear path from A to B. The study also provokes controversy in all aspects of relationship. Unless time is taken to foster and nurture all of these relationships

---

[20] Mason, "Complexity Theory and the Philosophy of Education," 14.
[21] Ibid., 15.
[22] Ibid.
[23] Robert W Kelly, *Educating for Creativity: A Global Conversation* (Calgary: Brush Education, 2012).

in a safe and caring environment, controversy can engage emotions in ways that are counter-productive to learning.

MacKeracher states that her students have convinced her, "very little happens without relationships of some sort."[24] My students continuously persuade me that relationships are at the core of learning; if I forget this for I moment, I am invited to listen to their snores. At least a few of the five aspects of relationship (self, peers, instructors, course content, learning) must be engaged at any given moment or the dissipation of energy in a class is palpable. Collaborative development, as the bedrock of creative development, is essential.[25]

A typical day can unfold as follows: stamping the doc-thing; entering Ba; deciding on the big questions of the day; moving into groups to explore the big questions, usually as big maps; snooping the explorations of other groups; excavating patterns that are trying to emerge; looking for ways to demonstrate the patterns that have been posited in the work of the group; watching a video about a contemporary artist and her work; returning to groups to locate the artist and her work in the mix; going on another snoop mission; excavating more patterns; locating these patterns in the work of each group. Students are frequently photographing their work-in-progress and posting the photos on our class' electronic Blackboard.

We usually end with a pause for quiet reflection, then work on a question such as, "So what did we do today?" or "What were you doing when you were really learning?" Strategies for both individual and group reflection could include the use of de Bono's Six Thinking Hats, Plus/Minus/Interesting, and Random Input, as well as a number of strategies that we have developed for ourselves including *Odd Human Out* and *Elephant in the Room*, for example; the titles of these are somewhat self-explanatory.[26] Although de Bono and his tools can be criticized as dated, I have not found other strategies that request reflection on the cognitive, affective, and creative domains of learning in as succinct and immediately useful a form.

When we are working as a large group, there is often a four-stage cycle in whatever we do: quiet, individual reflection; sharing reflections; finding patterns (commonalities, discontinuities); building models and metaphors as a group; then back to reflection again. We use speaking, reading, writing, drawing, model-making, mapping, metaphor constructing, singing (there was

---

[24] Dorothy. MacKeracher, *Making Sense of Adult Learning*, 2nd ed. (Toronto: University of Toronto Press, 2004), 151.
[25] Kelly, *Educating for Creativity: A Global Conversation*, 16.
[26] Edward de Bono, *Serious Creativity: Using the Power of Lateral Thinking to Create New Ideas* (New York: Penguin, 1992).

a Russian opera singer in a recent class who would erupt into a passage of opera that connected to whatever we were doing), and threats of interpretive dance. As a result, most intelligences have a voice. Because responding to the work of others is often conducted as a sticky-note conversation with notes placed on a group's work during a walkabout, introverts contribute as frequently as extroverts. As one particularly shy student wrote in her doc-thing about the sticky note process, "Finally, I have a voice!" Sticky-notes have become an essential tool to promote flexible thinking as we reposition and re-configure visual indicators. The instructor's work is to keep moving through the room, looking for shifts in the emotional terrain, in cognitive energy or ennui, in creative approaches, and in patterns of anything that may be emerging. Sometimes in post-secondary learning situations, there can be an assumption that we are heads on sticks and our bodies are conveyances for these. Over the years, my students have revealed to me the need for physicality in learning. Physical metaphors, such as actually using the body as a site for organizing information/ideas/questions, has spontaneously emerged several times in recent years. Students also, for instance, have moved out into the hallway to map ideas using their bodies, as locations to map an idea or theory. I am expecting greater growth in this domain of learning. Because we work in an open, non-linear process of learning, students know that there are no confines to how we can explore together. In my pedagogy of chaos and complexity in the post-secondary classroom, I have seen students arrive at so many new (sometimes to themselves, sometimes more broadly) understandings of big truths; they have then been able to represent these in forms that are brilliantly communicative, as will be explored in the student stories.

Collaborative Inquiry or Folding in the Egg Whites

It is not a comfortable metaphor to think of egg whites folded into the string art of relationships, but both sugar and egg whites can be used to give body to a thread structure. In most culinary mixtures, egg whites have to be folded in with care or they lose their frothy, leavening properties and fall in despair. Such is how collaborative inquiry can operate in a complex system: It can give it body, leaven it, and prevent it from falling into the despair of acting without purpose. Yorks outlines four dimensions of collaborative inquiry as follows:

- Involving co-inquiry among a collection of inquirers.
- Having the goal of producing new knowledge.
- Taking action in the 'world' as an important vehicle for learning.

- Being intentionally educative, useful and developmental for participants.[27]

The study of critical theory relates to reality above what is immediately apparent to our senses (trans-phenomenal), it leaks into a variety of disciplines (social sciences, education, politics, art, literature, science, history, math; ergo is trans-disciplinary), it delves into multiple frames of discourse (trans-discursive), it invites and welcomes ambiguity, and eschews single ways of knowing.[28] When using critical theories, as a set of lenses with which to engage in exploring works of contemporary art, discourse broadens even more widely. Exploration could become an exercise in breathing rare air in a small, and alienating, community of seekers without an opportunity to engage with others outside the knowing cohort. Hence, the Critical Theory Fair is born to, "take action in the world and be intentionally educative."[29]

The Critical Theory Fair or Ribbons Flutter in the Air

As I have created section titles somewhat intuitively, air, as a significant metaphor, has only revealed itself to me in editing. Air, for me, is a metaphor for the space for all to breathe together; it is a notion based on abundance rather than scarcity. There is enough air for everyone in the space we have created to now draw in the larger world to the active learning work of our class. The whole notion of a 'fair' as associated with the subject of critical theory is a little tongue-in-cheek; one could be perceived to be festive, the other dry and tedious. There is something about the perceived dissonance that opens the opportunity for 'play.' Our advertising for the event is often somewhere between playful and cheeky. The Critical Theory Fair grew out of our need to take action in the world as an important vehicle for learning; it is "intentionally educative, useful and developmental for participants."[30] The best way to describe how the Critical Theory Fair functions is to tell some stories as a way for students to reveal discovered truths about a specific issue. I have changed the names of the students to protect the privacy of the individuals.

Find the 'Post'

'Nancy' is a person of First Nations origin, who is in her thirties. She is a single mother of three little girls. She returned to school so she could learn to do

---

[27] Yorks, "Adult Learning and the Generation of New Knowledge and Meaning," 1219.
[28] Ibid.
[29] Ibid., 1218.
[30] Yorks, "Adult Learning and the Generation of New Knowledge and Meaning," 1218.

something that would make a better life for her children. She was studying to become a graphic designer. At the beginning of the Critical Theory course, she was just dipping her toe into 'discovering' her First Nations heritage because, although she grew up on a First Nations reserve, in a First Nations family, her education had been in off-reserve schools. At the time, it just seemed like a better idea to keep your head down and not talk about, or think about, heritage. By her own admission, she came out of high school looking down on her people and wanting to get as far away as possible from her heritage.

It was not until she was in her early thirties that she started to become more interested in her heritage, largely because she wanted her girls to know more about their heritage. Over the course of the term, Nancy was becoming bolder about self-identifying as First Nations and bolder about entering into discourse on the subject. We were exploring post-colonial theory and 'Nancy' said, "Honestly, in my experience, I can't find much 'post' in post-colonial. The colonizers haven't left yet." We talked clusters of meanings for 'post.' In Nancy's learning about her people's heritage in readings, discussions, and films that were explored in and out of class, many of the mysteries underlying why she grew up, how she grew up started to reveal themselves to her.

As a group of people learning together, we are looking out for each other for frames to shape individual projects for the Critical Theory Fair. Another student said to her, "I think you just found the seed for your project." Nancy did not say anything at the time, but she came to the second story meeting with her project exquisitely mapped (we have two story meetings per term during which the instructor meets with groups of approximately five students at a time, to discuss their final projects). Nancy had drawings, a site map of the College, and had written a very solid draft of her synthesis page.

Installed on the day of the Critical Theory Fair, the project was made from five sticks (trimmed tree branches), each about six feet tall. Attached to the top of the sticks were a number of leather thongs reaching down about three feet, each of which had a hook on the end of it. Attached to one of the hooks was an official-looking information card. She situated each of the posts at a different location in the College. At her table in the major traffic area, in which the Critical Theory Fair was located, she had a sign that said, "Find three posts and you will receive free bannock on a stick; just think of it as a corn-dog without the corn or the dog." Nancy sat there with a plate of bannock on sticks and a really good sense of humour, which she was just beginning to reveal.

The sticks referenced the poles used in the Sundance Ceremony, an Indigenous ceremony that had been banned in Canadian law in the late 19th century. It had to be performed in secret, if at all, until 1951 when it was re-legalized. In the Sundance Ceremony, young men would insert hooks into their chests and literally hang from these, on the thongs attached to the top of the poles. A spiritual practice of great power, it was performed as a right-of-passage for young men. It has now broadened, according to Jennifer Ashawasegai Windspeaker, "It's the ceremony of ceremonies, because it involves a sacrifice of self to give something to the Creator."[31]

The official-looking cards on the hooks had information taken from Statistics Canada and the Government of Alberta documents about First Nations peoples and education. For instance, the 'post' at the College Registration desk had statistics about the numbers of First Nations peoples that go on to post-secondary education. The 'post' at the College Library had statistics about the rates of illiteracy amongst First Nations peoples. The installation was a very clever and moving blend of banned practices of an oppressed people and statistical information provided by the offices of the oppressor. It was interactive and intriguing. Passersby took Nancy up on the challenge, found three 'posts' and collected their bannock on a stick. She shared with me afterwards that she felt bold, brave, empowered, and smart! She said these feelings were unfamiliar to her, but she really liked them.

Who's Your Jesus?

'Billie' is a big, African American man from Texas. He is in his early forties and is a single father of three girls. A long story landed him in Alberta and back at school. He had always worked in construction but knew he had highly visual sensibilities and wanted to become a designer. He also said his knees were too bad to last much longer in construction.

'Billie' was struggling with the critical theory readings and was very uncomfortable writing but came up with a very sound semiotic system for building his doc-thing. He was at first apologetic about his doc-thing, but as he found students crowding around him and saying things like, "Oh, now I get it!" he became more confident about developing and sharing his system. He came to the first story meeting without direction for his final project for the Critical Theory Fair. One of the other students reminded him of a topic he had brought up several times in previous art history courses. "Remember how you asked, hey, when did Jesus get blue eyes?" Billie had noticed that images of Jesus in works of art from about 500 CE to 1800 CE had shifted from a middle eastern looking man with very dark eyes to a light-brown haired, blue-eyed, fair-skinned man. During the story meeting the group tossed around ideas of how

---

[31] Jennifer Ashawasegai Windspeaker, "Sundance Is the Ceremony of Ceremonies," *Buffalo Spirit* 30, no. 6 (2012), https://ammsa.com/publications/buffalo-spirit/sundance-ceremony-ceremonies-0.

Billie could make this into an interactive piece of action research for the Critical Theory Fair.

Billie's final piece was a large poster mounted on foam-core, with images of Jesus from the history of art. The title at the top was *Who's Your Jesus?* 'Billie,' who is a great talker and a very friendly, engaging fellow, was able to draw in passersby to engage in this work. He asked them to look at the reproductions and put a red sticky dot on the Jesus image that most closely resembled their image of Jesus.

He drew in:

- middle-eastern students,
- Asian students,
- local students,
- a number of instructors
- college employees.

He drew a crowd. The greatest number of dots was accumulated on the fair-haired, blue-eyed Jesus reminiscent of Sunday school book illustrations that are thought to be based on an Albrecht Durer self-portrait from early 1500 CE.

Billie's synthesis page concentrated on cultural hegemony and semiotics, with a little deconstructionism thrown in for good measure. In the next class, when we were debriefing and reflecting on the Critical Theory Fair, Billie shared with the class how much fun he had at the Fair and how, "Critical theory is a blast!"

Glamour Anyone?

'Sasha' is a tall, beautiful, young woman in her mid-twenties. She worked as a window dresser for a few years but was returning to school to get some credentials that could lead her to work as a designer. She became very interested in feminisms and wanted to do a project that linked feminism, fashion and popular culture. It is interesting that at the beginnings of our explorations into feminisms, very few students self-identified as feminist. This state changed by the end of the course with most students, both male and female, identifying as such.

'Sasha' had collected a trunk-load of research in her doc-thing but was struggling with a clear direction for her Critical Theory Fair project. She had a number of ideas, but they were all verging on the polemic. Her fellow students pointed this out to her at the story meeting and suggested that she might want to keep it in the realm of discourse. 'Sasha' said something like, "I keep looking at my stack of Glamour magazines and waiting for inspiration." That started the ball rolling.

Sasha looked up Glamour magazine covers, for every month of the year, from the year 1962 (the year of Glamour's birth) and up to those from 2012. Fifty years of Glamour! From each cover, she documented all the words appearing on it. She then fed these into Wordle software. She made a bound magazine, in the dimensions of Glamour magazine, which contained a page with a reproduction of each cover for each month of the two chosen years (1962, 2012), a list of words that appeared on each cover, and several Wordle configurations of the words on each cover. She then made a large Wordle for each entire year using all the words and their number of occurrences. These two master Wordles were framed and put out for public reaction at the Critical Theory Fair with the question. "Which Wordle is 2012 and which 1962?" Passersby used sticky notes to weigh in with their choices. Interestingly, most people selected the reverse of the actual, i.e. they labelled 1962 as 2012 and 2012 and 1962. Some keywords that appeared on the 2012 Glamour covers were *sex, guys, surgery*, and references to celebrities. On the 1962 Glamour covers, the words *college, education, careers* came up frequently. Sasha, herself, had been surprised when she processed the words, their size, and frequency. She concluded that we need another big feminist wave right now. 'Sasha's' synthesis page drew from feminisms, deconstructionism (in the sense of relationships between text and meaning), and semiotics. She was particularly interested in feminist writers who wrote about images of the body. In the reflection class she said, "I am thinking more about what it means to be a human woman, in this place and time. I am alert." She also shared that she had not self-identified as a feminist a few weeks ago, but she sure was one now.

I Make Change

'Todd' is a twenty-something student with a great sense of humour and a snappy wit. He had been working at a big-box electronics store in sales and thought there might be more to life. He was great to have in the class because he could lighten a weighted atmosphere with a well-placed, clever remark that often acted to re-focus attention. He was very unsympathetic, however, to the feminist theories we were exploring. He did not see women as being in any way discriminated against or disadvantaged. When we looked at the Statistics Canada analysis of what women earn as compared with men and it was revealed that women make 70 cents on the dollar, he was skeptical, as were many other students of both genders. He said, "If this is true and I was getting 70 cents on the dollar, I'd be really mad."

What evolved into his Critical Theory Fair project was a very cleanly designed booth that stood beside a notoriously unfair drinks machine, situated beside an equally shady change machine. Both machines had been reported by students as never giving the right change. The sign on 'Todd's' booth said, *I*

Make Change. He sat there with a little cash box and made change for people who needed change for the drinks machine. If a female came up for change, he would make accurate change. If a male came up, he would give him 70 cents on every dollar. He would eventually make the right change but not before handing the 'change' a pamphlet with info about economic state of women in Canada; it even included a section on how many women sat in Canada's Parliament, the Alberta Legislature and on Boards of Directors of major companies. 'Todd', in his own way, *made change*, as was indicated in his clever title. At the reflection class afterwards, Todd said, "Ok, I'm a closet feminist."

These stories are examples of culminating truths that emerged out of collaborative inquiry in an atmosphere of creative complexity. The learning that took place was very much owned by each student and was self-directed in several aspects, but it emerged from the web of relationships in a safe, supportive, but highly charged and creative learning community. Many different kinds of transformations also took place, not out of the urging, direction, or expectation of the instructor, but as a function of the work of the collective. Influence was extended beyond the collective into the real world of the Critical Theory Fair.

Conclusion and the Missing Relationship

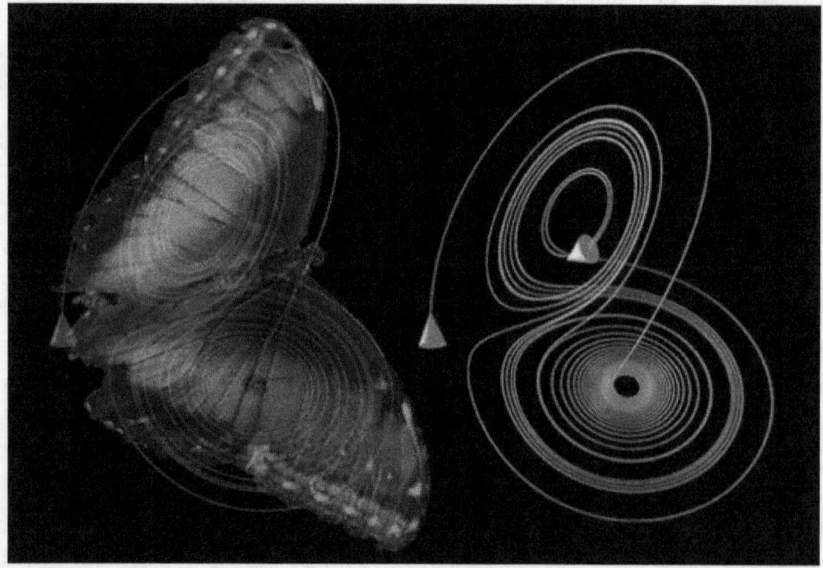

Figure 8.1. Morpho butterfly overlayed over one of two trajectories of the Lorenz attractor.

The starting point of the two trajectories differ by one-100,000th of a unit, and their paths start to diverge after 23 time steps. Credit: Creative Commons | Asturnut (butterfly), Creative Commons | Hellisp (attractors).

Entering into an unknown space places learner, educators included, in vulnerable, but exciting, positions. Embracing chaos and complexity heightens these qualities. By using a chaotic mix of metaphors and stories, this chapter seeks to reveal active learning in a collaborative and creative context of complexity. Over the course of the term, students and instructor alike find that their willingness to risk growth—they find it easier to accept a state of 'unknowing.' In the often-uncomfortable state of unknowing, everything seems equal—truths from sources that appear reliable, noise from sources that seem less so, personal experiences, feelings, opinions of others; they all congregate and start to form relationships. It is in using the processes (often visual and experiential) that allow most-likely truths to surface, that meaningful learning can take place, in ways that make sense to each student. Assessment in this chaos has not been discussed, but suffice to say it is an imperfectly translucent process of discourse and reflection on higher-order tasks, coupled with an exam for lower-order thinking or, in the words of Sergeant Joe Friday of Dragnet fame (television show of the mid-20th century), "Just the facts, Ma'am–nothing but the facts." Both could use some evaluation and revision.

Although I constantly reflect and create with my students, change and adapt as I go, I ache to have a colleague or two in the classroom; someone with whom to share the experience and co-construct different types of meaning. I think of the supposedly failed experiment of 'team teaching' of the 1970s and, would love to give it another whirl in the 21st century. I think it would look different and be informed with greater research into learning in all its domains. Collaboration as "active construction of mental illumination through cycles of brain-based, transformative learning," is something I yearn to engage in with another educator on a similar quest.[32] When something really exciting happens in a class I literally run to find one or two colleagues who share my interests in learning/teaching/learning. They do the same with me, but the description is not the experience, and is thinner in the telling. It is like travelling alone and sharing the photos on your return; as satisfying as it might be, sharing the actual experience with a loved one is so much richer.

---

[32] Daniel Glisczinski, "Lighting Up The Mind: Transforming Learning Through The Applied Scholarship of Cognitive Neuroscience," *International Journal for the Scholarship of Teaching and Learning* 5, no. 1 (2011): 11, https://doi.org/10.20429/ijsotl.2011.050124.

I must be patient and alert. Edward Lorenz, a father of modern chaos theory, posited in 1961, that when a butterfly flutters in Brazil it could cause a storm in Texas.[33] Relationships and chaos are delicate, nuanced, and only reveal their patterns in their many mysteries over time and space. Perhaps a butterfly is fluttering right now in Africa that will cause a storm of collegiality right where I sit.

References

Ball, Philip. *Critical Mass: How One Thing Leads to Another.* 1st Americ. New York: Farrar, Straus and Giroux, 2004.

Bennett, Barrie Brent, and Carol Rolheiser. *Beyond Monet: The Artful Science of Instructional Integration.* Toronto: Bookation, 2001.

de Bono, Edward. *Serious Creativity: Using the Power of Lateral Thinking to Create New Ideas.* New York: Penguin, 1992.

Doll Jr, William E. "Complexity and the Culture of Curriculum." *Complicity: An International Journal of Complexity and Education* 9, no. 1 (2012). https://doi.org/10.29173/cmplct16530.

Eoyang, Glenda Holladay. "Conditions for Self-Organizing in Human Systems." *The Union Institute and University*, 2001. https://capitalrevolution.typepad.com/a_free_enterprise/files/conditions_for_selforganizing_in_human_systems.pdf.

Glisczinski, Daniel. "Lighting Up The Mind: Transforming Learning Through The Applied Scholarship of Cognitive Neuroscience." *International Journal for the Scholarship of Teaching and Learning* 5, no. 1 (2011). https://doi.org/10.20429/ijsotl.2011.050124.

Kelly, Robert W. *Educating for Creativity: A Global Conversation.* Calgary: Brush Education, 2012.

Krathwohl, David R. "A Revision of Bloom's Taxonomy: An Overview." *Theory Into Practice* 41, no. 4 (2002): 212–18. https://doi.org/10.1207/s15430421tip4104_2.

Lorenz, Edward. *The Essence of Chaos.* Seattle: University of Washington Press, 1995.

MacKeracher, Dorothy. *Making Sense of Adult Learning.* 2nd ed. Toronto: University of Toronto Press, 2004.

Mason, Mark. "Complexity Theory and the Philosophy of Education." *Educational Philosophy and Theory* 40, no. 1 (2008): 4–18. https://doi.org/10.1111/j.1469-5812.2007.00412.x.

Ricca, Bernard. "Beyond Teaching Methods: A Complexity Approach." *Complicity: An International Journal of Complexity in Education* 9, no. 2 (2012): 31. https://doi.org/10.29173/cmplct17985.

Rosenberg, Brian. "Gould Promotes the Entity Theory of Evolution." *The Tech*, December 7, 1990. http://tech.mit.edu/V110/PDF/V110-N56.pdf.%0A%0A.

---

[33] Edward Lorenz, *The Essence of Chaos* (Seattle: University of Washington Press, 1995), 181.

Shimizu, Hiroshi. "Ba-Principle: New Logic for the Real-Time Emergence of Information." *Holonics* 1 (1995): 67–69.

Sullivan, Graeme. "Critical Interpretive Inquiry: A Qualitative Study of Five Contemporary Artists' Ways of Seeing." *Studies in Art Education* 37, no. 4 (1996): 210–25. https://doi.org/10.1080/00393541.1996.11650456.

Trygestad, JoAnn. "Chaos in the Classroom: An Application of Chaos Theory." In *Annual Meeting of the American Educational Research Association.* Chicago, Ill, 1997. https://files.eric.ed.gov/fulltext/ED413289.pdf.

Waldrop, M Mitchell. *Complexity: The Emerging Science at the Edge of Order and Chaos.* Toronto; Simon and Schuster, 1992.

Windspeaker, Jennifer Ashawasegai. "Sundance Is the Ceremony of Ceremonies." *Buffalo Spirit* 30, no. 6 (2012). https://ammsa.com/publications/buffalo-spirit/sundance-ceremony-ceremonies-0.

Yorks, Lyle. "Adult Learning and the Generation of New Knowledge and Meaning: Creating Liberating Spaces for Fostering Adult Learning Through Practitioner-Based Collaborative Action Inquiry." *Teachers College Record* 107, no. 6 (2005): 1217–44. https://doi.org/10.1111/j.1467-9620.2005.00511.x.

Chapter 9

Truth and Awe

Robert M. Randolph
Waynesburg University

Abstract

The value of Liberal Arts becomes apparent when approaching the idea of truth through the thinking of Carl Jung and John Cobb. Jung's belief in "art of the unconscious mind" posits imagistic meaning lying deeper than conscious reasoning. Growth of ego consciousness, and a more sophisticated understanding of meaning, occurs when such images are understood as symbols as Jung defines them, representations of what does not yet exist, of potential. The notion of truth becomes a process of growth through pondering deeply moving, sometimes disturbing, images, rather than being the result of a logical reasoning process. Viewed through the perspective of Process Theology, the process of truth involves an ever more complex grasp of harmony and beauty, more inclusiveness of life energy. The Liberal Arts provide the field of meaning for such imagery, and the permission and encouragement to understand awe as an appropriate goal of study.

Keywords: Truth, Image, Process, Jung, Cobb

***

I

Carl Jung identifies two basic creative impulses in the artist, depending on whether the art comes from the conscious mind or from the unconscious mind. In *The Spirit in Man, Art, and Literature*, he describes an artist working in the conscious mind in this way:

> He submits his material to a definite treatment with a definite aim in view; he adds to it and subtracts from it, emphasizing one effect, toning down another, laying on a touch of color here, another there, all the time carefully considering the over-all result and paying strict attention to the laws of form and style. He exercises the keenest judgment and chooses

his words with complete freedom. His material is entirely subordinated to his artistic purpose.[1]

In art of the conscious mind creativity is subordinated to the artist's ego, but in art of the unconscious, creativity comes from outside the artist. Art from the unconscious arrives on its own, asking to be realized by the artist. "One might almost describe it," Jung writes, "as a living being that uses man only as a nutrient medium:"

> The work brings with it its own form; anything he wants to add is rejected, and what he himself would like to reject is thrust back at him. While his conscious mind stands amazed and empty before this phenomenon, he is overwhelmed by a flood of thoughts and images which he never intended to create and which his own will could never have brought into being. Yet in spite of himself he is forced to admit that his own self is speaking, his own inner nature revealing itself and uttering things which he never would have entrusted to his tongue.[2]

Jung believes that the unconscious mind expresses itself solely in imagery, never through syntactical logic. In art of the unconscious, a-logically juxtaposed images carry paradoxical meaning without logical connection.

Because the meanings of images of the unconscious are not logical, they make the conscious mind uneasy: "We are astonished, confused, bewildered, put on our guard or even repelled; we demand commentaries and explanations. We are reminded of nothing in everyday life, but rather of dreams, night-time fears, and the dark, uncanny recesses of the human mind."[3] Images from the unconscious mind are so powerful, awful (eliciting awe), they can change, even destroy, the perspective of the ego encountering them.

On the other hand, these powerful images can cause profound growth and a new understanding of truth. How might one steer away from the destructive possibility and instead access the growth potential of these images? Jung argues that images from the unconscious can be understood if seen as symbolic, as he defines symbol. He sees the symbol as an embodiment of paradox.

A concise definition of Jung's idea of symbol is offered by Jolande Jacobi in *The Way of Individuation*. Jacobi writes that symbols "represent the

---

[1] Carl Gustav Jung, *The Spirit in Man, Art, and Literature*, trans. R. F. C. Hull (Princeton: Princeton University Press, 1972), 72.
[2] Jung, *The Spirit in Man, Art, and Literature*, 73.
[3] Ibid., 91.

fundamental order of the psyche, the union of its polaristic opposites."⁴ She continues:

> The criterion for symbols...is their numinosity. This is their constant characteristic, for they represent a coincidentia oppositorum, a union of opposites, in particular of conscious and unconscious contents, and thus transcend rational understanding. Through this union they bridge the dissociated portions of the psyche by creating a tertium, a 'third' thing supraordinate to both sides......All these symbols are the vehicles and at the same time the product of the 'transcendent function,' that is, of the psyche's symbol-making capacity, of its creative power.⁵

Jung understands the symbol as rooted in the future, not as reflective of the present. He writes, "A symbol is the intimation of a meaning beyond the level of our present powers of comprehension."⁶ These symbols from the unconscious mind, tied to the creativity of the psyche, stress loosening in the individual ego toward wholeness and interrelationship, rather than rigidifying toward perfection and category. Truths derived in relationship to these images/symbols moves toward inclusion rather than exclusion, toward wholeness rather than perfection.

John Sanford offers a concise amplification of the symbol-making characteristic of the unconscious, the process which Jung identifies as the 'transcendent function':

> The great mediator of our psychic conflicts is within, and begins to work in us as soon as the symbols of the unconscious are recognized and accepted by us as part of our inner reality. Such an acceptance allows the natural mediating power of the Self to operate, thereby producing the possibility for a reconciliation of the opposites, and the emergence of a hitherto unconscious totality. This symbol-making aspect of the unconscious is called by Jung the 'transcendent function' because it enables the psyche to transcend the conflict of the opposites, and permits consciousness to move out of a previously limited condition and emerge into a new life and vitality.⁷

---

⁴ Jolande Jacobi, *The Way of Individuation*, trans. R. F. C. Hull (N.P.: New American Library, 1983), 58.
⁵ Ibid., 59.
⁶ Ibid., 77.
⁷ John A. Sanford, *Healing and Wholeness* (New York: Paulist Press, 1977), 114.

The goal of the movement toward wholeness in the transcendent function Jung identifies as individuation, coming into one's unique individuality, which consists in the development of deeper consciousness.

The process is painful: "Wholeness results in the reorganization of the personality on a higher, more developed level. Since this kind of growth can never be achieved without the death of the old state of consciousness, there is, inevitably, in every instance in which someone begins to become whole, a considerable measure of pain and suffering."[8]

Images from the unconscious, through a painful process, can deepen consciousness. Jung says this is the goal of human life.

II

In *The Place of Creation*, Erich Neumann, drawing from a Jungian base, argues that images in great art can heal and redeem whole cultures. Neumann says that being itself consists of a unitary reality, a unitary field of meaning, but that "ego-consciousness represents a specifically restricted field of knowledge in which the world-continuum is broken up into constituent parts."[9] The emphasis and discrimination of ego-consciousness "tends to sunder the world-continuum into opposites."[10]

Because ego-consciousness builds polarity, the overall numinosity of the unitary reality is dimmed. The great elan vital of wholeness is lost in our discriminating, choice-making, nature. The increased discrimination necessary to develop *perfection* causes one to lose a sense *wholeness*. The ego, to protect itself in its own definition of perfection moves away from the awe before which the ego stands stunned. Seeking truth only through reasoning of the conscious mind prohibits the possibility of seeing a larger truth carried in images from the unconscious mind. Neumann writes that even though the world of our conscious mind "is the world of rationality and discrimination" and "its instrument is the separation of pairs into opposites,"[11] it is the mark of a creative person that he or she be open to the original wholeness.

Jung and Neumann both argue that the great image creators, the great artists, are essential to finding the truth. Neumann says, "In the uniqueness of every great work of art...the split in the reality of our conscious minds is overcome and abolished."[12] Therefore, what touches us is neither in the outside world or

---

[8] Ibid., 03.
[9] Erich Neumann, *The Place of Creation* (Princeton: Princeton University Press,1989), 9.
[10] Ibid., 13.
[11] Ibid., 97.
[12] Ibid., 108.

the inner world, but in a beyond "which emerges and speaks directly to our condition and, for blessed moments, actually redeems us."[13] We are redeemed because

> we return to the unitary reality that we had lost, because it had become to us an object, a kind of vis-a-vis. In art, the sympathy of all things—the way they belong to us and we to them—is brought back to life and becomes vivid and clear to us, clearer, in fact, than generally happens in the relations between ourselves and what we call nature and the world. What coalesces in a painting and manifests itself as sympathy is not things or copies of things but symbols, which in their essential suchness and in their togetherness with one another bear witness to something other than their simple existence.[14]

In essence, according to Neumann, in experiencing the powerful imagery in great art "a reunion takes place of those elements our ego is constrained to separate."[15] The experience of reunion is wondrous, "something in ourselves and something in the world appears as shaped, formed, centered, animated, and filled with meaning; both these things belong together and we find that they are grounded in a third thing, which is what we have called 'the unitary reality.'"[16] One might understand that as a sense of coming home to a larger selfhood.

Though these images in great art can heal us, canonizing them can block their power through a rigidity of set interpretations. We recognize the power of the images, but protect ourselves from feeling awe by distancing ourselves through standardized interpretations. Neumann writes:

> as the attitude of ego-consciousness becomes more extreme, it is protected by the erection of a cultural canon of acknowledged collective values and orientations and the 'immediate' experience of wholeness is inevitably excluded as too dangerous. In this way the tendency of the cultural canon only to admit newly emerging contents of the unconscious insofar as they conform to the cultural canon is reinforced.[17]

---

[13] Ibid.
[14] Ibid.
[15] Ibid., 109.
[16] Ibid., 113.
[17] Erich Neumann, *The Place of Creation* (Princeton: Princeton University Press, 1989), 136.

Of course, it is necessary for the conscious mind to find safe harbor against the flux of the unconscious, but a rigidified self-protection can become incarceration. Canonization of great art can be "a prison and consolidation can easily turn into rigidity."[18] To avoid that, one needs to keep alive 'heightened sensibility' and "a capacity and willingness to be deeply moved and impressed."[19] Regardless of the sacredness of the canonized artwork, an ongoing openness to awe in the face of it, and to deep transformation in unforeseen ways through it, must be maintained.

The reward of such openness is growth a call to action. Neumann says the symbolic image "includes within itself 'a way,' a transformation, something which has to be done; it never remains, in its essential nature, a 'vision,' but is always a guiding principle whose demands have to be fulfilled in life."[20]

III

To this point, this essay has suggested that awe-inspiring images rooted in the unconscious mind, found in dreams and art, require the ego to move to a more holistic perspective. The same process at work in the individual also operates in cultures, involving images from great art canonized by that culture. In either case, the change of perspective causes suffering because the narrower perspective wants to defend itself.

Years ago, while I was working on my M.A. and PhD in English, I came across Carl Jung's ideas, largely in connection to archetypal interpretations, although his idea of the transcendent function fascinated me as well. Sometime after I first started to read Jung, I worked with a Jungian analyst for about two years in the process I had read about, working with individuation in myself. As the course of my life made its way, I went to seminary (after receiving the PhD and teaching). There I encountered the ideas of Process Theology and saw parallels between that and Jung's thinking. Both call for change from a narrower to a more holistic perspective, change that feels dangerous, but Process Theology reimagines the suffering so that hope abides.

Process Theology is rooted in the thinking of the mathematician philosopher Alfred North Whitehead. At the end of his *Process and Reality*, Whitehead writes that God is "the poet of the world, with tender patience leading it by his vision of truth, beauty, and goodness."[21] In Process Theology human beings are called

---

[18] Ibid., 138.
[19] Ibid.
[20] Ibid.,176.
[21] Alfred North Whitehead, *Process and Reality*, ed. David Ray Griffin and Donald W. Sherburne (New York: The Free Press, 1978), 346.

to a life of creatively living those values of truth, beauty, and goodness while developing ever more complex harmony. If these were cast in Jungian terms, the holistic selfhood would include all things brought together harmoniously, even things from the past previously rejected.

For John Cobb, developing increasingly complex harmony can only be achieved through 'Christ energy' or 'Novelty' (Cobb's terms) which is a call to the creativity inherent in all human beings. We are called to be creative in the present in seeking harmony, and also in trying to include previously excluded elements from the past. Cobb writes, "Only as novelty enters creatively into an event can the many strands of potential contributions of the past be jointly realized."[22] This is a novelty "that allows maximum incorporation of elements from the past in a new synthesis."[23] In seeking such harmony, we align with God's will, and Christ's life.

There are parallels between Cobb's thinking and Jung's. Edward Edinger writes in *The Creation of Consciousness*, "The new psychological dispensation finds man's relation to God in the individual's relation to the unconscious."[24] For Cobb, however, the approach would involve finding the individual's relation to the unconscious as representative of a deeper connection—man's relation to God. Jung's idea of ego change from images of the unconscious parallels Cobb's idea of creative transformation bound to Christ energy.

Jung sees psychic growth as a result of that change. Cobb says that life itself depends on creative transformation from the creative transformation of Christ energy: "When the creative transformation ceases, the organism dies and its body decays. There can only be advance into novelty or else erosion of what has been attained."[25]

Jung sees that individuation change frightens the ego, and Cobb says the Novelty underlying creative transformation "must struggle for actualization against habit, anxiety, and defensiveness."[26] Both Jung and Cobb see that the change we fear is the change we need.

Cobb, however, argues that alignment with Christ offers hope during difficult, even drastic, change, because, in Cobb's words, "Christ is essentially bound up with hope."[27] For Cobb, Christ energy calls for genuinely threatening creative

---

[22] John B. Cobb, Jr., *Christ in a Pluralistic Age* (Philadelphia: Westminster, 1975), 70.
[23] Ibid., 76.
[24] Edward F. Edinger, *The Creation of Consciousness: Jung's Myth for Modern Man* (Toronto: Inner City Books, 1984), 90.
[25] John B. Cobb, Jr., *Christ in a Pluralistic Age*, 77.
[26] Ibid., 76.
[27] Ibid., 24.

transformation, but contextualizes it in hope, because it is in Christ already, luring us toward those divine standards of harmony, truth, beauty, and goodness.

If one looks at the crucifixion and resurrection images, arguably the most canonized images in the western world for thousands of years, the awful image of a good man nailed to a cross when connected to the empty tomb resurrection image, illustrates a process ending in transcendent new being. Cobb writes that the two images are a "field of force,"[28] and to enter that field, to be open to it, is to access "the efficacy of the salvation event."[29]

For Cobb, the cross and empty tomb images are canonized but not rigidified. In addition to remaining open to them, Cobb stresses finding new images in our time. He writes, "We must continue to work for images of hope that convince us,"[30] and he reminds us that "images of hope arise only through creative transformation."[31] Moreover, the hope found in these images would be guided by values of harmony and beauty, which suggests an aesthetic component embedded in truths that matter. Such understandings that matter would lead us to understanding increasingly complex harmonies in all things, with, as Whitehead would say, nothing left out.

This Process Theology idea of harmony parallels an idea offered by the Jungian thinker Lawrence Jaffe, who writes in *Liberating the Heart: Spirituality and Jungian Psychology*, that in years to come, "there will be a growing conviction that a kind of moral sense is an essential element in general intelligence,"[32] and he adds, "moral integrity is an essential ingredient of scientific creativity."[33]

IV

From a Jungian and Whiteheadian perspective it is wise to remember in our time of pluralistic truth making, that there is an abiding underlying truth, which is that there is a wholeness beyond any contemporary context. We are drawn to that holistic perspective through images that inspire awe and may appear paradoxical, but which intimate a harmony not yet realized. Axiomatically, all contextual truths remain partial within the abiding truth, the

---

[28] Ibid., 117.
[29] Ibid.
[30] Ibid., 244.
[31] Ibid., 256.
[32] Lawrence W. Jaffe, Liberating the Heart: Spirituality and Jungian Psychology (Toronto: Inner City Books, 1990), 36.
[33] Ibid., 37.

values of which are harmony and beauty, and the ongoing appropriation of which creates increased life energy.

The Liberal Arts are the storehouse and field for images of awe, and their study engages the process of truth-seeking at that deepest level. The way to approach them is to emphasize hope and creativity in a potentially frightening, even destructive, world. To be a teacher in the Liberal Arts, one would do well to stay open to canonical images in great art, be willing to be moved by powerful new ones from the unconscious of one's students, and to let one's students know that even the teacher is learning.

The author of this essay teaches at a Christian Liberal Arts University, as identified in the first sentence of its mission statement. Christian liberal arts universities have been criticized as offering a narrow, doctrinal, perspective—paralleling Neumann's critique of imprisonment by rigidifying canonized art. From Cobb's perspective, however, Christ's energy itself demands perpetual advance into the novum, perpetual creative transformation, perpetual work toward a more harmonious, more beautiful world. This vision is anything but looking through rose-colored glasses; it hurts to work toward it; one might feel crucified, but the truth is, for this writer at least, that a more holistic world is possible. The paradox of how to harmonize what seems, and has seemed, disparate, is our task.

In my own country, for example, how might one harmonize the image of the Statue of Liberty in New York harbor and a wall along the border with Mexico—how to harmonize the paradox of *you're welcome here* but *keep out*. The Liberal Arts teacher might invite students to look at powerful photos of the Great Wall of China (*National Geographic* Photo of the Day 1/9/2012)[34] and The Statue of Liberty (*National Geographic* Photo of the Day 10/1/2016,[35] and to read Robert Frost's poem "Mending Wall," which includes the lines, "Before I built a wall I'd ask to know / What I was walling in or walling out."[36] If the Statue of Liberty were the awe-inspiring image canonized by the culture, then the wall may be the image of defending the culture as it has rigidified into exclusion rather than inclusion. Those two identity images, seeming opposites, suggest a paradox. In terms of the transcendent function idea a new, transcendent identity might emerge perhaps disregardful of geographic boundaries. In terms of Process Theology that transcendent identity would be rooted in harmony, beauty, and good pressing to be known beyond geographical boundaries.

---

[34] National Geographic Photo of the Day, accessed February 28, 2019, https//www.nationalgeographic.com/photo-of-the-day/2012/1/climber-greatwall-china/
[35] National Geographic Photo of the Day, accessed February 28, 2019, https//www.nationalgeographic.com/photo-of-the-day/2016/10/statue-liberty-night/

V

During the three weeks that I had set aside to work on the final draft of this paper, we were discussing Michael Ondaatje's *The English Patient*, in a literature class I taught. As I thought about the last paragraph above, the idea of geographical boundaries, some of the novel's descriptions of the desert came to mind. The English Patient himself says, "The desert could not be claimed or owned—it was a piece of cloth carried by winds, never held down by stones."[36] After a dust storm, "the surface of the desert" was totally changed.[37] It is not fixed, which presents a profound conundrum for a passionate mapmaker/geographer, which the patient was. In the context of ever-changing landscape, the patient, as he explored, found himself letting go of national boundaries: "There were rivers of desert tribes, the most beautiful humans I've met in my life. We were German, English, Hungarian, African—all of us insignificant to them. Gradually we became nationless."[38] As measurable identities fell away, faith consciousness arose: "It was a place of faith. We disappeared into the landscape."[39] The consciousness which was lost in the landscape of flux developed faith. The process of surviving in such context requires ever new understanding: "In the desert to repeat something would be to fling more water into the earth."[40] Abiding in the new became a way of life in the desert.

The ideas of meaning composing itself in an endless process, of harmonizing human consciousness trying to figure things out inside that process, of finding faith inside that process, and of abiding in the Novum in order to survive in that process, all do suggest parallels to the ideas of this paper. Those would be surface parallels, and I would not say that Ondaatje's presentation of the desert represents a nuanced representation of the ideas of this paper. I will say that for me, however, certain ideas from Jung, Neumann, Whitehead, Cobb, and Ondaatje fold into a meaning I sense, the truth of which I hope unfolds itself to me. Maybe the next time I teach *The English Patient*, I will see the desert more deeply; maybe the next time I preach a sermon about faith I will sense a dimension of it that can only be found inside flux (i.e. outside the set creeds of doctrine); maybe I will be better able to identify others who are working on the same questions that I think about in my country, and this world, as we seem perhaps to have lost our way. Whatever truth may unfold, it will be about

---

[36] Michael Ondaatje, The English Patient (New York: Vintage International, 1993), 139
[37] Ibid., 137.
[38] Ibid., 138.
[39] Ibid., 139.
[40] Ibid., 231.

process. The Liberal Arts engages meaning holistically, contextualizing truth statements in a process of truth making.

References

Cobb, John B., Jr. *Christ in a Pluralistic Age*. Philadelphia: Westminster, 1975.

Edinger, Edward F. *The Creation of Consciousness: Jung's Myth for Modern Man*. Toronto: Inner City Books, 1984.

Jacobi, Jolande, *The Way of Individuation*, trans. R.F.C. Hull, N.P.: New American Library, 1983.

Jaffe, Lawrence W., *Liberating the Heart: Spirituality and Jungian Psychology*. Toronto: Inner City Books, 1990.

Jung, Carl Gustav, *The Spirit in Man, Art, and Literature*, trans. R.F.C. Hull. Princeton: Princeton U. P., 1972.

National Geographic Photo of the Day January 9, 2012. Accessed February 28, 2019. https//www.nationalgeographic.com/photo-of-the-day/2012/1/climber-great-wall-china/.

National Geographic Photo of the Day October 1, 2016. Accessed February 28, 2019 https//www.natonalgeographic.com/photo-of-the-day/2016/10/statue-liberty-night/.

Neumann, Erich, *The Place of Creation*. Princeton: Princeton U. P., 1989. Bollingen Series LXI:3.

Ondaatje, Michael, *The English Patient*. New York: Vintage International, 1993.

Sanford, John A., *Healing and Wholeness*. New York: Paulist Press, 1977.

Whitehead, Alfred North, *Process and Reality*, corrected edition, ed. David Ray Griffin and Donald W. Sherburne. NY: The Free Press, 1978.

About the Authors

James Cunningham, Ph.D. James is the chief tutor at Quick Thinking Tutoring, in Toronto, and teaches at Mount Royal University (MRU), Calgary. Prior to his association with Quick Thinking and MRU, James spent fourteen years as a philosophy instructor at Ryerson University (2000-2014), having first received his doctorate in philosophy of education at University of Toronto/OISE, in 1998. He has written articles on critical theory, existentialism and his primary concern, humanities education. When he is not tutoring, teaching, or writing, James enjoys his extreme old age in the company of his wife, children, and grandchildren.

Karim Dharamsi, PhD. Karim is a Professor of Philosophy and Chair of General Education at Mount Royal University. His scholarship has primarily been in the philosophy of history, the philosophy of education, and liberal education. Karim is the primary organizer of the Mount Royal University-Medicine Hat College Liberal Education Conferences, held between 2017 and 2019.

Deborah Forbes, M.Ed. - Deborah is an installation artist, educator at Medicine Hat College, guest curator, and public-school trustee. Her artwork has been shown in solo exhibitions across Canada. In addition to post-secondary instruction, Forbes has presented at many conferences in areas of visual art, art history, art education, creativity, design thinking, and chaos and complexity theory.

Ronald Glasberg, Ph.D. Ron is an Associate Professor at the University of Calgary. He teaches several history of ideas courses in the Department of Communication, Media and Film. His goal is to explore fundamental cultural assumptions as these have evolved throughout history in different cultural contexts.

Navneet Kumar, Ph.D. Navneet has a Ph.D. in Postcolonial Theory and Literatures from the University of Calgary and is presently teaching at Medicine Hat College, Alberta, Canada. He teaches courses in English literature, composition and liberal education. His areas of interest and research are race and refugee studies, genocide studies, pluralism, identity, religion, and violence.

Andrew Moore, Ph.D. Andrew is the Director and an Associate Professor of Great Books at St. Thomas University. His primary research interests are Shakespeare and early modern political thought. He is the author of *Shakespeare between Machiavelli and Hobbes: Dead Body Politics* (Lexington 2016). His writing on higher education and liberal arts pedagogy can be found in the *Journal of General Education, Transformative Dialogues, Times Higher Education,* and *University Affairs*.

David Ohreen, Ph.D. David earned his Doctoral Degree in Philosophy from the University of Wales, Lampeter, specializing in philosophical psychology. Before coming to General Education at Mount Royal University, he taught at the Bissett School of Business and the Faculty of Management, University of Lethbridge teaching a wide range of courses including social responsibility, business ethics, and environmental management. David's research interests bridge the complex interconnection between psychology and moral decision making. He is currently researching the motivations behind corporate funding of nonprofit organizations; the role of peer influence on moral decisions; and the extent to which empathy can be used to create good corporate citizens. He is the author of *Folk Psychology: It's Scope and Limits* and *An Introduction to Philosophy: Knowledge, God, Mind, and Morality* and has also published academic articles in psychology, ethics, and corporate social responsibility.

Jason Openo. Jason serves as the Director of Teaching and Learning at Medicine Hat College, and he teaches leadership and management principles as an Assistant Lecturer in the University of Alberta's online Graduate School of Library and Information Science. He co-authored *Assessment Strategies for Online Learning: Engagement and Authenticity,* published by Athabasca University Press in 2018. Jason received his Bachelor of Arts in Political Science from Albion College's Gerald R. Ford Institute for Leadership in Public Policy and Service, and his Master of Library and Information Science from the University of Washington's iSchool. He is now a doctoral candidate in Athabasca University's doctoral program in Distance Education. During his studies at Athabasca, he received the 2019 Outstanding Distinction Award for AU Graduate Students, and the 2016 Graduate Citizenship Award. His research interests include authentic assessment in digital contexts, faculty development for contingent faculty, and the ideology of technology.

Robert M. Randolph, B.A., M.A., M.A., M.A, Ph.D. Robert teaches English at Waynesburg University in Pennsylvania. He has been a Fulbright Scholar in Finland and Greece, has published poems in 50 journals, academic essays in ten more, and an award-winning book of poems. For 12 years he pastored a church close to the Monongahela River. As he was writing this, his daughter said he should add that his wife and daughter are "both super cool," which they are. They have a cairn terrier and a black Labrador retriever. For four of the last five years red tail hawks have nested in the tall pines in his back yard. He believes liberal arts open us to awe, profound self-reflection, and demand a creative response in working on the world's problems.

Bruce Umbaugh, Ph.D. Bruce became a philosopher to try to understand everything. He works on issues about how various technologies embody values and on issues about human reason and knowledge. Courses he teaches include Critical Thinking, The Scientific Revolution and the Enlightenment, Theory of Knowledge, Feminist Philosophy and Technology, Global Information Ethics, Making Decisions, and the Keystone Seminar Real World Survivor. He enjoys helping students discover new perspectives, make new intellectual connections, and formulate their own meaningful accounts of things. Bruce is (currently) the President of the Association of General and Liberal Studies.

Index

A

Arendt, Hannah, 60, 61
Aristotle, 114, 121

B

bullshit, ix, 3-5, 7, 8, 12, 45, 53-55, 57-67, 69-75

C

chaos, 6, 11, 122, 131, 132, 134, 135, 137, 140, 147-149
citizenship, x, xii, 46, 58
climate change, x, 7, 33, 39, 42, 43, 47, 51, 62, 63
Cobb, John, 151, 157
collaborative inquiry, 8, 135, 140, 146
complexity theory, 11, 131, 132, 134, 135, 137, 138, 148
criminalblackman, 128
Critical Theory Fair, 141-146
culture industry, 9, 77-82, 87, 89, 91, 92

D

dehumanization, 119
discourse analysis, 34, 51
discourse of crisis, 6, 33-37, 39, 41, 43, 44, 47, 48, 51
disruptive technology, 21

F

fake news, 3, 4, 5, 7, 8, 10, 24, 33, 37, 39, 53, 54, 55, 57, 59, 64, 67, 69, 70, 71, 73, 74
Frankfurt, Harry, 4, 5, 8, 53, 54

G

Gadamer, 77, 79, 82- 90, 92

H

higher education, i, 3, 5- 7, 12-15, 17-22, 24, 25, 27, 28, 30-39, 41-52, 68, 73

I

ideology, 33, 40, 44, 45, 66, 121, 122

J

Jung, Carl, 151, 152, 156, 161

L

liberal arts, xi, 7-9, 34, 36, 37, 46, 50, 67-69, 73, 74, 77-79, 90, 93-96, 97, 100, 102, 105, 107-109, 111-115, 131, 132, 152, 159
liberal education, i, x, xi, 3, 5-12, 13, 15, 19, 20, 27, 28, 33-39, 41-44, 46, 49, 53, 54, 58, 67, 68-70, 71, 77, 78, 79, 80, 81, 82, 91, 121, 122, 126, 128, 129

M

mass incarceration, 119-121, 126, 127, 129
metaphors, i, 13-15, 21, 29, 30, 40, 89, 139-141
myth of progress, 39, 40

O

Obama, Barack, 4

P

Plato, 9, 78-92
Process Theology, 151, 156, 158, 159
propaganda, ix, 10, 24, 30, 60, 61, 119, 120, 121, 122, 126, 128, 130
public discourse, 5, 6, 13, 14, 16, 17, 25, 28

S

Sophist, 81, 89, 90

T

Trump, Donald, 3, 53-59, 66, 72, 74, 78

W

Whitehead, Alfred North, 156, 161
Woolf, Virginia, 13, 25-31

www.ingramcontent.com/pod-product-compliance
Lightning Source LLC
Chambersburg PA
CBHW050638300426
44112CB00012B/1847